GOLD DAYS

Also from Westphalia Press

westphaliapress.org

GOLD DAYS

California During the Eventful Days of '49

by Owen Cochran Coy

WESTPHALIA PRESS

An imprint of Policy Studies Organization

Westphalia Press
An imprint of Policy Studies Organization
1527 New Hampshire Ave., NW
Washington, D.C. 20036
info@ipsonet.org

ISBN-13: 978-1-63391-175-8
ISBN-10: 1633911756

Cover design by Taillefer Long at Illuminated Stories:
www.illuminatedstories.com

Daniel Gutierrez-Sandoval, Executive Director
PSO and Westphalia Press

Rahima Schwenkbeck, Director of Media and Marketing
PSO and Westphalia Press

Updated material and comments on this edition
can be found at the Westphalia Press website:
www.westphaliapress.org

GOLD DAYS

By Owen Cochran Coy

Director, California State Historical Association; Author of *"The
Great Trek"; "Pictorial History
of California,"* Etc.

of the series
CALIFORNIA

Edited by
John Russell McCarthy

AUTOGRAPHS

Gold! Gold! Gold! California in '48. In '49 the "RUSH."

The one-time boys of that historic period are now veterans. Their number is few.

As a fitting recognition of what the modern state owes to the Argonauts, we take pleasure in publishing facsimile autographs, done with pen and ink, of men who knew the land before the thirty-first star had been added to the flag; men who enjoyed the romance of those colorful years; men who as citizens of the outpost of American civilization had a part in the molding of California's destiny. All hail!

FACSIMILE AUTOGRAPHS
of CALIFORNIA PIONEERS

Specially obtained for this work

Covered Wagon Babies

Born on the Trail in '48, '49, and the '50's

Mrs Caroline Ann Jones (1856)
516 Monterey St. Vallejo Calif

Mrs Jennie H. Davis Artello (1858)
541 Maryland St. Vallejo, Cal.

Mrs. Nettie E. Bush (1850)
2428 Prince St Berkeley Cal

Mrs Dana O. Moon (1854)
63. Yosemite ave. Oakland Cal

John Carson Grider (1859.)
2523 Hillegass ave. Berkeley Cal.

Mrs Permelia J Norris (1853)
564 - 39 St. Oakland, Cal.

Mrs Belle Louise Gavin (1859)
6409 - Filbert st, Oakland, Cal

Mrs Matilda Norton (1853)
3209 San Jose ave Alameda, Cal.

Gold Days

CONTENTS

ILLUSTRATIONS

Specially produced for this work

By Franz Geritz

*Left to right:
  TOP ROW—*Senator Wm. Gwin, Sam Brannan, Abel Stearns, Thomas O. Larkin.*
  SECOND ROW—*John Bidwell, John A. Sutter, Mariano Vallejo, Andrés Pico.*
  BOTTOM ROW—*Peter H. Burnett, First Governor; Dr. Robert Semple, Chairman; Pablo de la Guerra.*

PREFACE

The purpose of this volume is to depict life in California during the eventful days of 'Forty-nine. While wide use has been made of historical sources, this volume is not offered as a monographic study but rather as a popular presentation or interpretation of that period, the author having especially in mind the interests of the lay reader rather than the critical historical scholar. This will explain the omission of much of the paraphernalia of research, such as voluminous foot-notes.

In many places the author has found himself drawing more or less upon the work of earlier historians, to whom he has endeavored to give due credit. To the writings of Hubert Howe Bancroft and Theodore H. Hittell he is especially indebted, as sooner or later is every historian who works at all extensively in the field of California history. For further reading those interested should make a more extended study of the works of these men together with the many other volumes mentioned in the bibliography.

The author wishes also to acknowledge his obligation to the many writers who depicted early California life as observed in the gold region during the flush times. Frequent references will be found to Bayard Taylor who visited the mining area in 1849 and 1850 as a newspaper correspondent, and gave a pleasing account in his *Eldorado;* to J. D. Borthwick, the Englishman who spent some time in California during the early 'fifties; to William Taylor, the Methodist street-preacher of San Francisco, and to a host of others. The *Annals of San Francisco*, published in 1854, is a rich mine of information about life in the great metropolis of Gold Days. For the chapters dealing with the geological history and the more technical side of miners' activities, use has been made of the reports of the State Mining Bureau, and the United States Geological

Reports, especially Lindgren's *Tertiary Gravels of the Sierra Nevada*.

The first two chapters deal with the period before Marshall's discovery, giving a brief resumé of the various tales about California gold from the sixteenth century to the close of the Mexican period. They point out that while there always were claims and rumors of gold in California and gold mines were even worked in California before 1848, the great discovery was made by James Marshall just as the territory was being turned over to the United States. The story of Marshall's discovery and the effect this knowledge had upon California itself is told in three chapters. The geological history of the gold area showing how the modern miner benefited by nature's hoarding is here presented in its relation to the history of the period. Four chapters then take up the life of the miner and his method of handling economic and social affairs as well as the more serious difficulties due to the lack of governmental machinery. Three chapters are devoted to the consideration of the region outside of, but closely related to, the mining area; to the speculation in townsites, the development of the great metropolis at the Golden Gate and the dizzy whirl in that city during the days of the gold fever. In the final chapter the author endeavors to show the relation of the gold rush to the political development of the state and nation, pointing out that while there has been a tendency of many to look upon the Gold Days as a period of instability, and the 'Forty-niners as care-free gamblers and heavy drinkers, they were, on the whole, a body of typical American men who met this problem in a manly way and established the institutions from which the great State of California has developed.

The author wishes to express his thanks to the many persons who have so kindly assisted him in the preparation of the manuscript and in proof-reading. Miss Charlotte Brown, Librarian of the University of Southern California, and her staff have rendered valuable assistance in the compilation of the bibliography and in other ways; Miss Laura Cooley and other officers of the Los Angeles Public Library have been most helpful; to Dean Rockwell D. Hunt the author is especially indebted for valuable suggestions while the work was still in manuscript form. The artistic skill and poetic genius of Franz Geritz in his excellent woodcuts which so beautifully illustrate the volume will more than compensate for any shortcomings of the text. Finally the author wishes to express his deep appreciation to the publishers, particularly to Sidney M. Haskell, whose kindly interest and patience have made it possible for him to carry on the necessary research, and to John Russell McCarthy whose sympathetic aid, as editor of the work, has added materially to its readability.

OWEN C. COY

Los Angeles, February, 1929.

GOLD DAYS

CHAPTER I

California Gold in Fact and Fable

CALIFORNIA, A LAND OF GOLD, was the vision held by Hernando Cortés when in 1533 his men reported the discovery of a new and unexplored land lying to the north and west of Mexico. Just when the name was first applied to the southern peninsula is not recorded in history. It is interesting, however, to note that from the very beginning California has been thought of as a land of gold and that in spite of many disappointments the idea persisted until it became a tremendous reality in January, 1848, just on the eve of American annexation.

"Know that on the right hand of the Indies there is an island called California, very close to the side of the Terrestrial Paradise; and it was peopled by black women, without any man among them, for they lived in the fashion of the Amazons. They were of strong and hardy bodies, of ardent courage and great force. Their island was the strongest in all the world with its steep cliffs and rocky shores. Their arms were all of gold, and so was the harness of the wild beasts which they tamed to ride; for in the whole island there was no metal but gold."

Here in a popular Spanish novel appeared for the first

[1]

time the name California, referring, as is seen, to a land of romance and charm, a land abounding in gold. These words, penned by Garcí Ordóñez de Montalvo probably in the fifteenth or very early in the sixteenth century, were eagerly read by the story-loving Spaniards of that time, an age when life and romance were closely blended. When these words were written, California existed only in imagination and, even after the name had been applied to a newly discovered land, three centuries were to pass before men gained actual knowledge of the existence of gold.

During the decades immediately following the discovery of the new world by Columbus, the Spaniards turned their attention to seeking that wealth in which they had been led to believe India abounded. The conquest by Hernando Cortés of the land of Montezuma, bringing to the Spanish coffers a vast hoard of mineral wealth, intensified the passionate desire to be among the first to acquire great fortunes. To the wealth of Cortés was added that of Francisco Pizarro from the treasure houses of the Incas of Peru. Was it not probable that vastly greater wealth awaited some fortunate *conquistador?* The highly imaginative Spaniards readily accepted fabulous reports and hastened from place to place in the new world making explorations and discoveries, always firmly convinced that the land of gold was just beyond.

El Dorado (the gilded man) was believed to dwell among the equatorial plains of Orinoco or plateaus of Bogotá; La Florida was confidently believed to be a land "the richest of any which until then had been discovered"; Cabeza de Vaca, followed by Fray Marcos of Niza, brought fascinating tales of a wondrous new Mexico. It was during this time that Cortés was pushing his exploration northward and, upon discovering what appeared to be a new land, he bestowed upon it the name of Cali-

fornia, possibly in the hope that it might measure up in wealth to the fabled land depicted in Montalvo's *Deeds of Esplandián*. It is not surprising then that from the very first California has had a reputation as a land of gold. It is the purpose of this chapter to sketch briefly the development of that idea down to the time when gold was actually discovered.

During the summer of 1579 Upper California was visited by Captain Francis Drake, later Sir Francis, admiral of the Queen's Navy in the battle with the great Spanish Armada. Believing that he had reached a point farther north than any yet explored by the Spanish, he named the place New Albion, claimed the land for the English Queen, and enthusiastically proclaimed praises of the newly discovered country. Among other advantages:

"There is no part of earth," reads the record of Francis Fletcher, the chaplain of the expedition, "here to be taken up wherein there is not a reasonable quantity of gold or silver . . . . The earth of the country seemed to promise rich veins of gold and silver, some of the ore being constantly found on digging."

In view of the fact that Drake's land explorations appear to have been confined to a small area in modern Marin and Sonoma counties, and because no gold has since been discovered in this region, it would appear that Drake's chaplain possessed a vivid imagination and that his belief in the presence of gold was based more upon hope than fact.

This invasion of their vast empire by Drake aroused the Spanish to renewed explorations lest the English discover the supposed Strait of Anián, and possibly the rich Kingdom of Gran Quivira. Among these explorers was Sebastian Vizcaíno, who won fame by his discovery of Monterey Bay in 1602. The Spanish King in being urged to support further explorations and the extension

[5]

of settlement along this California coast was informed
that the Indians for some eight hundred leagues had
told Vizcaíno of "large settlements in the interior and
of silver and gold," and that "Vizcaíno was inclined to
believe that great riches may be discovered." It is to be
noted, however, that while reports of gold were common, the precious metal itself had not come within reach
of any whom they had met.

It is probable that Spain's occupation of Alta California would have been attempted in the early seventeenth
century had not rumors of gold in the Pacific led to a
dissipation of effort. Reports came of two islands off the
coast of Asia known as Rica de Oro (rich in gold), and
Rica de Plata (rich in silver). It was in the attempt to
discover these mythical isles that Spain's strength was
wasted at a time when her power was beginning to ebb.
The Spanish occupation of California was consequently
postponed nearly two centuries.

Early in the eighteenth century another Englishman
made his appearance on the California coast, and in the
book describing his voyage we find these words:

"The eastern coast of that part of California which I
had a sight of, appears to be mountainous, barren and
sandy, and very like some parts of Peru; but nevertheless,
the soil about Puerto Seguro, and very likely in most of
the valleys, is a rich, black mould, which as you turn it
fresh up to the sun appears as if intermingled with gold
dust, some of which we endeavored to wash and purify
from the dirt; but though we were a little prejudiced
against the thoughts that it could be possible that this
metal should be so promiscuously and universally mingled with common earth, yet we endeavored to cleanse
and wash the earth from some of it, and the more we did
the more it appeared like gold; but in order to be further

[6]

satisfied, I brought away some of it which we lost in our confusions in China."

This account taken from Shelvocke's book entitled *A Voyage Round the World in 1719-22* has repeatedly been quoted as reliable proof that gold had been known to exist in California. A study of his itinerary, however, shows that he never visited the shores of upper California at all, and that what he found must have been particles resembling gold in the sands of Baja California. Although two centuries have passed since Shelvocke's voyage, no one seems to have been so fortunate as to locate his "gold."

There are likewise many stories that the Russians knew of the existence of gold in the Sierra before their withdrawal from Bodega and Fort Ross. According to at least one writer, Sutter was led to locate his establishment in the Sacramento Valley because of the information given him by the Russians. Count Scala, writing in 1854, relates that in 1838 or 1839 a Russian merchant had shown Sutter a large amount of gold which he had obtained while on an excursion in the Sacramento Valley some five years before. Sutter was advised to give especial heed to the gold-bearing lands of this district in California. Scala then relates how Sutter, following these admonitions, explored the valley and carefully located his grant.

That the Russians knew of gold in the interior of California is not beyond the realm of possibility. They doubtless made many expeditions into the interior north of San Francisco Bay and may have acquired knowledge of gold from the natives. If they had this knowledge they would not have been inclined to announce it to the Californians. And that Sutter had learned from them of the presence of gold is extremely doubtful. Not only do his actions indicate that he did not know of the existence of gold before 1848, but he himself stated that he had had no previous knowledge of it.

Juan B. Alvarado, at one time governor of California, stated that he had evidence that the Russians knew of gold in the Sacramento Valley by 1814, for a Russian who had been thrown into jail at Monterey was found to have gold in his possession. Notwithstanding many interrogations he would not disclose the source whence he had obtained it, and he was soon afterward deported to Sitka. Alvarado goes on to say that the Mexicans "knew of the existence of gold deposits on the slopes of the northern mountains, but the Indians who were so much more numerous than we, prevented our exploring in that direction." The rings used at his wedding in August, 1831, Alvarado states, were made of California gold. General M. G. Vallejo also records that the Spanish people knew of the presence of gold but that the Indians interfered with their making use of this knowledge.

Many reports credit the missionaries of California with the knowledge of the presence of gold. Soon after the occupation of Alta California under Portolá and Serra, reports were current that the Jesuits had found gold mines and had secreted large deposits near their missions in Baja California. This caused much excitement, but careful search failed to reveal either mines or treasure hoards.

In subsequent years it was likewise claimed that the Franciscan Fathers knew of gold but endeavored to prevent the dissemination of the knowledge lest it bring ruin to their missionary endeavors. José Pico of San Luís Obispo reported that Father Martinez of San Luís Obispo Mission in 1829 gave to him and two other soldiers twenty ounces of gold. He believed that this had been obtained by the priest at some place near the mission and that the father had been secretly engaged in refining gold

[8]

with the aid of several Spaniards and the use of quicksilver and various materials and instruments.

More trustworthy probably is the record left by William Heath Davis in his *Sixty Years in California*. Mr. Davis first came to California in 1831. Writing in 1889 he relates this account of his conversation with Father Muro of Mission San José and Father Mercado of Mission Santa Clara.

"Father Muro, while I was visiting him along in 1843 or 1844, at the time I was agent for Paty, McKinlay & Company at Yerba Buena, mentioned to me his knowledge of the existence of gold in the Sacramento Valley as a great secret, requiring me to promise not to divulge it. I have never mentioned it to this day to anyone.

"Afterward, in conversation with Father Mercado, the same subject was gradually and cautiously broached, and he confided to me his knowledge of the existence of gold in the same locality. Both of the priests stated that their information was obtained from Indians.

"After he had imparted the news of gold in the Sacramento Valley, I would interrupt the discourse, and, for the sake of argument, suggest that it would be better to make the matter known, to induce Americans and others to come here, urging that with their enterprise and skill, they would rapidly open and develop the country, build towns and engage in numberless undertakings which would tend to the enrichment and prosperity of the country, increase the value of lands, enhance the price of cattle, and benefit the people.

"He would answer that immigration would be dangerous; that they would pour in by thousands and overrun the country; the work of the missions would be interfered with, and as the Californians had no means of defense, no navy nor army, the Americans would soon obtain supreme control; that they would undoubtedly at some

[9]

time come in force, and all this would happen; but if no inducements were offered the change might not take place in his time.

"I never heard from anyone, except the two priests, of gold in Northern California prior to its discovery in 1848 at Sutter's Mill."

Although the accounts hitherto mentioned have been either vague hopes or unconfirmed rumors regarding the existence of gold in California, the same cannot be said of the discovery made by Francisco López in San Feliciano Cañon, not far from the San Fernando Mission, probably in March, 1842. López and a companion were gathering wild onions when the former, who had acquired some knowledge of minerals in Mexico, noticed particles of what appeared to be gold clinging to the roots of the plants. Upon a further examination of the soil more of this mineral became apparent. A test showed that it was gold.

For several years this *placer* (a name applied to surface mines) was extensively worked by the native Californians and some foreigners and became of such importance, Castañares declared, that "it forms in California one of the most valuable resources which that department contains." By May, 1843, about one hundred men were engaged in mining in these gold mines. Ignacio del Valle, owner of a rancho in that vicinity, was appointed *juez de policia* with power to maintain peace, distribute land claims and collect taxes. Water was not plentiful and with its diminishing supply the number of miners declined. As the season advanced only a few remained, for the earnings did not exceed one or two dollars a day, and as a result of this condition del Valle refrained from levying any taxes. When visited by John Bidwell in 1845 there were only thirty-five men engaged in mining and their earnings were very small. These were largely Sonorans accustomed to placer mining in northern Mexico. The war between the United States and Mexico almost completely terminated these operations during the latter part of 1846.

Gold from the San Fernando placers was gathered by American traders, especially Abel Stearns, and shipped to the Philadelphia mint to be coined. The letters exchanged between Stearns and the officers of the mint were preserved in the collection of the Society of California Pioneers until destroyed by the fire of 1906. They showed, according to the report of the secretary of the society, that on November 22, 1842, Stearns sent twenty ounces of California placer gold to the Philadelphia mint.

In view of the San Fernando discovery it is not strange that there were persistent stories of gold in California just preceding and during the American Conquest, and it is but natural that after Marshall's discovery in 1848 these should be brought to the fore by the wise ones who had known all along of the existence of gold, but for reasons of their own did not profit by this superior knowledge.

The California boosters of that day seem to have been strangely lacking in their ability to exploit in publicity all the natural advantages of this region. L. W. Hastings was one of California's earliest and most ardent promoters during the period before 1846. One is therefore surprised at the self-restraint of the man when in 1845 he discusses the mineral resources of California in his *Emigrant's Guide*. He says:

"The information which I was able to acquire does not afford me sufficient data upon which to predicate any very accurate conclusions in reference to the mineral resources of California . . . but sufficient investigations have been made to determine that many portions of the mountainous regions abound with several kinds of miner-

[11]

als, such as gold, silver, iron, lead, and coal, but to what extent, the extreme newness and unexplored state of the country, utterly preclude all accurate determination."

Several scientific men, among them geologists and mineralogists, had visited California, and yet strangely enough they had failed to make the discovery of gold. One, a Doctor Sandels, spent several months during 1843, making geological investigations. During his visit he spent some days at New Helvetia. Captain Sutter, who greatly enjoyed the presence of this able man, suggested that he would be very happy should the scientist discover a gold mine for him; whereupon the geologist is said to have replied, "Captain Sutter, your best mine is in the soil." Dr. Sandels with John Bidwell and others explored the valley as far north as Chico Creek, including the Buttes, but the results seemed to indicate "that unless the mountains on the sides were richer than those in the valleys the mines would not pay to work."

Frequent reference is found to indicate that United States officials knew of the existence of gold before the conquest. The best authority is Thomas O. Larkin, consul and special diplomatic agent of the United States at Monterey. In a communication to Commander Montgomery dated May 2, 1846, Mr. Larkin reports:

"At San Fernando, near San Pedro, by washing the sand in a plate, any person can obtain from one to five dollars per day of gold that brings seventeen dollars per ounce in Boston. The gold has been gathered for two or three years, though but few have the patience to look for it. There is no doubt in my mind but that gold, silver, copper, quicksilver, lead, sulphur, and coal mines are to be found all over California."

That the American representatives to Mexico believed that minerals including gold must exist in such a large mountainous area later included in the Mexican cession is very probable; that they were well informed by Larkin and others regarding the discovery near San Fernando is evident, but that they knew of gold beyond the knowledge here indicated is extremely doubtful. The conquest of California was completed without any definite knowledge of its great mineral wealth.

That California was to be the Land of Gold seems to have been ordained at an early date, the very name bears a connotation with gold and romance. Many early explorers and writers expressed their opinion or stated as a fact that gold is to be found in great abundance, and yet in no case had any of them first-hand evidence. The San Fernando mines caused considerable excitement in the early 'forties, but their gold supply was meager and soon exhausted. Scientific observers and geologists examined the region to report the probability of gold and other minerals but without definite location of such deposits. Such was the condition at the beginning of 1848 when the authority of the United States was definitely recognized over this area.

Chapter II

CHAPTER II

John A. Sutter, Lord of New Helvetia

AT THE TIME of the acquisition of California by the United States probably no person in that territory commanded greater interest than did John A. Sutter. The strategic location of his establishment in the Sacramento Valley had given him a position of independence from the Mexican authorities, and therefore one of leadership among the ever increasing number of American immigrants.

John Augustus Sooter, as the name was then spelled, was born of Swiss parents in the Duchy of Baden, Germany, in 1803. Twenty years later he was graduated from a military college at Berne, Switzerland, and soon afterward married Miss Anna Dubelt. After some years in the army he engaged in commercial pursuits in Switzerland, but it appears that in these he was not financially successful.

He was, therefore, ready to heed the call of his romantic nature for adventure in the new world. Cutting loose from his old surroundings in order to seek life anew, Sutter arrived in New York in July, 1834, and immediately proceeded to the western frontier and stopped for a time in the vicinity of St. Charles on the Missouri River.

To the far west, two trails beckoned the adventurer on.

One led to the Rockies and thence to the Columbia River and the Oregon country, then just beginning to attract the attention of the American pioneers; the other turned to the southwest and to the Mexican settlements at Santa Fé. With the latter a very profitable trade had developed and caravans made annual trips in the interest of this commerce. Sutter joined the caravan to Santa Fé and profited by his speculations in fur trade and other commerce, especially with the natives. What is more important, he learned there of California, a land as yet but little known to the American frontiersmen. The reports praised this land so highly that Sutter decided to make it his goal and the seat of his further activities.

To reach California from Santa Fé, Sutter was forced to take a very roundabout route. Returning to St. Louis he went west in a company of fur trappers to the Rocky Mountains, thence with a smaller company to Fort Vancouver on the Columbia River, where he was kindly received by the Hudson's Bay Company's officials. Unable to cross the Siskiyou Mountains in the winter, and with no vessels running direct to California ports, he took ship to the Sandwich Islands, where he was hospitably received by both king and foreigners and where he made contacts which were valuable in the years to follow. From the islands he gained passage on a brig bound for Sitka. The Russians became close friends of the affable Sutter and not only furnished him with iron, tools, powder, and other articles, but also formed associations that were mutually beneficial. As the Russians were then planning to withdraw from California, Sutter purchased their claims to Fort Ross together with all their equipment in California. After his circuitous journey, Sutter arrived in San Francisco Bay, July 2, 1839.

His first mission took him to the capital at Monterey, where he presented letters of recommendation to Governor Juan B. Alvarado, together with a petition for a large tract of land as an *empresario de colonizacion*. Although Governor Alvarado was not in position to grant this petition at once, he advised Sutter to apply for naturalization papers and suggested that he select a tract of unoccupied land which might be granted to him one year later upon the completion of his naturalization.

Sutter adopted Alvarado's suggestion, and after taking out his first papers returned to Yerba Buena and thence proceeded to Sonoma, where he visited General M. G. Vallejo, Comandante of the Northern Frontier. Later he crossed to the coast to visit Rotchef, the Russian officer at Fort Ross. Vallejo endeavored to induce Sutter to settle in the vicinity of Sonoma, but the latter, following advice that he had received in the north, resolved to select a place in the great central valley, for among other advantages this would give him a position more independent of the Mexican officers. Although he was not unwilling to become a citizen of Mexico, since that was a prerequisite to securing a land grant, his plans could be worked out more readily if he were not too closely scrutinized by Mexican officials.

Early in August, 1839, Sutter with a fleet of two schooners and other small vessels, and with several Kanakas and other workers, made his way through the straits seeking a site upon the Sacramento River. More than a week was devoted to this exploration. The river was examined as far as the mouth of *el Rio de las Plumas*, Feather River, but no location appeared as good as that at the mouth of American River, *el Rio de los Americanos*. This name had been well bestowed, for here was to be established a stronghold of Anglo-American activity, on this river an American was soon to discover gold, here was later to be established the capital of an American state.

[19]

"Sutter was now left to carve his fortune in the wilderness," says Bancroft, "his companions being three white men whose names are not known, ten Kanakas, including two women, an Indian boy from Oregon, and a large bulldog from Oahu. A site for a permanent settlement was selected about a quarter of a mile from the landing on high ground, where two or three grass and tule houses were built by the Kanakas, more or less in Hawaiian style, on wooden frames put up by white men. Such were the primitive structures of California's later capital, and they were ready for their occupants early in September."

Work was immediately begun on more permanent structures, and before the winter had set in there had been erected an adobe building of three rooms, with a tule roof. This served Sutter as living quarters, kitchen and forge-shop. By judicious use of trinkets the Indians of the region were enticed to visit his establishment. When too bold they were awed into submission by use of his brass cannon. A herd of cattle was purchased on credit from neighboring ranchos, wild game was obtained by hunters, gardens were planted and the new settlement soon began to take on permanent form. In honor of his native land Sutter called his place *Nueva Helvecia*, New Helvetia.

At the end of a year Sutter received his final papers of citizenship together with the grant of eleven square leagues of land and a commission to represent the Mexican government upon the frontier. His title as he was wont to sign himself was "*Encargado de justicia y representante del goberno en las fronteras del Rio del Sacramento.*"

Sutter's Fort as thus established grew to be an institution of considerable importance upon the Sacramento frontier. The Indians who had been unfriendly to the Californians were not only induced to take a friendly

attitude toward the genial Swiss and his associates, but were even persuaded to come into his employ. In this manner Sutter was able to build up his establishment by use of inexpensive labor.

At the close of the war between the United States and Mexico eight years after the entrance of Sutter into Sacramento Valley, he controlled a veritable principality, measured in terms of the cramped areas of central Europe. His manor seat, known as Sutter's Fort, was upon a slight elevation on a small tributary of the American River. Surrounding it were large fields inclosed by ditches. These served the twofold purpose of drainage and of excluding cattle and wild horses that roamed the grassy plains. For the raising of garden truck and fruits some eight or ten acres were carefully laid out into gardens and orchards. Here were produced a large variety of garden stuff as well as grapes, apples, peaches, pears, olives, figs, and almonds.

The fort itself was constructed in the form of a quadrangle with heavy adobe walls and was provided with loopholes, bastions and a dozen or more pieces of ordnance. The enclosure measured 150 feet by 500 feet, the granaries, stores, workshops, and dwellings being arranged just within the outer walls, while within a large central building were located the headquarters of Captain Sutter himself.

The interior of the houses was crude, as one might expect from their construction. In the case of his reception room, however, as well as his own private quarters Sutter had obtained from the Russians at Fort Ross a California-made set of furniture built of native laurel; of this he was very proud, for it was quite superior to the crude furniture of the Mexican rancheros.

Sutter's Fort was a place of activity, for here were busily engaged Indian laborers, white mechanics and

Yankee traders. Newcomers from the eastern states sought Sutter's Fort as the end of the trail, for any who arrived without friends had no difficulty in securing employment with the generous lord of the manor. Thus we find at one time or another, men in the employ of Sutter who rose to places of importance in the history of California.

The white population in the vicinity of Sutter's Fort in December, 1847, numbered according to Sutter, two hundred and eighty-nine. Half-breeds, Kanakas, and negroes brought the number of foreigners to slightly over three hundred. Sutter had some four hundred and seventy-nine domesticated Indians more or less under his control. In and near the fort were about three score houses. There were also a tannery and several mills. His wheat fields yielded in 1847 over 2,200 bushels, but nearly three times that amount was expected the following season. Twelve thousand head of cattle and about as many sheep, one thousand hogs and about two thousand horses and mules were counted among his possessions. Although his land grant consisted of eleven square leagues, because of its peculiar boundaries it extended along the Sacramento, Feather, and American rivers in such a manner that it commanded a much larger area.

By the beginning of 1848 Sutter had many neighbors who likewise controlled large holdings. Across on the north side of the American River John Sinclair held El Paso Rancho of 44,000 acres; on the south side above Sutter's Fort Leidesdorff held 35,500. On the Feather River, Nicolaus Altgeier was located nearly opposite Sutter's Hock Farm. The latter was a secondary manor-seat where Sutter had about one half of his cattle, most of his herd of horses, besides a large acreage under cultivation. William Johnson held a place on Bear River, upon a portion of which the United States army soon afterward established Camp Far West both as protection from Indian disturbances and as an assistance to incoming trains. At the mouth of the Yuba River, on its north side, Theodore Cordua had settled in 1842 and operated a trading post. On Chico Creek, John Bidwell, formerly in the employ of Sutter, had begun to build up an independent settlement which was later to take the name of the creek. On Deer Creek, Peter Lassen, a Danish immigrant, had established a small place and conducted a blacksmith shop. Pierson B. Reading was the most northern of any of the settlers, being located on Cottonwood Creek near the northern end of the Sacramento Valley.

West of the Sacramento River, William B. Ide held forth near the present Colusa, while William Knight had established himself opposite the mouth of Feather River, and John R. Wolfskill had a place on Putah Creek. These men were probably the more important settlers, although located here and there throughout the valley were numerous other Anglo-Americans, who had settled with the intention of remaining permanently in the Sacramento Valley.

South of the American River, settlement had been less rapid. Due to the hostility of the Indians, the Spaniards had been reluctant to ask for land grants in that region. During the 'forties, however, several grants had been allotted. Charles M. Weber, a native of Germany, had recently established himself upon French Camp Rancho. This had received its name because the French-Canadian trappers of the Hudson's Bay Company's brigades had used it annually as a place of encampment. His attempt to promote a town under the name of Tuleburg had as yet not been entirely successful. South of Weber's place on the Stanislaus River the Mormons under Samuel Brannan had recently laid out a town known as New

Hope, but this likewise was not thriving. On the Cosumnes River and Dry Creek between Weber's and Sutter's establishments were located a number of settlers.

The ranches were widely scattered, for land was reckoned in square leagues rather than acres. These large holdings had been acquired before the war between the United States and Mexico, but as the success of the American arms became manifest many new settlers had come in. The newcomers were creating a demand for more land as well as for various articles of commerce. As the population grew, Sutter's position gradually lost some of its preeminence from a military point of view, for the protection offered by his fort became less necessary; yet until the American Conquest the fort remained a source of strength to the foreign settlers, who looked with covetous eyes upon the fertile lands of California but with few exceptions had little confidence in the friendly attitude of the Mexican officials.

Even though Sutter's Fort were to lose its importance from a military point of view, Sutter was determined that New Helvetia should maintain its place economically and socially. To this end he endeavored to build up its industry and commerce. Three miles from the Fort on the Sacramento River was Suttersville, from whose boat landing the sloop *Amelia* made regular trips down-river to San Francisco Bay. Other boats also plied back and forth, and a ferry had recently been established across the Sacramento River at this place. At Brighton, on the American River six miles from the Fort, discharged Mormon soldiers were busy erecting for Sutter a grist mill with four runs of stones, an extensive plant upon which Sutter was expending $20,000 to $25,000. Sun-dried bricks of adobe served for building materials for native Californians, but the incoming Anglo-Americans demanded lumber. Sutter recognized the value of being prepared to meet this demand also. In his employ was a wheel-wright named James W. Marshall, who in 1845 had come into California from Oregon, seeking employment. He was a good mechanic who had established a small ranch on Butte Creek; but during the Mexican War most of his stock became scattered and he was now again without means. Sutter consulted with Marshall and it was agreed that together they would erect a sawmill. Marshall was to supervise the selection of a site and the erection of the mill. After several trips to the mountains, in May, 1847, he reported a suitable mill site about forty miles up the South Fork of the American River in a little valley called by the Indians "*Culuma*." The needed water power was available, good pine timber was near at hand, and, what was equally important, a way thither could easily be prepared for oxcarts.

With the coming of the new year, 1848, the prospects for New Helvetia were brighter than ever. The crops promised well, a flour mill was almost completed, a saw-mill would be ready within the new season. When the great party of new immigrants would arrive from the States, and they were sure to come as soon as the melting snows opened the passes across the Rockies and the Sierra, the Lord of New Helvetia would be prepared to meet all their demands. Surely at last his dreams were about to be realized.

Chapter III

CHAPTER III

Gold! Gold! Gold!

"Monday 24th, this day some kind of mettle was found in the tail race that looks like goald, first discovered by James Martial, the Boss of the Mill."

THESE simple words, quoted from the diary of a young Mormon laborer at the mill, Henry W. Bigler by name, describe an event of such momentous consequence as to change the current of history; not only did Marshall's memorable discovery affect the history of California—its influence was felt throughout the civilized world.

In accordance with the plans of John A. Sutter, a sawmill was being constructed on the South Fork of the American River. James W. Marshall, a partner with Sutter in this project, had almost completed the task of construction. Assisting him were Peter L. Wimmer, foreman, his wife, Elizabeth Jane, and two sons, John and Martin Wimmer; Charles Bennett, William Scott, Henry W. Bigler, Azariah Smith, James S. Brown, Alexander Stephens, William Johnson, and James Berger. The last six were young Mormon soldiers recently discharged from the Mormon Battalion which had marched into California under General Kearny. In addition to these whites there were a number of Indians; about ten of these were from New Helvetia and some could speak Spanish.

The work upon the mill, begun the previous August, had been carried on all winter and was nearly completed. It was found, however, that the mill race, which was an old channel of the river, was not deep and wide enough to permit the water to pass the wheel as rapidly as it should. In order to remedy this condition the gravel was worked loose, the wheel hoisted out of gear, and the channel left to be flushed out each night by the action of the current.

Little did the men realize that they were using the miner's method of operation known as "ground sluicing," but it was not long before the results became evident. Early in the afternoon of Monday, January 24, 1848, Marshall was watching the work of the water upon the mill race when his attention was directed to shining yellow particles mixed in the loose dirt. These at first did not impress him seriously but as he saw still more he decided to investigate further. Calling one of the Indian boys at work near by, Marshall sent him to James Brown for a tin plate. Brown, who was then working at the top of the saw pit, jumped down and brought the plate, but with the surprised query: "I wonder what Marshall wants with a tin plate?"

After Marshall had secured the pan, he washed out a small amount of gold dust—about as much as would cover a dime. Later in the evening while Bigler and Brown were in their cabin, Marshall came in, and during the evening, in his queer way, remarked casually, "Boys, I believe I have found a gold mine." "I reckon not," was the reply, "no such luck."

Nevertheless, Marshall instructed his men to shut down the headgate of the mill race at daybreak and to pack leaves and mud closely around it to prevent leakage.

His instructions were followed and Marshall himself was early on the job. While the others were at breakfast he was down in the mill race to see what would be revealed.

As the men gathered at the mill, Marshall approached them with a very pleasant expression. In his hands he carried his old white hat. James Brown, whose curiosity had been especially aroused, was the first to see what Marshall was carrying on his hat crown. There were ten or twelve small pieces of what appeared to be gold. Picking up one of the pieces he tested it with his teeth and, finding it was malleable, he exclaimed, "Gold, boys, gold!" Whereupon all dropped their tools and hastened to gather around Marshall.

The metal was next tested upon the anvil and later in the forge. It seemed to stand all the tests of gold. Azariah Smith had in his pocket a five-dollar piece from his army pay and produced it for purposes of comparison. Since Mrs. Wimmer was then engaged in making soap, it was decided to subject it to vinegar and then to leave it for a while in the lye of the soap cauldrons.

Not many days afterward, Marshall, taking with him samples of the gold, made his way down to Sutter's Fort. He had been there within a fortnight, and inasmuch as Sutter had just sent up to the mill all supplies asked for, the appearance of Marshall was entirely unexpected. His nervous manner also indicated that something extraordinary must have happened at the mill. He asked for a private interview with Sutter, and after the doors were locked drew out a bag containing about three ounces of mineral dust. Since Sutter had scales and acids among his apothecary supplies they were able to subject the dust to a more severe test. The encyclopedia was also brought into use. When all known tests had been applied, it seemed evident that it was pure gold. Marshall desired Sutter to return with him to the mill and the latter agreed to do so as soon as possible. Marshall, however, could not wait but set out for the mill immediately. Shortly afterward Sutter made his way to the mill, where he was met by Marshall.

Marshall was anxious to make a good impression upon Sutter, and according to the story of Bigler appeared at the cabin of the men with the word that Sutter had arrived at the mill that evening. "Now, boys," Bigler reports Marshall as saying, "we have all got a little gold dust. I motion that we all give Henry [Bigler] some, and in the morning when he shuts off the water, let him take it down and sprinkle it all over the base rock. Not let on to the old Gentleman and it will excite him that he will set out his bottle and treat, for he always carries a bottle with him."

Bigler and the men did as Marshall proposed, and of course were much interested when, as they were finishing breakfast, Sutter, accompanied by Marshall and Wimmer, passed their cabin door. Sutter shook hands all around and invited the men to go with him, which, of course, they gladly did. Imagine then their feelings when at this juncture one of the Wimmer boys, not knowing what was planned, ran on ahead and, having picked up nearly every particle of gold, came running back exclaiming, "See here how much I have found!" Although he had about fifty dollars' worth the men did not dare say a word lest the joke be found out. Their chief disappointment seems to have been that they lost their liquor.

"I went in the race," related Sutter, "and picked up several pieces of gold, several of the laborers gave me some which they had picked up, and from Marshall I received a part. I told them I would get a ring made of this gold as soon as it could be done in California; and I had a heavy ring made with my family's coat of arms engraved on the outside, and on the inside is engraved, 'The first gold, discovered in January, 1848.'"

Sutter spent two days prospecting in the vicinity of Coloma and then returned to the Fort. Before leaving he called all hands together and requested that they keep the discovery a secret if for only six weeks, when not only could the sawmill be completed but also his flour mill at Brighton, which was almost built. Notwithstanding that the men made the promise, Sutter seemed to realize that events about to take place were beyond his power to control. Fortune had been carrying him on as by a rising tide, but now might not that tide become a veritable flood and sweep him away?

Notwithstanding that evidence now seems quite clear in regard to the fundamental facts relating to the gold discovery, they have in the past been subject to much dispute. Even the actual date of discovery has been in question and only within the past few years has the Marshall monument at Coloma set forth the correct date.

Both January 19 and January 24 have been claimed as the correct date for Marshall's discovery. The discrepancy arose quite naturally and was rectified only by careful search for more complete and correct data. The first attempt in print to establish the date seems to have been in a statement made by Marshall to Mr. J. M. Hutchings in 1857 and published by the latter in his *California Magazine* of November of that year. It reads as follows:

"On or about the 19th day of January—I am not quite certain to a day, but it was between the 18th and the 20th of the month, 1848. The first piece of gold which I found weighed about fifty cents."

For nearly thirty years the date was accepted as January 19, but there were many discrepancies in the documents tending to discredit this date. Marshall said in his statement elsewhere that four days after the discovery he went to Sutter's Fort to determine the genuineness of the gold. Now Sutter kept a diary and in it are to be found entries as follows:

"Friday, January 28th 1848 . . . Mr. Marshall arrived from the Mountains on very important business . . . .

"Saturday, January 29th 1848 . . . Marshall left for the Mountains."

The dates given there seem to show either that the gold discovery had taken place at a later date than the nineteenth or that more than a week had elapsed before Marshall's trip to the Fort. John S. Hittell, in his historical research, became interested in determining with more certainty the exact date. He found that among the young Mormons at Coloma both Azariah Smith and Henry W. Bigler had kept diaries. He first found the diary of Smith, but unfortunately that youth wrote in his diary only on Sundays. Although not as exact as might be hoped, its entries helped to determine the week of discovery. His first entry referring to the gold find is as follows:

"Sun. Jany the 30th . . . Mr. Marshall having arived; we got liberty of him, and built a small house, down by the Mill, and last Sun. we moved into it in order to get rid of the Brawling; Partial, Mistress and Cook for'ourselves. This week, Mr. Marshall Found some peaces of, (as we all suppose), Gold, and he has gone to the Fort for the purpose of finding out. It is found in the raceway in Small peaces. Some have been found that would weigh five dollars."

Since this diary was written at the time the events were taking place it cannot easily be disputed. It is apparent then the date of the discovery must have been after Sunday, January 23, for otherwise Smith would have recorded the event with the entries of that Sunday.

Comparing this with Marshall's statement we find that while it calls in question the date of the 19th, on the other hand, it places the discovery nearer the date indicated in the Sutter diary. It was not, however, until the diary of Henry W. Bigler was produced that all question as to the exact date was set at rest. On Monday, January 24, 1848, he recorded as a happening of that day the fact of the discovery, as given in the opening of this chapter. It is interesting to observe that even in such important matters as the date of the gold discovery the unsupported memory of one who was a participant was exceedingly unreliable when compared with the evidence set forth in contemporaneous documents such as the diaries of Sutter, Smith and Bigler.

Another point of uncertainty has been in regard to the final disposal of the first piece of gold discovered at Coloma. This has even become at times a matter of acrimonious controversy, and in spite of rather conclusive evidence there are still those who are unwilling to accept the facts. Some have declared that it was converted into the heavy ring made for and worn by Sutter and having the inscription, "The first gold discovered in January, 1848." Others have maintained that it is the Wimmer nugget, still on display. Facts seem to show that neither of these contentions was correct. Fortunately the research of Mr. Phil B. Bekeart, who has done so much to bring to light the facts regarding the early life at Coloma, has contributed also to the solution of this problem.

In an earlier paragraph it has been related how, upon his first visit to the gold fields, Sutter had been able to gather a considerable amount of gold which later he had had made into a signet ring. That this was actually the first gold discovered is not necessarily implied in his inscription. That it was some of the first gold taken out of the mill race at Coloma no one was inclined to dispute, but

[39]

that the ring was made of the very first piece of gold picked up by Marshall even Sutter did not claim.

As the years passed and memories were less reliable, another piece of gold was brought before the public eye and this from time to time has been urged as the identical first piece of gold found at Coloma. This is usually referred to as the Wimmer Nugget by reason of the fact that for many years it was in the possession of that family. Wimmer was employed as foreman and was busy especially with the Indian laborers, while Mrs. Wimmer served as housekeeper for the mill workers. They are described as very respectable people and naturally were closely associated with events taking place at the sawmill at the time of the discovery.

Since the discussion of the Wimmer Nugget partakes of the nature of a controversy it may be desirable to review briefly what appear to be the facts in so far as they are now ascertainable. That Peter Wimmer considered himself the real discoverer of gold was not extensively claimed until about eight years after the discovery. The *Alta California* of January 5, 1856, makes mention of the fact "that lately the first discovery has been claimed for Peter Wimmer." This does not seem at the time to have been seriously considered by those familiar with the facts. After this, as time bedimmed the memory of all the participants, it seems that the Wimmers became possessed of the idea that they had taken a far more prominent part in the gold discovery than had usually been accorded them. Furthermore, did they not have in their possession the original piece of gold picked up in the tailrace, by Marshall and Wimmer? Outside of his immediate family there appears to be no evidence that Wimmer was even present when Marshall first brought his gold up to show to the mill men, but rather that he soon afterward came from the house and joined in the excitement that ensued. Efforts on the part of Mr. and Mrs. Wimmer to dispose of this nugget to the Society of California Pioneers, or with their help to the State of California, did not meet with success because the Pioneers were unwilling to accept the evidence supporting their extravagant claims. In 1877 the Wimmers finally disposed of the nugget to a Mr. Allen, and in 1885 gave him signed affidavits stating that this gold was the first picked up by Marshall. In 1893, these were printed in the *California Gold Book*, published by Allen and Avery.

There are furthermore certain discrepancies between the appearance and size of the Wimmer Nugget and the description of the small flake of gold first discovered by Marshall. This probably as much as anything else caused the Pioneers, who were familiar with the facts, to hesitate to accept the story of the Wimmers at full value. This nugget is described as being about the size and shape of a small walnut or, as Mrs. Wimmer herself said, like a piece of chewing gum after the latter had been used for its intended purpose. It weighs about six pennyweights, eleven grains, which gives it a real value of five dollars and ten cents. On the other hand, Marshall's flake of gold was worth only about fifty cents and was a small thin piece worn smooth by water action in the bed of the river. No gold taken from a stream bed would be apt to have rough corrugated surfaces, for such pieces of gold are found only in the higher gravel banks known as dry diggings.

That the Wimmer Nugget has real historical value, aside from the exaggerated claims set up for it, is very probable, for undoubtedly it was one of the first if not the first large piece of gold found by Marshall, in 1848. Upon this point we are fortunate to have the statement of Jules F. Bekeart, an intimate companion of Marshall from 1849 until his death in 1885. He says:

"As regards this nugget of gold, Marshall has told me many times, that after his first discovery of gold, he was prospecting and mining at Kelsey's dry diggings over the ridge from Coloma, and found that Wimmer nugget. He prized it much, he said, for he wished and intended to send it to his mother in New Jersey. Marshall was a great friend of the Indians, some of whom had slain white men (for tampering with their squaws, probably) . . . . Marshall thought best to remove, which he did, going prospecting; but before going, he hid his sack of gold dust and specimens, the big one included, under Wimmer's door stoop. When the passengers of the 'California' and the 'Oregon' steamships arrived, they came up and settled at Sutter's Mill. Marshall, feeling that danger was over by reason of Eastern invaders with their ideas of civilization, returned, dug up his sack, but found his pretty specimen gone, gone . . . ! The slip you send says that one of Wimmer's sons discovered it."

In considering these points of difference it must be remembered that in events of this kind no one person is able to command the total knowledge of what is taking place. Some of the witnesses are less reliable than others and all are apt to become confused as time passes and other issues becloud the memory.

"There is little wonder that the statements are conflicting," is the opinion of Bancroft, who made a careful study of the points at issue, "when no one saw it all, and each was able to describe correctly only those parts of which he was an eye-witness. And after innumerable repetitions and disputings, confusion arose. Some even denied that Marshall was the first discoverer at Coloma, but this assertion is not worthy of consideration. Then there was a controversy over the first piece found, and what became of it, more senseless than the rest. Sutter, at Litiz, showed me a ring upon which was engraved on the outside, his coat of arms, and on the inside, 'The first gold discovered in January, 1848.' And yet it was not, speaking with exactness, the first gold discovered; for Sutter says in his statement that some of it he picked up himself, and some was given him by the men then present. The ring weighed an ounce and a half. Then Mrs. Weimer claimed to have had in her possession for many years the very first piece picked up, and which Marshall gave her. This cannot be true, as according to Marshall's testimony the first piece weighed fifty cents, whereas Mrs. Weimer's piece was equal to five dollars and twelve cents. It is safe to conclude that the destiny of this first piece is lost to history."

Fortunately the statement made by Bancroft is not final, for subsequent research has apparently revealed the location of that first flake of gold. For information on this point great credit is due Mr. Phil B. Bekeart, who, following suggestions made to him by his father, has recently pursued careful investigations with the result that all reasonable doubt regarding this piece of gold is now removed. Following up a statement that this piece of gold had been sent in 1848 to Washington to be placed in the Smithsonian Institution, Mr. Bekeart in 1914 wrote the secretary of the Institution asking that an investigation be made to ascertain whether or not there was to be found there an item meeting the description of Marshall's first gold.

The reply was most interesting, for not only did the Institution have samples of gold to meet the description of Marshall's first flake, but also had documents which practically establish the fact that the first gold flake found by Marshall has been safely preserved in the National Museum. An extract from the minutes of the National

Institute (a predecessor of the Smithsonian Institution), for January 15, 1849, contains these entries:

"The Corr. Secretary announced a donation of California minerals from Capt. J. L. Folsom, U. S. A.

"Prof. Johnson made some remarks on the specimens of California minerals this evening presented to the Institute, stated that according to the accompanying memoranda, No. 1 was the first piece of gold ever discovered in the northern part of Upper California. It was found by J. W. Marshall, at the saw-mill of John A. Sutter."

Accompanying one of the gold specimens which seems to be the one described above is an autographic memorandum signed by J. L. Folsom which reads as follows:

> "Quartermaster's Office,
> San Francisco, U. C.,
> August 23, 1848.

> "This paper contains the first piece of gold ever discovered in the northern part of Upper California. It was found in February, 1848, by James W. Marshall, in the race of Captain John A. Sutter's sawmill, about 45 miles from Sutter's Fort on the south branch of the American Fork. It was beaten out with a hammer by Mr. Marshall to test its malleability.
>
> "It is presented to the National Institute, Washington, D. C.
> "(signed) J. L. Folsom,
> "Asst. Q. M."

Inasmuch as the question naturally arises as to how the gold came into the possession of Captain Folsom, Mr. Bekeart's interpretation of this is timely. Folsom arrived in San Francisco, March 6, 1847, with other members of Stevenson's Regiment of New York Volunteers. He was appointed Assistant Quartermaster in charge of the port of San Francisco and during the summer of 1848 made one or more trips from San Francisco to Sutter's Fort. It is not improbable that Sutter, realizing the value of that piece of gold which had been beaten and flattened by the men in making the first tests, should have preserved it carefully and given it to Captain Folsom in July, 1848, to send to the National Institute. Since Folsom was only a subordinate officer he did not make public the fact that he possessed the gold but sent it directly to the Museum rather than have it handled by his commander, Colonel R. B. Mason. In view of the fact that none of the samples sent by Mason were preserved in their identity, it is fortunate that Folsom took this independent action. For the evidence seems conclusive that the Smithsonian Institution still has the gold sent east by him within a few months after its discovery and that in all probability it may be, what is claimed for it, the identical original flake of gold first discovered by Marshall on January 24, 1848.

Chapter IV

CHAPTER IV

The Secret Broadcast

"'Mein Gott,' says Sutter, in his Swiss German accent, to Marshall, 'if the boys find out there is gold there, there is no more work at our mill. It will be all up—gone to the dyfel.'"

THUS DID SUTTER express himself when it was ascertained that what Marshall had brought down to the fort was really gold. A strange premonition came to him that this great scene in world drama would have an unhappy ending for the actors at that time taking the leading rôles. Let us now see in what manner the discovery became known, and note the immediate results this knowledge produced in California.

As related previously, Sutter and Marshall exacted from the men employed at the mill the promise that for a period of six weeks they would maintain secrecy and continue their work upon the mill. To those thrifty youths, this was probably no great hardship, for were they not receiving good wages?—and who knew whether any more gold would be found after the few small flakes in the mill race were gathered up? The fact that a few small particles of gold were to be found was after all nothing to make one excited, at least not to the point of giving up a paying job. Doubtless, moreover, the fact that they were numbered among the "Saints," as members of the

Mormon faith were commonly called, caused them to think too strongly of their contract with Sutter and Marshall to be led aside for filthy lucre. Whatever the motive, we find that work at the mill continued without any sudden break even after the discovery was a recognized fact.

Meanwhile, some plan had to be worked by Sutter and Marshall whereby they could control the forces soon to be set in motion. The site upon which the mill stood was public land. Sutter's claim of eleven square leagues, while stretching widely through the valley, was scarcely expected to include this area, even under the Mexican régime where exactness in land titles was not required. For the purposes of a sawmill no further title was deemed necessary, for would not the timber be exhausted within a short time, anyway? But since the very land upon which the mill stood was now seen to contain gold, no one could foresee what the consequences might be.

In California hostilities between the forces of the United States and Mexico had ceased more than a year previous to Marshall's discovery, yet in so far as was known no treaty of peace had yet been signed. Without doubt this treaty would provide that California be transferred permanently to the United States. In view of these circumstances, what should be the procedure in securing a more definite title to this land? In the light of the long period of confusion regarding land titles during the years to follow, it is no wonder Sutter and Marshall were puzzled.

An idea occurred to Sutter. The land hitherto had been held by the Indians. Would it not be a prudent step to secure from them a concession of the land about the mill? Precedent for this could be found in early American colonial history and even in California in case of the Russians at Fort Ross. Marshall's attitude toward the natives made it easy to negotiate with them. The Culumas, as they called themselves, were assembled in council and a proposition was placed before them. As a result, in return for shirts, hats, handkerchiefs, flour, and other articles of trifling value, Sutter and Marshall were given a three-year lease to an area of from one hundred to one hundred and fifty square miles. One of the older chiefs, we are told by Kemble, did not hesitate to warn his white friends that the yellow metal they were so eagerly seeking was very "bad medicine"; that his ancestors had known about it; that it existed all through the mountains but that it belonged to a demon, who devoured all who searched for it.

Since there were grave doubts in Sutter's mind that the Indian title would be sufficient, it was decided that an appeal be made to Colonel R. B. Mason, military governor of California. A petition was to be presented for the title to the land surrounding the mill, including the pasture and mining privileges. In reference to mining rights, it was suggested that it be explained that there appeared to be lead and silver mixed in the soil. Charles Bennett, a faithful employee of Sutter's, was selected to bear this petition to Governor Mason at Monterey.

The primary purpose of Bennett's mission was not achieved. Inasmuch as Governor Mason had received no instruction other than that he was to hold California until the close of the war, meanwhile continuing such government as necessity demanded, he had no authority over land matters and so declined to act upon Sutter's petition, explaining that, as he understood it, "California was yet a Mexican province, simply held by us as a conquest; that no laws of the United States yet applied to it, much less the land laws or preemption laws, which could only apply after a public survey."

Back at the mill the men, true to their promise, remained at work, although it was probably with a somewhat enlivened pace that they pushed its construction to completion. On Sundays and at odd hours when their time was their own they employed themselves in the mill race digging for gold with knives and other implements. Sometimes they were rewarded with as much as half an ounce. None of the men had ever had any practical experience in mining, and so all were unfamiliar with the process of washing gold to separate it from other materials. Their only method was to pick each separate particle out of the rock or gravel.

Henry Bigler seems to have been more possessed by the urge to dig gold than the others, and since he was frequently delegated to hunt game for the common table he had especially good opportunities to follow the impulse. During the week following the first discovery he and the others, according to his diary, "pict up more than a hundred dollars worth." On the second Sunday he announced his intention of crossing to a gravel bar opposite the mill. One of the others accompanied him. They were rewarded by finding gold there also; in fact this day Bigler brought back about ten dollars' worth.

Whenever he went hunting he was on the lookout for indications of gold, and during the following week he located what appeared a suitable deposit about a mile down the river across from the mill. Although the following Sunday was rainy and the mill hands remained under cover, Bigler, without announcing his purpose, made his way down the river and enriched himself by adding another half ounce to his pile. The following Sunday he again sought his favorite spot and returned with an ounce and a half. When February 22nd came, a fall of snow covered the ground and prevented the work laid out for the day. Marshall, therefore, gave the men the day off. All were ready to accept the offer. Bigler unconcernedly suggested that he might take the gun and hunt. He did not, however, spend much time hunting for game but soon made his way across the river to his gravel bar. But this day the river was especially cold, and after wading the stream, so benumbed were his hands and fingers that he could hardly work. Nevertheless, he stayed at the task picking out the gold particles and putting them into his cap. Night came far too soon. When he tried to straighten up, he thought he would die of pain. To wade back was unthinkable, so he made his way up-stream and when opposite the milldam hailed one of the men to cross with the raft. What was Bigler doing across the river? This was the question all asked. Why had he not asked to be ferried over in the morning when he started hunting? Bigler saw that now he could no longer keep his find from the men, so he produced, tied securely in a corner of his shirt, his day's accumulation, worth about twenty-five dollars. Needless to say, on later occasions, Bigler did not get off unaccompanied.

Even before this, Bigler had come to the conclusion that since gold was so plentiful it was very selfish of those at the mill not to let their Mormon brethren know of the blessings the Lord had bestowed upon his faithful children. Bigler had, therefore, written a note to some of his mates on the Mormon Battalion who were working on the Brighton flour mill near the fort. On the last Sunday of February three of these boys appeared at the sawmill, explaining that they wanted to visit their companions and shoot a few deer. Marshall received them kindly and talked freely of the prospects, even giving them permission to dig for gold in the mill race. Some three days later they departed for the fort with Coloma gold in their pockets and many ideas in their heads. Shortly after their return to Brighton they lost interest in their ordinary work and turned their attention to a gravel bar up the river, which, because of the success these young Mormons attained there, became known as Mormon Island. By the middle of April, mining was carried on along the American River in a very serious manner by nearly all who had heard of the discovery.

Bigler's letter to his Mormon friends was not the only means whereby the news escaped. Sutter had hoped that by isolating the sawmill the secret might be retained. This, however, was but a temporary expedient, for within a few weeks the supplies at the mill were exhausted and had to be replenished. To carry these supplies Sutter selected several Indians in the charge of a Swiss teamster whom he considered particularly trustworthy. Before the teamster had halted his horses at Coloma one of the Wimmer boys enthusiastically announced to him, "We have found gold up here!" Since the teamster was inclined to scoff at the youth's statement, his mother came to his rescue and vindicated the veracity of her boy by bringing forth some of the gold dust they had accumulated. She even gave some of it to the Swiss, who at once became convinced and converted. This particular teamster had a weakness for strong liquors and too often had nothing with which to pay the barkeeper. It therefore was the policy not to serve him with liquor without cash payment. Upon his return from the mill he betook himself almost immediately to the bar and with great dignity demanded to be served with whisky. In order to show his ability to pay he placed upon the counter the gold dust. Now gold dust was not yet recognized as an article of exchange and the barkeeper refused to accept it. As a compromise an appeal was made to Captain Sutter. Sutter was forced to admit that the teamster's statement was correct, that the stuff was really gold. Henceforth, the discovery was not a secret at Sutter's Fort.

As already recorded, Sutter and Marshall had dispatched Charles Bennett to Monterey to secure the land grant from Governor Mason. With him Bennett took some six ounces of gold dust. Upon reaching Benicia he found himself surrounded by a group of men who were engaged in an enthusiastic discussion regarding the mineral possibilities of California, due to the fact that what appeared to be valuable deposits of coal had been discovered upon the slopes of Mount Diablo. This discussion about coal was too much for Bennett's human nature to endure. "Coal!" said he with disdain, "I have something here which will beat coal." As proof of his statement he produced his bag of gold dust. The discussion regarding coal immediately took second place. On reaching San Francisco, Bennett learned that a Georgia miner named Isaac Humphrey was there. Surely he could give Bennett some useful suggestions. He was found and, of course, examined eagerly Bennett's gold specimens. Needless to say, at both Benicia and San Francisco there were henceforth many people to whom the gold discovery was no longer a secret.

Notwithstanding that San Francisco was informed of the gold discovery through so many different channels, the full realization of what the discovery meant came very slowly. The first notice in the San Francisco papers was published in the *Californian* of March 15, 1848, and reads as follows:

"Gold Mine Found.—In the newly made raceway of the Saw Mill recently erected by Captain Sutter, on the American Fork, gold has been found in considerable quantities. One person brought thirty dollars' worth to New Helvetia, gathered there in a short time. California, no doubt, is rich in mineral wealth, great chances here for scientific capitalists. Gold has been found in almost every part of the country."

Having made this preliminary account, the *Californian* had but little more to say regarding the new mines. The people of San Francisco paid little heed and went on actively building up their ambitious young city. Robert Semple at Benicia, one of the founders of the *Californian*, is reported to have said, "I would give more for a good coal mine than for all the gold mines in the universe." Likewise General Vallejo at Sonoma paid but little attention to reports reaching him.

The columns of the *California Star*, owned by Sam Brannan and edited by E. C. Kemble, illustrate well the attitude of the metropolis toward the new development. On March 18th, it mentioned that gold had been found near New Helvetia, and a week later reported that the quantity of gold was so great that it was becoming an article of traffic in that vicinity. The same issue also carries an editorial in which Kemble suggests facetiously that if the property holders of San Francisco who had no intention of improving their land would see that the lots were plowed and cultivated, it might not only put to work many who were then idlers about the saloons, but that some hidden treasure might be unearthed, for there were many reports of precious metals to be found in the ground of California. Nearly a month passed before the readers of the *Star* were furnished with more news from the gold fields. This merely reported new finds in the gold district of still more extensive and valuable mines.

Men who were unwilling to accept these persistent reports for full value were nevertheless inclined now to slip off quietly to the American River and investigate for themselves. This, the editor of the *Star* decided to do, and he announced in the issue of April 15th that he was going to "ruralize among the rustics of the country for a few weeks." The editor "ruralized" around Sutter's mill, but whether he went with a prejudice so deeply rooted that he could not see the facts or whether James Marshall, who was subject to queer moods, purposely misled Kemble into believing the gold talk was largely

misrepresentation, is not known. In the issue of May 6th, just after his return, he observes: "Great country, fine climate; visit this great valley, we would advise all who have not yet done so. See it now. Full flowing streams, mighty timber, large crops, luxuriant clover, fragrant flowers, gold and silver."

But Kemble was not the only one to visit the gold fields and to come back to report. The storekeeper at Sutter's Fort who served the Swiss teamster was a partner of Samuel Brannan, the proprietor of Kemble's paper. When Brannan heard that gold was being exchanged for merchandise at his store he immediately started up the river to investigate more thoroughly. Now Brannan was a different type of man from Kemble. There was no activity that he was not in, and when Brannan was connected with a thing he took a leading part. Brannan found gold; furthermore, he found it in such abundance that his enthusiasm was thoroughly aroused. His return to San Francisco came a few days after that of Kemble, and the result was similar to that of an electric spark in a powder magazine, for in his characteristic manner he made his way up the street swinging his hat in one hand, in the other holding aloft a bottle of gold dust, and shouting: "*Gold!* GOLD! GOLD from the American River!!!"

If San Francisco had assumed a skeptical attitude hitherto, that mask was now cast aside completely. Undoubtedly there was gold. But how abundant? Would there be enough for all, or must they not hurry before the supply was exhausted? Miners returning with gold increased the frenzy of excitement. J. H. Carson gives an account of his own experience. He says:

"I looked on for a moment, a frenzy seized my soul; unbidden my legs performed some entirely new movements of Polka steps—I took several—houses were too small for me to stay in; I was soon in the street in search of necessary outfits; piles of gold rose before me at every step; castles of marble, dazzling the eye with their rich appliances . . . were among the fancies of my fevered imagination. The Rothchilds, Girards, and Astors appeared to me but poor people; in short, I had a very violent attack of the gold fever."

San Francisco lost one fourth of her population to the mines during the month of May, 1848. Still Kemble refused to become enthusiastic. "Fleets of launches left this place on Sunday and Monday," he reports in the *Star* of May 20th, then adds, "Was there ever anything so superlatively silly?" As the population continued to leave, Kemble weakened and then made an effort to recover his ground by declaring he had never intended to discourage in any way "the employment in which over two thirds of the white population" of the country were engaged.

The *Californian*, which had had but little to say regarding the new mines, gave place in its columns to a correspondent who expressed himself in no uncertain terms:

"I doubt, sir, if ever the sun shone upon such a farce as is now being enacted in California, though I fear it may prove a tragedy before the curtain drops. I consider it your duty, Mr. Editor, as a conservator of the public morals and welfare, to raise your voice against the thing. It is to be hoped that General Mason will dispatch the volunteers to the scene of action, and send these unfortunate people to their homes, and prevent others from going hither."

In spite of protests from those whose interests were opposed to the exodus from the metropolis, the movement continued unabated. During June it reached its height, for by the middle of that month San Francisco was practically deserted—three fourths of the men were in the mines. The thriving young city found its growth suddenly stopped. Land values dropped more than fifty per cent and all goods not used in the mines became a drug on the market. Laborers could not be had except at exorbitant prices. Many places of business were closed with placards posted reading:

"Gone to the Diggings"

Vessels in the harbor were deserted by their crews. Of some one hundred new buildings in the process of construction late in May, according to one witness, men continued working on a meager half dozen. Alcalde Townsend closed his office and for a time even the sittings of the town council came to an end.

Stubbornly the two papers had endeavored to stem the tide, but the fight was an uneven one. On May 29th, the *Californian* sang its swan song: "The whole country from San Francisco to Los Angeles and from the seashore to the base of the Sierra Nevada resounds to the sordid cry of gold! gold!! gold!!! While the field is left half planted, the house half built, and everything neglected but the manufacture of shovels and pick axes, and the means of transportation to the spot where one man obtained $128 worth of the real stuff in one day's washing, and the average for all is $20 per diem." The *Star*, now the only paper, continued to struggle for existence. On May 27th, it urged its subscribers, "Pay up before you go—everybody knows where. Papers can be forwarded to Sutter's Fort with all regularity. But pay the printer, if you please, all you in arrears." On the fourteenth of June San Francisco's only remaining paper was suspended.

Other towns of California were drained by the flow of population to the mines. San José, usually spoken of as "the pueblo," proudly maintained a position of prominence in spite of the ambitions of the new rival on the bay. Its population of seven hundred contained a much larger percentage of the Spanish element. The gold fever epidemic struck San José, Monterey and the southern towns soon after it hit San Francisco.

"May had not wholly passed," says Bancroft, "when at San José the merchant closed his store, or if the stock was perishable left open the doors that people might help themselves, and incontinently set out upon the pilgrimage. So the judge abandoned his bench and the doctor his patients; even the alcalde dropped the reins of government and went away with his subjects. Criminals slipped their fetters and hastened northward; captors followed in pursuit, if indeed they had not preceded, but they took care not to find them. Soldiers fled their posts; others were sent for them but none returned. Valuable land grants were surrendered and farms left tenantless; waving fields of grain stood abandoned, perchance open to roaming cattle, and gardens were left to run to waste. The country seemed as if smitten by a plague."

During the excitement at San José, Henry Bee, the keeper of the jail, found himself with the custody of ten Indian prisoners, two of them charged with murder. To go to the mines immediately was imperative, but how to dispose of his prisoners was an enigma. He might have turned them over to the alcalde had not that officer already gone to the gold fields. To turn them loose with so many women and children undefended would be out of the question. The one thing left for him to do was to take the prisoners to the mines with him, where all worked together, netting Bee a neat sum before other miners, aroused by jealousy, interfered with his arrangement.

When the full purport of the discovery made its impress upon Monterey, the capital city was affected as were the other towns. Walter Colton, alcalde of Monterey, has given us the following graphic description of the conditions there: "My messenger, sent to the mines, has returned with specimens of the gold; he dismounted in a sea of upturned faces. As he drew forth the yellow lumps from his pockets, and passed them around among the eager crowd, the doubts, which had lingered till now, fled. All admitted they were gold, except one old man, who still persisted they were some Yankee invention, got up to reconcile the people to the change of flag. The excitement produced was intense; and many were soon busy in their hasty preparations for a departure for the mines. The family who had kept house for me caught the moving infection. Husband and wife were both packing up; the blacksmith dropped his hammer, the carpenter his plane, the mason his trowel, the farmer his sickle, the baker his loaf, and the tapster his bottle. All were off for the mines, some on horses, some on carts, and some on crutches and one went in a litter. An American woman, who had recently established a boarding-house here, pulled up stakes, and was off before her lodgers had even time to pay their bills . . . . The gold fever has reached every servant in Monterey; none are to be trusted in their engagement beyond a week . . . . General Mason, Lieutenant Lanman, and myself, form a mess; we have a house, and all the table furniture and culinary apparatus requisite; but our servants have run, one after another, till we are almost in despair; even Sambo, who we thought would stick by from laziness, if no other cause, ran last night; and this morning, for the fortieth time, we had to take to the kitchen, and cook our own breakfast. A general of the United States Army, the commander of a man-of-war, and the Alcalde of Monterey, in a smoking kitchen grinding coffee, toasting a herring, and peeling onions."

Across from San Francisco on the *contra costa* lived one man who was unperturbed by all this gold excitement. This was old Luis Peralta, owner of Rancho San Antonio, covering some 45,000 acres. While others were deserting their farms and herds he called his three sons

and gave them this advice: "My sons, God has given
this gold to the Americans. Had he desired us to have
it, he would have given it to us ere now. Therefore go
not after it, but let others go. Plant your lands,
and reap; these be your best gold fields,
for all must eat while they live."

Chapter V

CHAPTER V

Gold Fields of 1848

WHAT'S THE shortest route to Sutter's Fort?" This was the query on the lips of thousands during the summer of 1848, for time was an important factor. If people had been slow to accept as true the reports that gold had been discovered in amounts worthy of their consideration, now that they had accepted this as an established fact they did not intend to be outdistanced by others in arriving at the gold fields. Would there still be gold enough for them? There was no doubt that those who arrived first would have the best chance at the gold-bearing gravel bars; late comers might even find the claims all taken up or, still worse, the gold entirely exhausted. Haste was the one essential; other things must be left to adjust themselves. It was this apprehension that explained the rapid depletion in the population of San José, Monterey, and San Francisco.

It was the same force that led farmers, trappers, and herdsmen as well as clerks, merchants and professional men to leave their usual places of occupation. One writer tells us that, as he made his way toward Sutter's Fort in June, "along the whole route mills were lying idle, fields of wheat were open to cattle and horses, houses vacant and farms going to waste . . . people, before engaged in cul-

tivating their small patches of ground and guarding their
herds of cattle and horses, have all gone to the mines, or
are on their way thither; laborers of every trade have left
their work benches, and tradesmen their shops." Nothing
should be allowed to hinder one in making the quickest
time to the gold mines. We are told of a stable-keeper
whose two brothers, already in the mines, urged him to
come immediately and bring his family. "Burn the barn
if you cannot dispose of it otherwise," was their advice.

From the Bay District there were several routes open to
the mines. First there was the water route through Car-
quínez Straits and up the Sacramento River. To follow
this one must naturally have water craft. Immediately,
therefore, there was a demand for passage on some vessel
making the trip up the river, or to buy small vessels and
boats. Under this demand, rowboats, formerly worth fifty
dollars, now sold for four hundred or five hundred dollars.
Every available craft was soon brought into use.

For those who preferred to travel by land there was a
choice of routes, one leading north of the bay through
Sausalito and Sonoma, thence to the west bank of the
Sacramento River and across to Sutter's Fort. Except for
those located north of the bay this required crossing from
San Francisco by launch or other vessel and a second ferry
at the Sacramento. The other route led through the mountains by Mission San José and Livermore's Ranch. Once
the San Joaquin River was crossed, there was no further
great barrier to progress for mule or ox-teams before reaching the "diggings." Other variations of these routes were
soon discovered or developed. Robert Semple of Benicia
had established a ferry between his town and the rancho
of Martinez on the opposite shore. Ordinarily traffic had
been negligible but the desirability of this route, as it
considerably shortened the distance, soon caused the ferry
to be entirely inadequate to meet the demands. By the

middle of May one miner found two hundred wagons awaiting their turn to cross the straits. A committee of miners took upon themselves the registration of new arrivals and each had to take his turn. Soon an old scow was brought into service and a rival ferry established with the result that transit was more rapid. At various other places ferries were established to facilitate travel and roads were soon worn where only faint trails had been before.

Upon investigation it was found that gold was not limited to the tailrace of Sutter's mill. Henry Bigler during the early weeks in February had already found other deposits thereabouts. This led to wider search which in turn was rewarded by further discoveries. Marshall, giving his recollections some years later, said that the "second place where gold was discovered, was in the gulch near the Mountaineer House, on the road to Sacramento. The third place was on a bar on the south fork of the American River, a little above the junction of the middle and south forks."

In these explorations the mill hands, augmented by some of their Mormon associates and the others employed around Sutter's Fort, took the leading parts. Mention has been made of the "visit" at Sutter's mill of those Mormons from the Brighton flour mill attracted up the river by Bigler's letter. They learned much about the appearance of gold, and while on their return somewhat carefully explored the river bed for gold deposits. Upon an island just above the mouth of the South Fork they came upon a gravel bar from which they obtained gold but not in sufficient quantity to create any great enthusiasm among them. Their friends at Brighton, however, were so aroused over the tales told of the gold at Coloma that they implored the travelers to return with them to the gravel bar in order that they also might try their luck. Further examination showed that this spot was exceedingly rich in gold-bearing gravel. In fact the men from Brighton soon decided to turn their attention exclusively to gold-digging. Thus, early in March, began the operations at Mormon Island. By July, this had become a place of no small pretention as a gold center. Governor Richard B. Mason speaks of it thus: "On the 5th [of July] resumed the journey and proceeded twenty-five miles up the American Fork to a point on it now known as the lower mines or Mormon diggings. The hillsides were thickly strewn with canvas tents and bush arbors. A store was erected, and several boarding shanties in operation. The day was intensely hot; yet about 200 men were at work in the full glare of the sun washing for gold, some with tin pans, some with close-woven Indian baskets, but the greater part had a rude machine known as the cradle."

During the spring, settlers living in the vicinity of New Helvetia had decided to try their hand at gold-digging. Many of them were owners of large ranches held under Mexican grants. These men, following the example of Sutter, had found the Indians useful in performing much of their physical labor. It had been their policy, therefore, to be on good terms with the native Indian population. After the gold discovery it was seen by many of the valley men that native help would be of great assistance in gathering the valuable particles of gold from the river bars. John Sinclair, Sutter's neighbor on the north, was one of these men. Mason found him at work on the North Fork just above its junction with South Fork. Under him were some fifty Indians who washed the gold in baskets closely woven of willow. He had been working for about five weeks and had accumulated about $16,000. During the previous week the amount was fourteen pounds of clean gold.

With the increase in the number of miners the area oc-

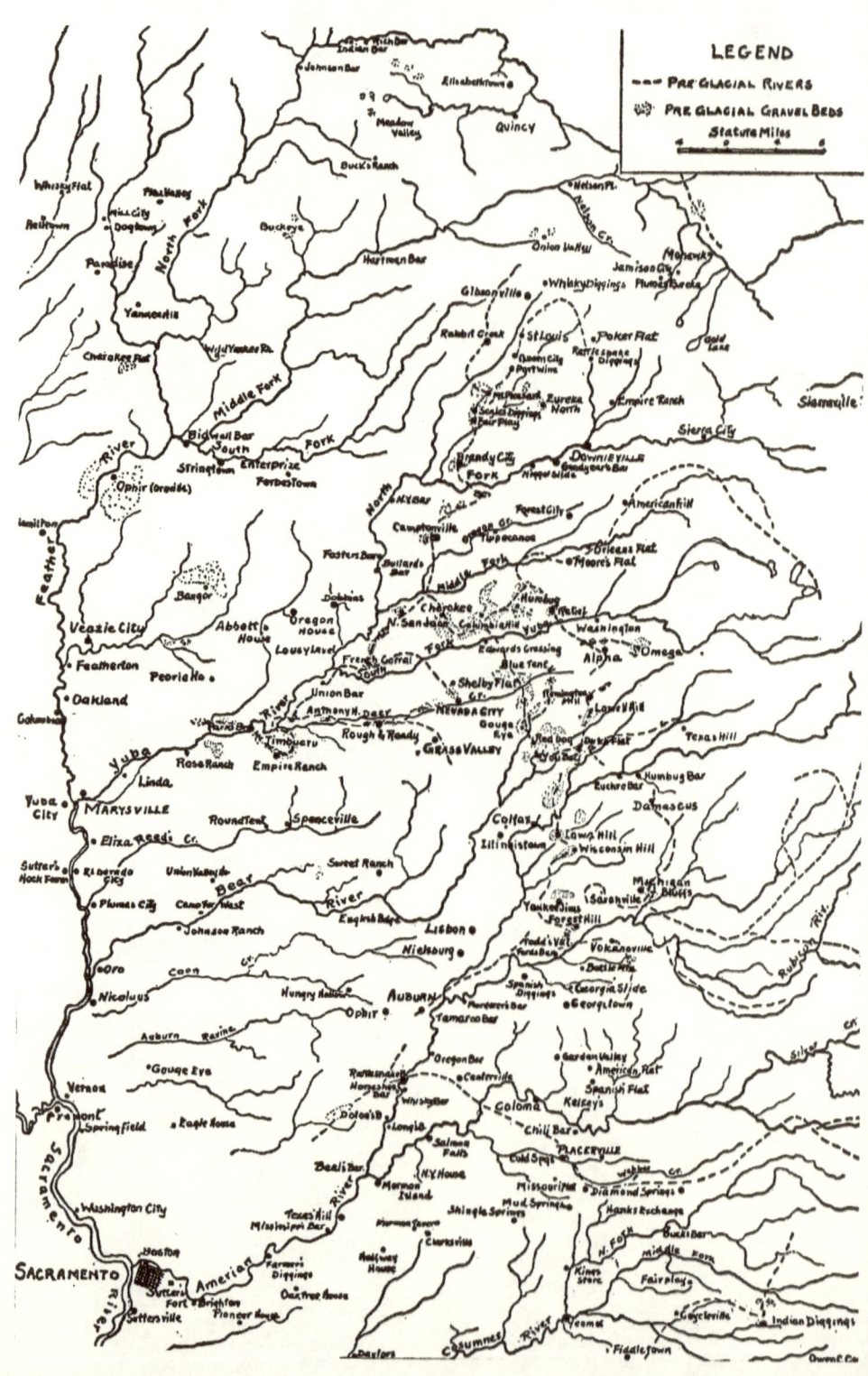

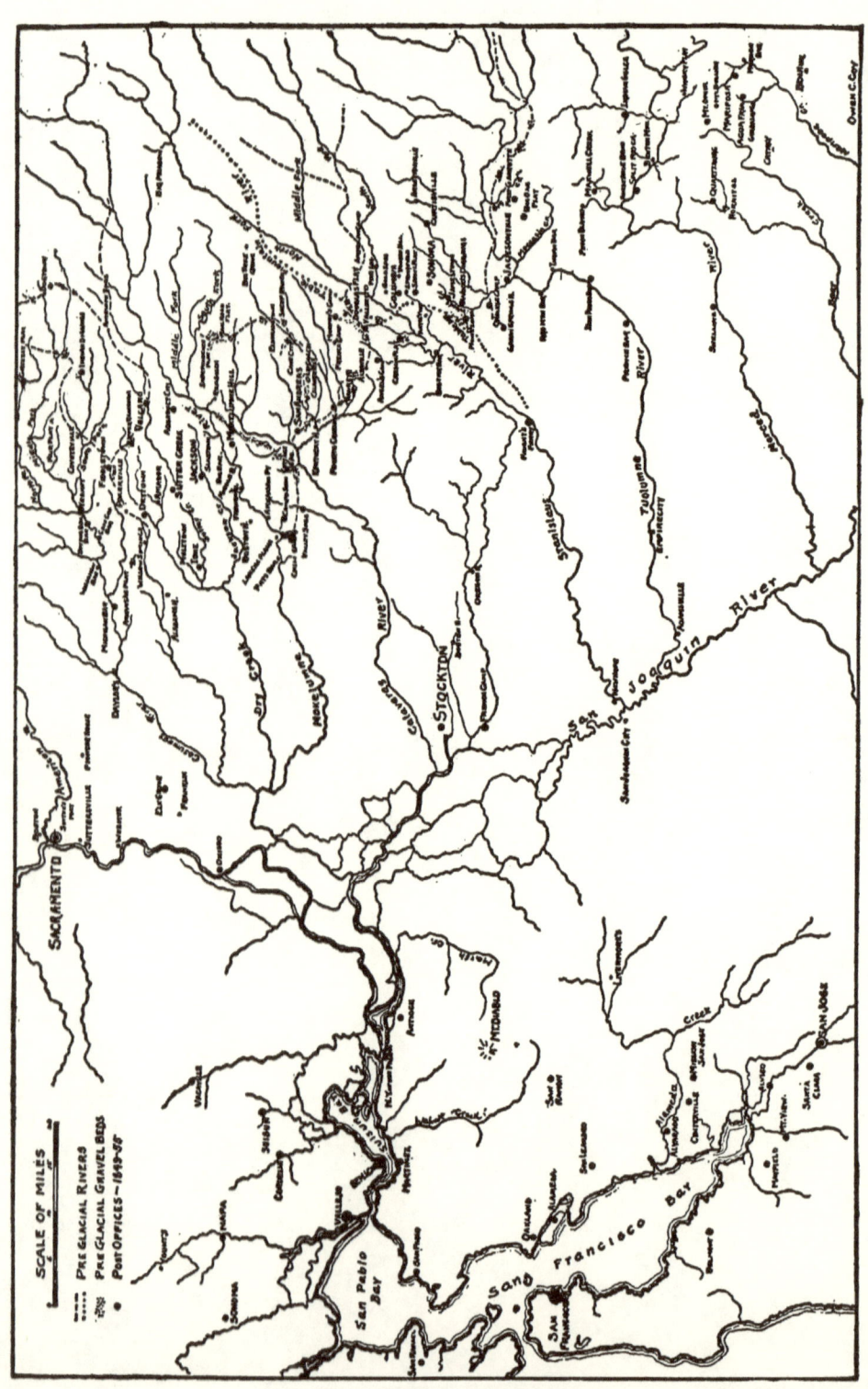

cupied also expanded rapidly. In various places all along the American Fork gold had now been found, at Coloma, at Mormon Island, at a point just above the junction on North Fork, on Leidesdorff's ranch a few miles above Brighton Mill and elsewhere. Above Sutter's mill, Kelsey led the way and discovered a rich placer which was subsequently known as Kelsey's Diggings. By May, it was estimated that there were eight hundred men engaged in washing for gold in the streams and ravines around Coloma and that they had explored and found gold along the American River for a distance of at least thirty miles on each side of the mill. During the first part of June Thomas O. Larkin estimated that the number had reached two thousand. A month later Mason stated that there were not less than four thousand engaged in the mines. This may have included, however, the Indians employed by white miners.

The expansion of the gold area up the North Fork of the American River is usually credited to a son of the Emerald Isle who, because of his strong Celtic disposition, had become known in a humorous way as "Yankee Jim." The place of his chief activity took the name assigned to him and became very famous as a rich mining center. Farther north, gold was soon afterward found at Iowa Hill, and at Illinoistown in the vicinity of the present Colfax, and at Todd's Valley, south of Yankee Jim's. In the later division of counties these fell into Placer County.

In the same vicinity, but further down-stream, Claude Chana, a Frenchman, had discovered gold in a dry ravine, thus bringing into existence a settlement which became the future Auburn. Early in May, Chana had visited Sutter's mill, and he was so impressed with the gold deposits that he organized a company of men and started to return to Coloma. Stopping overnight in a ravine on the west side of North Fork, Chana tried his hand at washing for gold. He was surprised and well rewarded by discovering thereby what was soon called Rich Dry Diggings, or North Fork Dry Diggings. Here in August, 1848, it is said that one man took out $16,000 in five cartloads of dirt and that many were able to collect from $800 to $15,000 a day. In the fall of 1849 the camp was given the name of Auburn.

The Middle Fork of the American River also made valuable contributions to the gold produce of 1848. Probably the most important point along this stream was Spanish Bar, which a little later produced more than a million dollars. The gold here was coarser than in many other places and therefore profits were larger. Above Spanish Bar was Ford's Bar where, according to report, a man named Ford took out large amounts of gold during the summer of 1848.

Captain Charles M. Weber, of the French Camp Rancho on the San Joaquin River, and the unsuccessful promoter of Tuleburg, organized a mining company with Tuleburg as headquarters. This company included several of the more prominent men. It was known as the Stockton Mining Company and employed such Indian labor as was available. After visiting the American River diggings the company turned its attention to a tributary since known as Weber (Webber) Creek. About the time of their arrival on this stream, William Daylor, a ranch owner on the Cosumnes River not far from New Helvetia, had already discovered rich deposits. These, because of the scarcity of water, were known by the descriptive name of Old Dry Diggings, but later became distinguished as Hangtown, or Placerville. The deposit here was very rich, the ordinary day's yield per man during this early period being two ounces. Mason saw here one small ravine only four feet wide and about one hundred yards in length where

William Daylor and Perry McCoon had but shortly before taken out $17,000 in a single week.

The mines extending southward from Weber Creek came in time to form what were known as the Southern Mines. For the opening of this vast area much credit is due the local Indians. On the Stanislaus River near what later became the site of Knight's Ferry lived José Jesus, an ex-Mission Indian. Displeased with his treatment at the hands of the authorities at Mission San José, this Indian fled to the valley and became chief of his tribe. While he had no love for the Mexicans, he was friendly with the Anglo-Americans. In response, therefore, to an appeal from Captain Weber and his company for Indians who would act as gold-diggers, José Jesus sent twenty-five men. It was arranged that after learning the process they should seek for gold in the Stanislaus region and should bring the results to the headquarters of the company, where the dust would be accepted in exchange for articles that would delight the Indian fancy.

The explorations of these Indians were even more successful than Weber's men had anticipated. Gold was found in larger particles than ever before. In fact it is reported that one nugget was found that weighed ten and one half pounds and sold for three thousand dollars. In view of these prospects the Stockton Company decided to abandon Weber Creek for the mines farther south. Captain Weber saw, too, that the opportune time for pushing the town of Tuleburg had arrived; so, severing his connection with the mining company, he henceforth gave his full attention to his town. From this time, under the name of Stockton, it began to rise to importance as a depot for the mines in the southern back country.

With the increase in mining population the southern mines developed rapidly. By August, when the best locations along the American River seemingly had been taken up by early arrivals, the rumor that rich mines had just been discovered on the streams farther south resulted in a general rush to Cosumnes, Mokelumne, Stanislaus, and Tuolumne rivers and their tributaries. In this district many of the places still bear names of pioneers of 1848, such as Murphy's and Angel's Camp, Jamestown, Sullivan Bar, Carson Creek, Sutter Creek, and Wood's Creek. William Knight established a trading post and operated a ferry where the Stockton trail crossed the Stanislaus River, which accounts for the origin of Knight's Ferry.

In July, 1848, Captain Sutter, who had been operating with about two hundred and fifty Indians and Sandwich Islanders on the South Fork near the mouth of Weber Creek, moved south and came to a tributary of Dry Creek to which was given the name Sutter Creek. Shortly afterward Sutter's men were followed by a company of native Spanish Californians from San Luís Obispo under José Pico, who mined on Arroyo Seco, or Dry Creek. Other developments followed rapidly, for about this time John M. Murphy established Murphy's Camp, and Angel started operations on Angel Creek, the beginnings of Angel's Camp. During this same period J. H. Carson, led by friendly Indians, took up a position on Carson Creek and, according to his report, panned out one hundred and eighty ounces of gold in ten days.

The Mokelumne mines were discovered and brought into importance during the fall of 1848. Big Bar of the Mokelumne River became the center of extensive operation. As an adjunct to the river-mining operation, a store was opened in November on a hill about a mile from the river bottom. This gave rise to a town known as Mokelumne Hill, itself the scene of much mining activity, and at one time an aspirant for the state capital.

Farther south on the Tuolumne, James Woods led a party of prospectors, among them James Savage, famous

in connection with the discovery of Yosemite Valley. They established themselves on Woods' Creek in what is now Tuolumne County, Wood's Crossing being the first place of settlement. This area constituted the southern frontier of mining operations at the close of 1848. Because of its proximity to the parts settled by Mexicans this region had a larger proportion of Spanish-speaking population, a fact which has been perpetuated in its nomenclature, one of the camps being called Sonorian Camp, later shortened to Sonora. Among the native Mexican-Californians engaged in these southern mines were Antonio Coronel, later mayor of Los Angeles, and Dolores Sepulveda, who in August of 1848 with a party of thirty struck out for the gold placers. By means of the Indians who knew of the richest deposits, this party was able to make a rich strike.

Not only did the mining district expand southward from the American River but very rich mines were also found farther north. Gold was found on the Middle and North forks of the American River as the miners spread northward from Coloma. The northward movement was especially advanced by settlers living in the northern portions of the Sacramento Valley, who were impelled to examine the river beds near their own places of residence.

One of the first visitors to Sutter's Mill after the discovery became known was John Bidwell, for some time associated with Sutter and at one time *mayordomo* of his Hock Farm. In 1845 Bidwell had acquired a grant on Chico Creek, far to the north. During the month of March, 1848, he visited the Coloma diggings. The appearance of the ground and gravel banks was so similar to what Bidwell had seen along the Feather River that he made up his mind to hasten with explorations nearer home. On his way back he spent the night at the site of

Hamilton, on the west bank of the Feather River near the point where his route turned off to Chico. Here in the river gravel he found particles of gold.

Satisfied that further up-stream gold would be found in larger amounts, he organized a party of miners and, taking with him a number of Indians, made his way up the river. Some time was thus spent in prospecting. The gold was found to be in small particles and difficult to separate. Some became discouraged with the results and all returned after a short time to their ranches. Bidwell and others, however, soon struck out again and located paying gravel at what became known as Bidwell's Bar, to which were soon attracted many other miners. Near at hand, across from Bidwell's, Potter's Bar was discovered, and farther down-stream Long Bar, Adamsville, and Thomson Flat also soon sprang into existence.

South of Feather River, Yuba and Bear rivers were also found to be rich in gold. A company of men including Patrick McChristian, Jasper O'Farrell and Jacob P. Leese, all from Sonoma, made their way to Yuba River during July, 1848. In three months' time, it is reported, they took out $75,000 in gold dust. At Park's Bar, Long Bar and Foster's Bar the men made regularly from sixty to one hundred dollars a day even with poor equipment. Of these bars the first was named for Parks, a recent arrival across the plains that year. It had been discovered previously, but was given the newcomer's name because of the fact that he had a family, and women and children were rare in the mines.

Shortly after Bidwell's visit, Major P. B. Reading, who had the distinction of owning the most northerly of the Mexican land grants, paid a visit to Sutter in order to ascertain the facts in reference to the gold discovery. He studied the situation along the American River and then returned to the north determined to examine the streams near at home for gold deposits. On Clear Creek near his rancho he discovered gold-bearing gravel which he proceeded to work by the aid of his Indian servants. Having encountered similar geological formations across the mountains west of the valley, Reading took a company of his Indians over the Trinity Mountains to the waters of Trinity River. This stream had been so named upon the assumption that it flowed into the ocean at or near Trinidad Bay, a place shown upon old Spanish maps. Rich deposits were discovered and Reading was making good profits when he encountered the opposition of a company of Oregon men on their way south from the Willamette Valley. Their recent experiences with the Oregon Indians had engendered within them a very antagonistic attitude toward the red men; this antagonism, combined with avarice, was sufficient excuse to cause them to drive Reading and his Indians from his newly discovered gold deposits; not, however, until he had established the fact that gold was to be found along the streams flowing westward directly into the Pacific.

Enough has been said to indicate something of the progress and methods of the miners of 1848. In view of the fact that the great influx to the mines came the next year, with consequent rapid development along various lines, it is fitting to call attention to a few features which characterize the mining operations of this first year.

Quite naturally the area was more restricted than in later times, and yet to one who looks into the regions explored during the summer and fall of 1848, the impression is one of surprise that a few men in so short a time should have covered the vast area extending from Trinity River in the north to the Tuolumne in the south.

One characteristic of 1848 which stands out in contrast with the next year and following years, is that those in the gold fields during the months of 1848 were largely a group of friends and neighbors; they were pioneer settlers who had become accustomed to frontier life, or native Californians from the ranchos and pueblos. Many of the names of leaders of exploring parties are already familiar to us for they were men well known in all parts of California.

Life in California before 1848 was largely, if not almost exclusively, pastoral. The large rancheros relied chiefly upon the Indians for such labor as was required. This was a heritage from the mission days passed down by the care-free native Spanish-Americans. Furthermore, with such an abundance of free land it was not possible to maintain laborers except from among the Indians; every white man had an opportunity to acquire land or otherwise establish his economic independence. Under those conditions, when the vast amount of mineral wealth was found on all sides, the natural thing for a Californian was to take with him to the gold fields all the men whose services he could command. Thus Sutter and Marshall began operation along the South Fork with one hundred Indians and fifty Kanakas; John Sinclair moved his Indians to the North Fork; Charles M. Weber secured the services of the Stanislaus Indians; and P. B. Reading made use of the natives on the streams at the far northern end of the valley and across the summit of the Coast Range. With the coming multitude of miners early in 1849, Indian as well as negro labor was taboo. Every man was entitled to the gold he himself could secure legitimately, but no man was to be permitted to exploit the services of others, at least not of Indians or negroes.

Even when the Indians worked independent of the whites they were not able to prevent the latter from obtaining undue advantages. To the red man the avaricious desire of the white man for these shining rocks was foolishness. They could not serve the immediate needs of the

[84]

savage either for food, clothing, or shelter. As a medium of exchange gold had no value except as the white man wanted it. Buffum tells of worn blankets selling to Indians for an equal weight in gold. Others tell of raisins and other foods bringing a like price. Later the Indians learned by observation that the white men, among themselves, weighed their gold; and thenceforth demanded that they be treated in like manner. Even then the untutored savage was no equal to a shrewd Yankee. A schedule of prices was adopted for the Indian, far above those in ordinary trade; calico cloth at twenty dollars per yard, white blankets at one hundred dollars, colored handkerchiefs at two ounces each, and pretty beads at their weight in gold. Moreover, the scales used for weighing the Indian's gold were equipped with heavy leaden weights to represent a "digger ounce." Although the Indian was very careful that he did not give over the exact amount to balance the scale, it can readily be seen that the odds were greatly against him.

Inasmuch as mining was relatively a new industry in California we are not surprised to find that methods of operation at first were exceedingly crude. There were two reasons for this: lack of experience and scarcity of equipment. When Bigler and his companions began to search for gold they were greatly handicapped; for digging tools their pocket knives were practically all they had. At first they pursued the policy of digging out and collecting only such flakes of pure gold as they might be able to see in the ground or in crevices in the rocks. This was painfully slow even where gold was plentiful. Soon, however, they learned to wash the gold from the sand and dirt. But this required pans, whereas at the mill an inventory recorded but one pan, a wooden wash bowl, and a chopping tray! All were requisitioned, and each served a good purpose. Later, it was found that Indian baskets of willow could be used to advantage and these were employed when they could be procured.

When Charles Bennett was returning from Monterey he was very much interested to meet, as before recorded, an experienced miner from Georgia named Isaac Humphrey. It is needless to say that being shown virgin gold from an unworked mine was invitation enough for Humphrey to proceed to Sutter's mill with Bennett. Humphrey arrived at Coloma early in March and after a short period of prospecting began the construction of a rocker or cradle. About the same time, there came to the mill a French-Canadian trapper, Jean Baptiste Ruelle, who had been engaged in mining in Mexico. He was employed by Sutter at the time at a whipsaw on Weber Creek. Some give him, instead of Humphrey, the credit of being first to use the rocker. These two men did much to assist the inexperienced miners in acquiring the knowledge necessary to attain success.

In spite of lack of experience and the inability to secure the necessary tools for effective work, the profits of 1848 were large. Governor Mason reports: "I see no laboring man from the mines who does not show his two, three and four pounds of gold. A soldier of the artillery company returned here a few days ago from the mines, having been absent on furlough twenty days; he made by trading and working during the time $1,500. During these twenty days he was traveling ten or eleven days leaving but a week in which he made a sum of money greater than he receives in pay, clothes and rations during a whole enlistment of five years. These statements seem incredible, but they are true."

Everywhere Mason went he found evidence of great success. Captain Weber, with four white men and about one hundred Indians, cleared $10,000 in one week's time. Sinclair, with his Indians, washed out fourteen pounds of gold in one week; Dye's party on Feather River, with the aid of fifty Indians, took out two hundred and seventy-three pounds of gold and averaged nearly forty pounds for each of the men of the company. John Sullivan enriched himself by $26,000 from Sullivan's Diggings on the Stanislaus. On the Middle Yuba from an area about four feet square one man is said to have picked out nearly thirty pounds of gold within three weeks. Amador, a native Californian, reports that he visited diggings that yielded as much as eight dollars per spoonful. Numerous other examples might be given.

The actual gold yield for 1848 is difficult to estimate, for no accurate check was made. Bancroft places the figure at $10,000,000 gathered by a population of 8,000 to 10,000 or an average of about $1,000 for each man for the season. The official report for the year was $2,000,000, but this is undoubtedly far too low. At the other extreme, the authors of the *Annals of San Francisco* give the figures at $48,000,000. It must be remembered that the season of 1848 was short; many did not begin work until July and all had to suspend after the beginning of the rainy season about October.

A natural result of this abundance of gold was to upset all standards of value as shown in prices current. Not only were the Indians at a loss to know what value to place upon gold, but even the white miners had their difficulties, for when food and necessary supplies are lacking, of what value is mere gold? The result was that prices soared. A man must eat. It would not be extravagance for him to pay $800 a barrel for flour, $400 for sugar, coffee or pork, or three dollars each for eggs, if the possession of these supplies would make possible profits in excess of costs. If the results of a day's work would net him several hundred dollars he could not afford to refuse to rent a team and wagon for fifty dollars per day, or a rocker for one hundred and fifty. Only very extraordinary conditions justified these prices, which were actually reported in the mines during the latter part of 1848.

The gold excitement had developed so unexpectedly in 1848 and was so unprecedented that it was difficult for the ordinary forms of society and government to keep pace. Some of the early miners, as in the case of Weber's Stockton Company, operated for a few months as an organized body. As a rule, however, mining activities were carried on by men as individuals who might associate with others for a brief time for a specific purpose. As the mining population increased, especially through immigration from without the province, it became necessary for the miners of each camp to come to an understanding regarding claims and other matters. Some such mining camp regulations were adopted in 1848. This, however, was a development more properly related to the period soon to follow.

Since the mining population of 1848 was composed so largely of people who had for some time resided within the borders of California, there was but little disorder and practically no crime. One or two speak of the large percentage of foreigners, but this class could by no means have been large. To be sure, there were large numbers of Indians and many native Californians, and these may inaccurately have been classed as foreign. Governor Mason, upon whom rested the responsibility of preserving order in the newly acquired territory, was very favorably impressed with the condition in the mining region.

"I was surprised to learn that crime of any kind was very unfrequent," was his report, "and that no thefts or robberies had been committed in the gold district. All live in tents, in bush houses, or in the open air, and men have frequently about their persons thousands of dollars' worth of this gold; and it was to me a matter of surprise that so peaceful and quiet a state of things should continue to exist."

Mason was not only the acting governor of California but, pending the action of Congress and the national administration at Washington, he was also the custodian of the rights of the Federal government in California. Just previous to the gold discovery he had decreed that the Mexican system of "denouncing" mines should be abolished. Under this practice any man discovering a mineral deposit could by public announcement declare his discovery, by virtue of which, and regardless of the ownership of the land, he had the right to mine for mineral provided he paid to the government its share, which amounted to one fifth of the mineral acquired. That the miners should pay the government for the opportunity to exploit its gold seemed very evident to Governor Mason, and yet how to secure this compensation was a problem he could not solve. "The entire gold district, with very few exceptions of grants made some years ago by the [Mexican] authorities, is on land belonging to the Americans. It was a matter of serious reflection with me how I could secure to the Government certain rents or fees for the privilege of securing this gold; but, upon considering the large extent of country, the character of the people engaged, and the small scattered force at my command, I resolved not to interfere, but permit all to work freely, unless broils and crimes should call for interference."

That this policy was the only one he could wisely have followed is apparent. The discovery had wrought havoc in the forces of the army under his command. Twenty-six soldiers, he reports, had deserted from the post at Sonoma; twenty-four from San Francisco, and the same number from Monterey. In fact he had difficulty in preventing his garrison from deserting in a body and to send even a few men to apprehend the deserters would result in merely adding to their number.

At the close of 1848 conditions in California were very different from what they had been twelve months before. The treaty of Guadalupe-Hidalgo had definitely transferred this land to the United States, but the apparent results from this transfer were small compared with the economic and social effects brought about by Marshall's discovery of gold. The "Americanization" of California proceeded at a pace which entirely bewildered the conservative native Californians. Practical democracy took the place of the quasi-aristocracy of the Spanish ranchero with his vaqueros and Indian retainers. The digging for gold was open to all with the advantage in favor of the humbler man who was accustomed to physical labor. The native rancheros made their way to the mines but soon returned when the physical exertion proved more than they had anticipated.

But a return to the rancho was not a return to former conditions. The vaqueros, too, had gone to the mines and had no intention of returning to their humble pursuits. With no herders, what was to become of the cattle? With Indian servants gone, what chance was there for a man to enjoy a life of ease upon his square miles of land? Alas, the California of the idle 'forties was fast passing into oblivion. On top of these undesirable changes others even greater were near at hand, for with the coming of the foreign miner from over the mountains and across the sea, not only would the risk of losing stock be increased many fold but the newcomers would even seek to dispossess the rancheros of the land itself if opportunity were offered.

With the sudden shift in population towns began to grow as if by magic at certain strategic centers. Some of them were among the mountain cañons, inaccessible places but yielding great riches; others grew up on the banks of the larger rivers where vessels dropped anchor, laden with supplies for the miners in the mountains beyond. In this manner during the year 1848 began the settlements from which emerged the mountain towns of Bidwell's Bar, Auburn, Coloma, Placerville, Sutter Creek, Mokelumne Hill, and Sonora, all in the gold region. At the same time, along the rivers, two rival cities were just beginning to rise to importance. As a depot for the southern mines, Charles M. Weber had turned his attention to the promotion of Tuleburg, rechristened Stockton, while further north upon the low country at the mouth of the American River, the town of Sacramento seemed to grow up spontaneously.

Sutter's Fort was removed from the Sacramento River some two miles or more. It was necessary, therefore, for goods to be freighted across to the fort, which by common consent came to be the immediate objective point of all the gold seekers during the months just following the discovery. Here were obtained supplies for the mines on the American River. Of the scene along the embarcadero and at the fort, one observer in 1848 gives us this picture: "Boatmen were shouting and swearing; waggoners were whistling and hallooing, and cracking their whips at their straining horses, as they toiled along with heavily laden wagons to the different stores within the building; groups of horsemen were riding to and fro, and crowds of people were moving about on foot. It was evident that the gold fever increased as the eagerly longed-for El Dorado was approached. Every store and shed was being crammed with bales of goods, barrels of flour, and a thousand other things for which a demand had suddenly sprung up. The captain's own house was like a hotel crowded with more visitors than it could accommodate."

It was soon found that Sutter's Fort could not accommodate the coming throng. Consequently along the river there arose a camp of miners which grew rapidly into a town. This was, to be sure, on land claimed by Sutter, but since it was not used by him for any practical purposes, the miners did not scruple to put their needs before his claims.

The effect of the gold rush upon Marshall and Sutter is a pathetic story, for neither was able to cope with the complicated problems and revolutionary conditions imposed. Their plan to hold the Mormon workmen at the mill until its completion was successful, largely due to the high character of the men themselves; but their attempt to keep the news a secret was doomed to failure, partly because of their own actions. By the aid of Indians and Sandwich Islanders Sutter mined large quantities of gold on the South Fork and later at Sutter's Creek, but the gold seems not to have been retained. The influx of miners brought men far too shrewd for even the scheming Swiss who had so successfully competed with the Mexican officials. The loss of laborers was in reality the greatest calamity to Sutter, for soon his flour mill was left in an unfinished state; his fields were forced to go untilled; leather was left to rot in the tanning vats. The sawmill at Coloma was run for a short time, when Sutter disposed of his interest and withdrew. The new life and confusion around the fort was distasteful to the lord of the manor, who sought retirement at Hock Farm on the Feather River.

With Marshall the results were even more keenly felt than with Sutter. He was lacking in practicality and was utterly unable to adjust himself to the unusual conditions among which he suddenly found himself. His discovery of gold, as we have seen, had been entirely accidental; he merely happened to be the agent by which the existence of gold became known. While it may be urged that he is deserving of no extraordinary credit for this epoch-making event, it is nevertheless unfortunate that he should not have received greater consideration from the gold-seekers who crowded in upon his rights. Although the claims of Sutter and Marshall to the lands at Coloma had not been recognized by Governor Mason, they attempted during the summer of 1848 to collect a fee from all who desired to mine there. For a time this demand was paid, but later it was refused.

Because of Indian troubles elsewhere, late arrivals assumed a hostile attitude toward the Indians employed by Marshall. In defending these he incurred the wrath of the miners and was even forced temporarily to leave Coloma. Upon his return things were not the same. Invading miners not only occupied the river bars but had even cut down the standing timber, thus ruining the prospects for the mill, which was soon abandoned.

This unfortunate treatment of Marshall caused him to become despondent and misanthropic. His remarkable tales of his ability to discover gold, together with his ideas of spiritualism, caused him even further trouble. Many were led to believe that he had occult powers of discovery, and when he failed to produce the results expected of him he not only lost the support but even incurred the animosity of his erstwhile friends. Under the hallucination that all the great benefits of the gold deposits to mankind were the direct outcome of his personal achievement, he came to feel that the public was greatly indebted to him. In fact, due to a lack of business sense made worse by a strong impulse to treat generously anyone apparently less fortunate than himself, he was not able to husband even the resources he already had. In

1872 the state legislature appropriated for him a pension of two hundred dollars per month. In 1874 this was cut to one hundred dollars and was not continued in 1876. His later life was spent as a gardener in the vicinity of Kelsey and Coloma where he died in 1885. His end was truly pathetic, but due more to his own weakness than to any ingratitude on the part of his fellow-men. Great riches were within his grasp, but he lacked the ability to retain them.

Chapter VI

CHAPTER VI

Nature's Treasure-Trove

WITH THE discovery of gold, the Sierra Nevada suddenly assumed a new rôle in the drama of history. Hitherto its chief purpose seemed to have been to serve as a great Wall of China—a barrier to shut out immigration from the East. Its snow-covered peaks were high, its passes exceptionally few and many there had been who had sacrificed property and even life in the attempt to cross its granite barrier. Furthermore, here was the refuge for the savage Indian, the lair of the grizzly bear and mountain lion. Happy was the emigrant when this mighty mountain range had been left behind him. But now things were different—the eyes of the world were turned with new interest toward these same mountains, for within their bosom was hidden that most coveted element—gold.

The Sierra Nevada is one of the dominant physical features of California. Its value is now no longer measured in terms of its mineral wealth alone; its raging streams furnish hydro-electric power to run the industry of distant towns, its snowy mountain tops furnish life-giving waters to desert farms and thirsty cities. Its scenic beauties are known the world over and it is fast becoming the great playground for California and her thousands of tourists. Its Alpine heights arouse the admiration of all, for clustered here are the highest peaks in the United States: one hundred and twenty of them over 9,000 feet; forty over 12,000 feet; fifteen over 14,000 feet and Mount Whitney, 14,501—the loftiest peak in the United States. Seven active glaciers move slowly down these mountain sides and glacial lakes are numbered by the hundreds.

The geologists tell us that this massive range is a great diastrophic block or section of the earth's crust, which has been upheaved bodily and tilted toward the west. On the east, its lofty summits tower high above the great interior basin, a short distance away; while to the west for nearly one hundred miles, dashing mountain streams gather and unite to form great river systems which have carved out scenic cañons through which they flow before they reach the distant plains. The life history of this range is plainly inscribed in tablets of stone far antedating those of the human hand. These the geologist reads with interest and thus interprets for us the happenings of eons long past. While this wonderful story does not fall within the scope of our present interest we are, nevertheless, concerned with that part of it which may help to answer the question: Whence came the gold of the Sierra Nevada, and by what method was it distributed?

In order to think in terms of geological eras, it becomes necessary for us to remember that man's existence has occupied but a short portion of the earth's history. On the slopes of the Sierra are to be found the giant Sequoias which rightfully arouse our wonder and admiration. Botanists tell us that four milleniums have passed since these giant trees began their growth. In terms of human life this long period is almost beyond comprehension; yet before even the soil was prepared to give these trees a bed in which to grow, ages upon ages had already passed away and from a geological point of view these ancient

[98]

trees, the world's oldest living objects, are to be classed in the most recent period.

Back in what the geologists term the Paleozoic era, they tell us there appears to have been a land area in what is now Nevada, extending westward to the present crest of the Sierra Nevada. This was later depressed and for a long period a shallow sea covered the whole surface from the Pacific Ocean as far east as central or eastern Nevada. Great amounts of earth, washed from the Rocky Mountains on the east, laid down deep deposits on the floor of this sea. This period is referred to as the Juratrias Age and this body of water as the Jurassic Sea.

As other ages passed, internal forces caused further changes in the earth's surface. It was then that the Sierra Nevada was heaved upward and probably the Coast Range also formed, leaving an extensive gulf lying between the two ranges. This upheaval was the result of great pressure and strain. The deposits upon the floor of the old Jurassic Sea were compressed into rock formation known as slate, shale and schists. The extreme heat changed the nature of this rock into a semi-fluid state, while great masses of liquid granite were forced upward leaving great granite intrusions among the slate and schists. These rocks thus acted upon are referred to as bed-rock formation in order to distinguish them from the rocks laid down at later periods. Since this area, formerly a sea bottom, had been uplifted bodily, its surface was fairly even; but along the western slope, more gentle than at present, the forces of nature soon began their work of disintegration. Streams became rivers with definite channels and valleys, gravel bars and deltas. To the geologist these are known as Neocene or Tertiary rivers. Inasmuch as gold was quite generally scattered through the great mass of the bed-rock series, the gravel beds of these ancient streams came to be great treasure houses of gold, which when it had once been torn from the bed-rock, sought a resting place in the lowest parts of the river beds.

The geologist, working with the miner in his tunnel and shaft, has in many cases reconstructed the great drainage system of this period of long ago. While not all the present rivers had Neocene ancestors, several of the ancient rivers followed courses so similar to the present streams that they are designated by the present-day names. Thus there were the Neocene ancestors of the Yuba, American, Mokelumne, Calaveras and Tuolumne rivers. Of these rivers the ancient Yuba was by far the most important, for it drained the westward slopes of the Neocene mountains of the present area of Sierra, Placer and the northern portion of El Dorado counties. The Neocene Calaveras also drained a large area, including not only the present Calaveras but southern Amador and northern Tuolumne counties as well. On the other hand, there seem to have been no large rivers to correspond to the present Feather or Bear River; the Neocene American River was not much greater than South Fork of the present stream, while the early Mokelumne was more like the later Cosumnes, a portion of whose area it drained. South of the primeval Calaveras River flowed the Neocene Tuolumne, following much the present course of that river from its source near Mt. Dana to the foothills in western Tuolumne County.

It is noted that their descent was less marked than that of the later streams. This would mean that greater time would be required to cut out channels, but on the other hand there would be a tendency to deposit their load along their courses rather than to carry it on to the inland gulf that occupied the present Great Valley. From the enormous amount of debris deposited by these streams, it is evident that their work was continued through vast periods of time.

As ages passed, the earth's forces once again were set in motion. The ridges of the Sierra Nevada were now heaved skyward until a mighty mountain range effectively shut off the interior basin, while internal convulsions caused great masses of molten lava to flow out of the fissures along the fault lines near the mountain crest. The mountains were built up higher still as this liquid rock flowed down the slopes filling the ancient river cañons and seeming to cover for all time the golden treasure lying in their beds. The Sierra Nevada, with sloping sides of hardening lava rock, now stood a towering, defiant mass, twenty thousand feet above the level of the sea.

But nature builds up only to tear down and to work over anew. These mountain heights caught the moisture-laden winds from off the sea and packed their summits deep with ice and snow. As time went on, this frozen mass accumulated until at last it began to move slowly down in great rivers of ice. These glacial giants, tearing rocks from the mountain sides and holding them securely in their frozen grasp, used them as planes and chisels to smooth off obtruding heights or to sculpture out the gigantic U-shaped cañons which are now so common in the High Sierra. As the ice melted it took the form of torrential streams which swept pell-mell down the mountain slopes, carrying with them in their mad rush the decomposing lava and rock formations and cutting new channels down through the rock until at last these rivers had cut deep into the mountain mass, leaving the wonderful V-shaped cañons that are the delight and admiration of the mountain lover. Thus were formed the deep cañons of Feather, Yuba, American, Mokelumne, Tuolumne, Merced and many other Sierra Nevada rivers.

Since the lava deposits had in many cases completely obliterated the ancient river channels, these later, or Pleistocene, rivers could not follow the exact course of their ancestral streams and often new and independent channels were carved out. The forces which elevated the Sierra Nevada ridge naturally raised the sources of rivers, so that the present streams, because of steeper descent, were able to cut more rapidly than were the ancient rivers. It would also appear that during this later transformation the slope of the mountain was changed more to the southwest rather than west. The newer streams all had a decided tendency to follow a southwesterly direction, while the Neocene river channels pursued a westerly course. This is especially noticeable in considering the Neocene Yuba and Calaveras rivers, which occupied territory now drained by the north forks of their neighboring streams to the south. This change of direction of incline caused the new rivers in many cases to cut new channels obliquely across the former river beds which lay buried beneath the lava. Inasmuch as the steeper incline gave these later rivers extraordinary erosive power, they not only cut their way down to the beds of the former rivers, but went deeper still, until now portions of the gravel of the old Neocene rivers are to be found under a cap of hardened lava, far up the sides of the present mountain cañons, while other portions have been swept away by the later rivers to be deposited in gravel bars along their channels or in the alluvium of the plains and lowlands below.

These forces that built the great Sierra Nevada were the agencies that gave California her most valuable golden treasures. The principal gold belt of California lies within the area of the Sierra Nevada and occupies about nine thousand square miles. However, gold has been found in other parts of the state, and not all of the area of the Sierra Nevada has been found to produce gold. In the northern portion of the Sierra, gold is found over nearly the whole width of the range, but the gold producing area narrows in width at its southern part. While gold is to be found in the extreme northern portion of the Sierra Nevada, the great lava fields lying between Mt. Lassen and Mt. Shasta have effectively covered it. The gold fields of the Trinity and Klamath district are probably an extension of the same great gold belt. Further south, gold has been found to exist in the granite bedrock that makes up the southern portion of the Sierra Nevada range, but it has been in relatively small quantities.

Much of the gold-bearing gravel, as we have seen, was deposited during the Neocene period. In some parts of the gold region these gravel deposits are much more noticeable than in others. One of the richest districts lies east of Nevada City and Grass Valley, in Nevada County. These gravel beds have been exposed by the erosion of the more recent streams and often lie high above the beds of the present rivers, for in many cases the river channels have cut through these old gravel beds and in places have entirely removed them.

Geologists and mining engineers have divided these gravel deposits into five classes: first, deep gravel; second, bench gravel; third, gravel of the rhyolitic or early volcanic epoch; fourth, gravel of the inter-volcanic epoch; and fifth, gravel of later andesitic lava. The deeper gravels are well-worn pebbles and cobblestones of the bedrock materials, usually very coarse and compact and are found near the bottom of the river channel. They are usually rich in gold, especially when near the bedrock. Bench gravels lie above the deep gravels, sometimes to a depth of two hundred to three hundred feet, and are frequently spread out over the floors of the main valleys for a great distance. In them are to be found many quartz pebbles but none of lava, while sand and clay are usually mixed with these gravels and cover them. The early volcanic eruption in the Sierra Nevada was made up of rhyolitic lava which dammed up many of the streams, causing them to deposit their load of rock and sand. Immediately the streams began their attack upon this recently deposited softer rock, with the consequence that mixed with the gold-bearing gravel are also to be found pebbles of rhyolitic lava. As these lava deposits increase the relative quantity of gold decreases.

These ancient rivers, as in the case of modern ones, deposited their debris in depressions some of which are narrow and deep, others broad and shallow. When not too greatly eroded by recent streams the old channels may be followed along regular courses, which indicate that they were once continuous gravel-filled streams. On the lower levels the flood plains of these streams were wide and extensive, but as they are traced toward the summit of the Sierra they are found to become smaller and less distinct.

Thus far attention has been directed especially toward the consideration of gold-bearing gravels, but gold is also found implanted within the bedrock itself. There it appears in quartz which has been deposited in veins or fissures by water action. While quartz veins may be found in any of those rocks known in the gold region as the bedrock series, they are especially found in the slate, sandstone, serpentine and other rocks making up certain formations. The fissures which are found to contain the gold-bearing quartz are not of uniform size, for they may be large or small, irregular or straight or split up into many smaller veins. They are seldom very long, two or three miles being an extraordinary length. The larger ones, however, are usually located in fissures running in general parallel series. These veins are of great importance, for without doubt the gold-bearing gravels all were originally from this source.

The principal gold quartz belt of the Sierra Nevada is known as the Mother Lode. This series of veins appears to underlie the greater part of the gold belt, but north of the middle fork of the American River it splits up into a number of seams and cannot be described as one belt or lode. As a consequence the name is usually restricted to a series of gold quartz veins lying south of the Cosumnes River, especially from Plymouth, Amador County, in a southeasterly direction into Mariposa County near the town of Coulterville. The length of the Mother Lode is about seventy miles.

Thus runs the story of the Sierra Nevada as read in the accounts left us by the Neocene rivers and the Mother Lode. Whether or not the Sierra of the Neocene period was richer in gold than the mountains of our recent epoch may be a matter of dispute, but of this we are certain: that through long ages the ancient rivers were patiently digging from the mountain sides their golden pebbles, storing them away upon the bedrock at the bottom of the channels, while at the same time sub-terranean streams were likewise at work gathering up particles of gold and stowing them one by one in the crevices of the rocks to make up the marvelous wealth of the Mother Lode. Here indeed was Nature's own treasure-trove, the accumu-lation of ages which was to give to California the unassailable title of Land of Gold.

Chapter VII

CHAPTER VII

The Miner at Work

"Iron is heaped in mountain piles,
And gluts the laggard forges;
But gold-flakes gleam in dim defiles
And lonely gorges."
— *Holland*

THE TASK before the men of Gold Days was twofold: first to find the precious metal, and second to extract it from the gravel beds and quartz rock. The search for gold, or rather for the richest gold deposits, was a most important factor in mining life and gave to the whole region a restlessness not to be found in other communities. This restlessness aided greatly in the rapid exploration of the Sierra Nevada during the Gold Days. The uneasiness was the natural result of the conditions in which the men found themselves. They had been torn from their usual occupations by a mad desire to become rich, to secure a fortune in as short a time as possible. Not only did this mean an occupation new to most of these men, but the country itself was also strange and their whole environment new. Under these circumstances we should not be surprised to find men uncertain that their immediate location offered them the best chance for riches.

Because of this uncertainty, explorers or "prospectors" covered the cañons and mountain sides of the Sierra Nevada much like ants working around a disturbed hill, in their feverish desire to be the first to discover rich diggings. Sometimes they went singly, but frequently a small company of men would start out, each laden with a pick and shovel on his shoulder, a gold pan in hand, and armed with revolver and knife in his belt. Upon his back he would often carry several days' supply of food, frying-pan, blankets and other necessary articles. Sometimes he took a mule to help carry his packs, but an animal was frequently more a cause for anxiety than a help, for if the trails were steep and the cañons dangerous the animal was apt to fall and break its back or neck. If snow was to be crossed the hoofs of the mule would sink beneath his weight; also, with an animal along, a foot-log could not serve as a bridge across a rushing mountain stream.

During the early part of the gold rush the rivers were considered the most likely places for finding gold, consequently the prospector directed his attention especially to river beds, cañons and gulches. When he had located a spot that appeared desirable he would begin with pick, shovel and pan. If the first panful proved to be promising he would consider that he had found "pay-dirt" and continue his operations. Every particle of gold found in the pan was called "color." If there were even a few particles of gold he had "found color." The value of a gold deposit was determined by the prospector in accordance with the result from one or more panfuls of gold "prospect." He might estimate it at "ten cents to the pan," "one dollar to the pan" or whatever the value might be.

One of the first things done by a miner who had discovered a location which appeared to be profitable was to stake off a "claim," which would include the amount of ground allowed him under the laws and customs of the

locality. He would then be ready to begin active operations developing his mine. If the "prospects" were not indicative of sufficient richness he moved on to another place.

During the early Gold Days in California practically all the miners confined their attention to what were known as "placer mines." Placer mining has been defined as the gathering, by mechanical means, of native or free gold found in alluvial deposits on or near the earth's surface. Because of the mixture of gold with other materials the first operation necessary was that of digging, hence the mines became referred to as "the diggings." They were divided into two kinds: first, those along the stream banks or in the river bars which were referred to as "wet diggings," or as "bars"; second, those located upon flats or the beds of gullies which for a large portion of the year were without running water. These later mines were known as "dry diggings." Practically all the operations of placer mining are based upon the principle that gold has a greater specific gravity than most elements, a quality which causes it to be less easily transported by the stream-currents which carry along with them the detritus torn from the mountain sides by their erosive force. Gold, then, is frequently to be found among the sand, gravel and rocks at the very bottom of the streams, usually upon the bedrock itself.

With this elemental knowledge the men of 'Forty-nine followed up the river channels searching them carefully for gold deposits, even turning aside the streams in order to clean the gravel beds lying under the usual water courses. Their method of search was simple, so at first were also the means employed in separating the gold from the baser materials. Soon more effective methods of washing gold were sought by the hard-working miners and Yankee ingenuity was not long in finding mechanical means of performing this task. Thus, there developed a rapid evolution of mining methods and appliances which made the process more economical and efficient. The first operation began with the miner's pan, then came the "rocker" or "cradle," followed by the "long tom," then the "sluice" or "riffle-box" and later "ground sluicing" and hydraulic mining in which the force of water is made to perform both the digging and washing processes.

The men at Sutter's mill during the early weeks of 1848 knew practically nothing regarding the properties of gold or of mining methods. Soon, however, use was made of the simplest of the mechanical means of washing gold, namely the pan. In the rush to find equipment suitable for washing gold, any kind of a pan or basin was brought into use, even wooden bowls and Indian baskets found their place; but when conditions became adjusted so that the demand could in some proper measure be met, the miner's pan came to assume certain standard proportions. It was constructed of the best of iron, if possible stamped out of one single sheet. In shape it was similar to a common milk pan familiar to former generations, but with sides more flaring. The usual dimensions were about ten inches in diameter at the bottom, sixteen inches at the top with a depth of about two and one fourth inches. Usually a heavy iron wire rim strengthened the top of the pan.

The experienced miner came by habit to divide the operation of washing gold into several steps. After having selected the dirt or gravel he desired to wash, he placed a portion of it in his pan and, kneeling by the side of a stream, he filled the pan with water; the pan was then placed upon the ground while the lumps of dirt were broken up and the contents stirred with his fingers until a soft mass was formed. The pan was again submerged and the mud and lighter particles allowed to be washed away. This action was assisted by a gentle agitation of the pan. Thus the finer and lighter particles were carried off while the gravel and coarse sand sank to the bottom. When all the mud or "slickens" had been removed by the water, the larger pebbles and gravel in the bottom of the pan were then carefully examined and, if found to contain no gold, they were thrown out. More water was used and carefully the coarsest particles were separated and rejected. If the operations had been done skilfully the contents of the pan would have been greatly reduced but without the loss of any of the gold which lay hidden at the bottom of the vessel. More skill was then required to see that even this remaining coarser material be separated from the gold. With the pan partly under water the miner slowly agitated the particles so that the coarse sand was slowly washed out in a very thin stream over the rim of the pan, every particle passing under the vigilant eye of the miner. If properly done but little foreign matter had been left in the pan with the gold. Then with a very little water the gold and sand were separated in a skilful manner, leaving only the gold in the bottom of the pan. Inasmuch as a black sand of igneous origin has a specific gravity similar to that of gold, it was sometimes very hard to separate by water action. In that case the residue was allowed to dry and the black sand removed by the use of a magnet or other means.

Ryan, who visited the southern mines during 1849, describes a variation of this process which he calls "dry washing":

"I came up next with a group of three Sonorans, or inhabitants of Sonora, busily engaged on a small sandy flat —the only one I had observed—at the bottom of the ravine. There was no water near, although I noticed several holes which had evidently been sunk in quest of it. These men were actively pursuing a process that is termed 'dry-washing.' One was shovelling up the sand into a large cloth, stretched out upon the ground, and which, when it was tolerably well covered, he took up by the corners, and shook until the pebbles and larger particles of stone and dirt came to the surface. These he brushed away carefully with his hand, repeating the process of shaking and clearing until the residue was sufficiently fine for the next operation. This was performed by the other men, who, depositing the sand in large bowls hewn out of a solid block of wood, which they held in their hands, dexterously cast the contents up before them, about four feet into the air, catching the sand again very cleverly, and blowing at it as it descended. This process being repeated, the sand gradually disappeared; and from two to three ounces of pure gold remained at the bottom of the bowl. Easy as the operation appeared to me to be, I learned, from inquiry, that to perform it successfully required the nicest management, the greatest perseverance, and especially robust lungs."

The pan was still retained by the "prospector" even after it had been discarded by efficient miners for more rapid methods. It was estimated that an industrious man could wash out fifty pans of gold in a day.

The first improvement over the pan was made in the introduction of the "rocker" or "cradle." It is said that these were introduced into the California mines during 1848 either by Isaac Humphrey, a Georgia miner, or by Ruelle, a Frenchman in Sutter's employ. The rocker is described as an oblong box about four feet long, two feet wide and nine inches deep at the higher end. A bar divided the box in the middle, the lower end being left with a very low end-board. The top of the rocker, which was inclined at an angle to cause the water to flow freely, was open. Another box with perforated sheet-iron bottom was made to fit into the upper half. This was known as the "hopper." Its depth was about four inches. Beneath

the hopper was a canvas "apron," placed at an angle of about thirty degrees with its lower end near the upper part of the cradle. The apron was so placed that the dirt in being washed through the water would have to pass over this apron and down onto the floor of the cradle. Much fine gold was caught by the apron itself, and it was made so that it could be readily removed for cleaning. The box was mounted on rockers so that by means of a handle fastened to its side it could be rocked back and forth like a child's cradle.

The method of operation was simple and in many ways similar to the work with the pan. The cradle operator dipped water from a near-by stream and poured it upon the mass in the hopper with one hand while he gently rocked the cradle with the other. The rocking of the cradle served both to aid the water in dissolving the dirt in the hopper and also by its constant motion kept the sand on the bottom agitated so that the lighter elements could be separated from the gold. As the water dissolved the gold-bearing material, it dropped through onto the apron which threw it back near the upper end of the cradle floor across which were fixed cleats about one inch in height to form a "riffle-bar." The lighter sand and dirt passed over these but the gold was caught and held.

After the mass had been thoroughly washed, the coarse gravel and boulders would be thrown away and the hopper was ready for another load. Whenever the miner thought necessary, he would clean the sand and gold from the apron, riffle-bars and bottom. When the claim was especially rich this might be done several times a day, the greatest amount of gold usually being found on the canvas apron. While the cradle was a great improvement over the pan, it was not economical or efficient, for much of the gold was lost, and so it was in turn soon displaced for more advanced methods of operation. It long remained, however, a favorite machine for the Chinese even after it had been discarded by the American.

Since both the pan and cradle were essentially adapted to the operation of one man, they were too slow for the eager miners. Some more expeditious method was necessary. As a result of this demand there was developed the "long tom," which for a time at least promised to fill all the needs of placer mining as an economical, efficient and convenient method of washing gold, when used by a company of from three to five men.

The early toms were little else than troughs constructed from hollowed logs. But they rapidly developed in form and soon came to be built of lumber and lined with sheet iron. The toms were not of uniform size but were varied according to the number of men to make use of them. The average tom was, however, a trough about twelve to fourteen feet in length open at the top and at both ends. It was about eight to ten inches in depth and its width varied from one to two feet at the upper end to three or four feet at the lower end. This lower portion of the tom was spoken of as the "riddle" and took the place of the hopper in the rocker, for it was equipped with a heavy perforated sheet-iron bottom which permitted the mass of earth and water to pass through to a riffle-box similar to, but larger than, that of the cradle.

When ready for use, the tom was placed in a position near the dirt or gravel to be washed, and a small stream of water turned into the upper end of the trough. The amount of the water required was spoken of as a "tom-head," which became a definite unit for the measurement of water. While two or three men shovelled dirt into the tom to be washed down by the force of the water, another with shovel or other implement kept the dirt and gravel constantly agitated so that it would dissolve and pass through the riddle to the riffle-box below. As the stones and boulders accumulated they would be cast aside. The gold itself was caught in the riffle-box where the water action kept the sand and mud in constant state of agitation. Since the gold sank to the bottom, it was held by the cross-cleats while the "tailings" or waste sand and gravel were being washed out at the lower end of the tom.

The next development after the long tom was the "sluice box." This was especially adapted to those places where large quantities of dirt were to be washed out and where water was plentiful and the descent was both steep and long enough to permit the operation with advantage.

The "sluice box" was merely an uncovered trough constructed in sections of about twelve feet in length. It was usually constructed of three planks, one each for the bottom and two sides. The height of the sides was about ten inches but the bottom varied in width from one foot to forty inches. It was usually sawed so as to be two or more inches wider at the upper than at the lower end. Cleats at both top and bottom prevented the trough from spreading or splitting. Any number of these boxes could be fitted together each into the end of the other and when supported on the ground or on trestle work would provide a continuous waterway or sluice from fifty to one hundred feet in length, as might be desired. Inasmuch as the sluice could be extended indefinitely, the additional length gave added action upon the dirt and made possible the separating and securing of more gold. This then came to be the accepted method for placer mining whenever it could be applied.

The sluice, if efficiently used, required the operation of several men, the number depending upon the amount of water and the nature of the dirt, because the current must not become clogged by overloading. The force of the water carried dirt, sand, gravel and boulders all before it down the sluice, but this action had to be assisted by men with their shovels and hoes as in the case of the long tom. To prevent the gold from being washed through the sluice, riffle-boxes or false bottoms were placed at intervals along the box. These were wooden cleats which lay crosswise to arrest the gold and the heavier particles. Quicksilver was usually also placed in the boxes above the riffles to catch the gold as it was washed about by the stream. Quicksilver has such an affinity for gold that it soon collected many of the smaller particles forming them into an amalgam.

The sluice could run for a week without cleaning, which became a favorite task for Sunday. In the meanwhile it was necessary to guard carefully the sluice boxes, for the temptation to thieves was very great, although the miner had little mercy for any suspicious character found in the vicinity of the sluice boxes at night. The clean-up was simple. Water was run down the sluice until all sediment disappeared, then a small stream was allowed to continue while the upper riffle-boxes were removed, one at a time, the stream, meanwhile, washing the remaining sand, gold and amalgam on down to the lower boxes. In this way all the gold-laden material was removed to be more carefully cleaned by means of the miner's pan. The next task was to separate the quicksilver from the gold dust. To do this the gold and quicksilver were gathered into a buckskin bag and as much of the mercury squeezed out as possible, then by treating the remaining amalgam in a retort the mercury would be drawn off and recondensed, leaving the pure gold.

Space does not permit a discussion of the many fake and useless devices and appliances suggested or tried during the earlier Gold Days. Without any practical knowledge of the conditions of the mines, many inventive Yankees had created contrivances which they believed would make their fortunes secure as soon as they had reached the gold mines. One of these is described by William Shaw as "The Patent Centrifugal Gold-Washer and California Chrysolite," which he says was a great unwieldy tub which the manufacturers had brought to San Francisco early in 1849. This, he says, was but one of many similar contraptions that could be purchased "as cheap as stinking mackerel." On the banks of the Sacramento River many other gold machines were abandoned for pick, shovel and pan.

While the early miners had dreams of mountains of gold, they found their greatest profits were to be obtained from the river beds and in the gravel bars along the channel of the favored streams. A river bar occurs at any place where the movement of the current is sufficiently slowed up to permit the deposit of gravel or sand. Bars are also to be found at the bends of the river where the eddying current has made deposits on the inner or concave bank of the curve. These river bars along the Sierra Nevada were usually rich in gold which had been gathered and stored away by the streams as they cut their channels through the quartz veins or auriferous gravels of the ancient pre-glacial rivers. The gold itself was found in the gravel and usually near the bedrock or in crevices or pockets within the bedrock itself. Since this mining was done in or along the river beds it was known as "river mining." Although the gravel bars along the river banks were first to receive the attention of the miners, when these had been washed of their gold, attention was turned to the bed of the stream. Since these stream beds were found to be rich in gold, the men of 'Forty-nine, in their eagerness and inexperience, exploited them with "far greater energy than judgment." How to secure the gold from the stream beds was a problem. William Kelly, who writes of his "Stroll through the Diggings," relates the following:

"I saw some Kanakas (who are perhaps the most expert divers in the world) go down and bring up fine chunks, which suggested the construction of a dredging machine; but it could not be got to work with effect, from the inequalities of the bottom. Diving-bells were also thought of, but I never saw any in use."

The diving apparatus here referred to was actually used during 1849 along the American River, but not with success. It was not satisfactorily explained whether the failure was due to any fault of the equipment or to the inability of the operator. The results, however, seemed to be always the same. The diver came up more dead than alive and without any gold. We may easily imagine that the weight of the diving helmet together with the swiftness of the current were a great hindrance to the effective mining operations that would be required on the stream bed.

The usual method was to divert the current by means of "wing dams." These were built of stone, brush and dirt and extended only a part of the way across, then down the stream and back, thus confining the water to a narrow channel and leaving exposed a part of the river bed. Sometimes the entire stream would be dammed and the water turned aside through a ditch or flume.

Mrs. Eliza Farnham was especially impressed by the way the miners turned the streams out of their channels to get at the golden gravels. She wrote:

"It is curious to see, in these regions, how nature is forced out of her lawful ways. Some of the largest mountain streams of California are now lifted from their beds for miles, and the earth, over which they have rolled since the edict 'Thus far and no farther' was spoken to them, is being searched and researched, washed and rewashed, one year after another.

"As you approach them, the noise of the toms and of the swift current rushing through the narrow artificial channels into which it is forced, the hum of voices and

the clink of spades among the gravel, rise up from the deep chasms to the very tops of the mountains that almost overhang them."

These works were of course only temporary and could be used only during the low-water season late in the summer. Because of the hazard of early rains the labor of construction was often entirely lost before any profits could be realized. The stupendous amount of labor expended upon these river claims cannot be estimated. Great companies of miners would join together to try their luck. Heavy logs would be cut and transported for use in the dam construction; flumes from one hundred yards to a mile or more in length would be built of planks and canvas and carried on supports down the river cañon; numerous wheel contrivances would be rigged up to pump the water from the bottom of the excavation.

These pumps were queer-looking contrivances but served their purpose admirably. The wheels which revolved by force of the current were connected by pulleys to belts upon which were attached buckets or other containers which filled, and lifted the water from the depression. Other necessary equipment consisted of tramway, trestles, sluices, rockers and other tools besides the workshops and cabin. The cost would reach thousands of dollars. Since the season at best was short the work was rushed at the greatest speed in order to obtain all the results possible before the river would rise too high to be controlled by dam and flume. Too often before the anxious miners had completed their work the angry waters would rush down upon them and carry all their labor as so much refuse before it. The occasional great profits caused many miners to cooperate in such schemes for the first few years, but it is doubtful whether the net returns greatly exceeded the labor cost.

River mining was not always certain even when not

damaged by early floods. In 1849 a number of men decided
to turn the Mokelumne River from its course. More than
13,000 feet of lumber was consumed in the building of a
flume. After a great amount of labor had been expended
on dam and flume and the miners were looking for many
thousands of dollars in reward for their labor, the entire
gold deposit was found in the spot first prospected and
amounted to but $160. The scheme had been projected on
the basis of the gold found in that one place along the
stream.

From Delano's description of his experiences upon the
Feather River, we can see some of the difficulties of the
miner:

"When the river was low enough, in June and July following, we reassembled, and began the work of building
the dams. I then had charge of the work at Stringtown,
while Billinghurst took that of the Ottawa bar. After
finally finishing my work, at an expense of sixteen thousand dollars, and getting into the bed of the stream, we
did not get the first farthing for our labor and our pains.
The unprecedented high waters of 1850 rendered it impossible to drain the water on the Ottawa bar, and we
were obliged to abandon it, or starve; but we had the
satisfaction of learning that in 1851, when the water was
very low, a company of Chinese took possession of it, and
took out from fifty to a hundred dollars a day for many
days. So that the harvest, which was almost within our
reach, was reaped by others, and they foreigners and
aliens . . . .

"For forty miles along the South Fork of Feather River,
the stream was dammed whenever it was practicable,
some of the dams costing, in labor and necessary expenditures, fifty to eighty thousand dollars, and not one paid a
moiety of its cost. Below Stringtown dam about a mile,
an energetic and enterprising company erected a splendid

dam, and dug a race at an expense of thirty-two thousand dollars, expending four thousand dollars which they had dug the previous fall, and all that they got when completed was fifteen cents! They were completely wrecked, and their company broke up hopelessly in debt, a portion of which was for the provisions on which they had subsisted during the winter."

Even aside from the uncertainty and risks involved, work in the river mines was not without its hardships, as is to be seen from the following words of a physician who visited the mines in 1849:

"At the bottom of steep rocky glens or ravines, through which a small stream flows, with banks so high and precipitous that you can not walk over them, except on the little dusty paths worn in their sides, and up to his knees in muddy water, with which his clothes are well bedabbled, plying a pickax or shovel, or rocking a washer, behold the gold-seeker! The sun pours his scorching rays upon his devoted head. Sometimes he will work, day after day and week after week, in a stooping posture, at as severe toil and great exposure as man ever felt or knew, and scarcely get a return for his labor.

"On the rivers, shut in as they are by high, steep, rocky and almost impassable hills, much sickness prevails among the miners during the summer and fall months. The latter is the most productive season, as the waters are then low, and the fine particles of gold deposited, can be reached and washed out of the sand, mud, and rocks, where they are found on the bars and in the bed of the streams. Scarcely a breath of air penetrates these deep cañons, while the sun shines with unclouded fervor, frequently bringing the thermometer to 110° in the shade. This to the miner, at his arduous and unaccustomed toil, is dreadfully severe and almost necessarily results in brain-fever or a billious-typhoid. Care and prudence could to some extent obviate these difficulties. But who is careful or who is prudent in the pursuit of gold in California?"

Although the earliest mining was along the river beds, the men of the Gold Days soon came to find gold in "dry diggings" as well. The discovery of these gold deposits followed naturally, for the gravel banks of the ancient rivers were very similar to the deposits of the later streams, even though often far removed from any present-day stream. While the river bars could be worked with success only during the season of low water, these other deposits were most easily operated when the winter rains filled the cañons with numerous lesser streams. Thus it was that when work in the streams was no longer possible the attention of the miner was turned to the cañons and gulches and gravel bars which were still exposed. These mines became known as "dry diggings." The winter season furnished an excellent opportunity for work on these claims. The winter of 1849 was a very wet season, and as a result many camps were established where in seasons of less rainfall it was not possible to operate. In the early days the miner often carried the rich dirt on his back or by mule cart to a convenient waterway for washing, or the summer's labor might be expended gathering the dirt in some spot to be washed out when the rains would have supplied the needed water. As time went on flumes were constructed and water carried for miles along mountain sides and across deep ravines to thirsty dry diggings, and later still the hydraulic process furnished a more efficient means for operating this class of mines.

"Hydraulic mining" is a term applied to the mining process whereby large streams of water under heavy pressure are thrown against gravel banks with such force that they are washed away, permitting the segregation of the heavier gold-bearing gravel from the lighter materials. This process came about quite naturally, for when men began to use the sluice it was found that in some kinds of material flumes could in part be dispensed with and the water current itself made to help strip off the top dirt.

In operating by this method a channel would be dug through the earth that was to be washed away. Sometimes this would be equipped with a sluice box and riffles at its lower end, but frequently not. The water action would be used to wear away the soil and gravel which would then be carried through the "ground sluice," or ditch prepared to catch the heavier material. If any gold passed through, the miner trusted that it would collect at the bottom of the channel in the natural way. Frequently he would place boulders along the bottom of the waterway to arrest the heavier particles and gold. After washing the claim in this manner attention would be turned to the floor of the ground sluice which would show whether gold had been collected or not. This would be ascertained by the use of rocker, long tom or wooden sluice box.

At times miners used a variation of this method known as "booming," which consisted of restraining the waters of the stream behind a dam until they could be turned loose at one time with a much accumulated force. The impact of the great mass of water would be effective in tearing down gravel banks and even in removing very large boulders. This method was of course wasteful as the finer gold would be apt to be carried off down-stream.

Hydraulic mining proper has been defined as "the art of extracting gold from gold-bearing detritus, that is, surface deposits of gravel and other material, by means of water under great pressure discharged through pipes against the auriferous material." Several conditions were necessary to success: an abundance of free or cheap water readily at hand, loose earth or gravel containing sufficient amount of gold to pay for working it, bed-rock within reach, high lands near the claim so that water might be conducted advantageously, and a channel through which the débris from the washings might be discharged.

Nevada County claims the distinction of having made the first use of hydraulic mining. It is said that Edward E. Mathewson, a Connecticut Yankee, first employed the use of water to wear away the gravel banks in 1852. The means were crude compared with later methods, for the power was limited, being but twenty-five to fifty inches of water which was played through a canvas hose and nozzle after a fall of from forty to sixty feet. Its force was not greater than that of a stream at the nozzle of an ordinary fire-hose, nevertheless it was far superior to the old pick and shovel method when gravel banks of any size were to be washed down.

As may be seen, hydraulic mines, by their very nature, required a great supply of water. This it was necessary to obtain from sources sufficiently high above the mines not only to allow for transporting to the mines, but also with sufficient fall to give a force that might be used effectively. In order to secure this water the early miners performed many interesting engineering feats. Inasmuch as metal piping was not available for their purpose they were required to resort to the use of "flumes." To carry the water along the mountain sides and across deep ravines often required great mechanical skill, and it was no uncommon sight to see wooden flumes held upon trestles one hundred feet or more from the ground. The later miners were able to make use of iron pipes and found many of their problems greatly simplified because the pipes withstood heavy pressure when it became necessary to conduct water down and up across an intervening cañon.

The demand for water soon led to the formation of water companies, the forerunners of our present water and hydro-electric companies. This led to problems of distribution and sale of water. In order to fix a rate for sale of water, units of measure became necessary. Mention has already been made of the use of the term, "tom head," as defining the amount of water used by a long tom. With hydraulic mining the "miner's inch" became the unit. This varied in different camps, but it was generally understood to mean the amount of water that would flow through a hole one inch square during a period of ten hours, the opening being in a vertical position and six inches under water. There were many variations from this standard, depending upon conditions, such as whether it was to be under six, seven, or ten inches' pressure, and whether it ran for a ten, twelve, or twenty-four hour period. The average miner's inch was the equivalent to about one hundred cubic feet of water per hour.

Hydraulic mining was most successful where the great gravel banks of the Neocene rivers were to be found. In this manner much of the gold of Nevada and Placer counties was obtained. Great mountains of gravel were quickly reduced and the gold successfully extracted.

But hydraulic mining, while an economical way of obtaining gold from auriferous gravels, had very decided disadvantages which soon became manifest and led to disputes between the miners and their neighbors in the valleys below. Under the process of "placer mining" whereby great numbers of men worked with pick, shovel, pan and rocker, only very moderate amounts of earth were disturbed by their operations. This would discolor the streams for a short distance, but the refuse was soon deposited along the river course and forgotten. When, however, activities of the hydraulic miners were in full operation hundreds of monitors, or heavy stationary nozzles, were played against the ancient gravel beds and shortly the streams were filled with boulders, gravel, sand and mud. This soon increased to enormous proportions.

The amount of débris was estimated in scores of millions of cubic feet each year. The heavier and coarser boulders found lodgment in the cañons near at hand, the gravel and sand were deposited in the small valleys of the mountains and foothills, while the finer silt was carried on down the river channels, thence to the bay and ocean. As the rivers became clogged, opposition to the hydraulic operations grew, but still the miners continued to wash down the mountains of gravel. During seasons of heavy rainfall the coarser materials were washed farther downstream and as time went on the river beds became more and more choked with the heavy débris from the hydraulic mines. In time these boulders and masses of gravel effectively buried many of the old mining bars so famous in the days of 'forty-nine.

The winter of 1862 was one of torrential rains which produced extraordinary floods and showed very plainly the dangers of unrestricted hydraulic mining. A crisis soon came in the struggle between the miner on the one side and the valley farmer on the other. Since the filling of the river beds not only caused the surrounding land to be flooded but also effectively hindered water navigation, the farmer found allies to his cause. Eventually, in 1892, Congress established a commission with power to regulate hydraulic mining. A state commissioner was likewise appointed. Under license of these bodies hydraulic mining was restricted to conditions which did not permit interference with navigable waterways or work detriment to agricultural lands. While these regulations did not forbid hydraulic mining, they did curb it in such a way that it was not economically profitable except in certain limited localities. At present Trinity and Siskiyou counties are the only parts of the state in which this kind of mining is carried on at all effectively.

While the earliest mining operations were confined

largely to the gravel bars along the river channels and at various dry diggings, the miners were constantly looking for the source of the gold supply. Their ideas of what constituted this source were exceedingly vague; it seemed not at all improbable to some of them that near the summits of the Sierra Nevada there might be mountains of pure gold awaiting the lucky discoverer. These fanciful visions were slowly dispelled, but good fortune did reward the searcher by displaying the gold imbedded in the quartz veins of the bedrock.

The fact that gold in the beds of the rivers was frequently found in quartz gravel had led the more intelligent miners to believe that gold and quartz were commonly associated; if so, why might it not be found in the quartz which was so often seen exposed along the cañons of the rivers? During 1850 and 1851 attention was directed to the possibilities of mining operations in the quartz veins directly. The first quartz vein seems to have been discovered on the Frémont Grant in Mariposa County in 1849, but other developments quickly followed at numerous points in the gold region. Here again Nevada County claims to be the pioneer, for at Gold Hill, near Grass Valley, there was discovered one of the richest of mineral veins, and here was established the first quartz mill.

While scientific knowledge was useful in locating quartz veins, accident played a very important part in the early years. Many are the stories told of veins discovered by men while hunting or engaged in other pursuits than prospecting for gold. It is related that in the Mariposa region a miner when attacked by a robber made most expert use of his gun. He killed the robber, but was more interested to note that a stray bullet which had struck a rock near at hand produced a bright sparkling scar. An examination revealed that it had struck a gold vein in the quartz rock. Another account tells of a hunter in

Tuolumne County who killed a bear, which rolled down the mountain side and hung upon a projecting ledge of rock. The hunter followed to skin the bear and found that the rock was gold-bearing quartz. In Nevada County, we are told, two discouraged miners on one last spree before leaving the mines pried loose a great boulder and set it rolling down the mountain side. In its mad rush it struck a rock ledge with such terrific force that it broke it into fragments, exposing auriferous quartz. Sobered by this discovery the miners forgot their discouragement and began operations upon the quartz vein, which was very rich.

The first quartz mine in what is now Amador County was discovered in February, 1851, by a Baptist minister named Davidson, who was mining here with a number of other men of the same profession. Their claim, known as the "ministers' claim," was located on the south side of Amador Creek near the present town of that name.

Capital was enlisted and the Spring Hill Company organized. About the same time the original Amador Mine was located on the same vein on the north side of the creek. This was the beginning of quartz mining on the "Mother Lode," a name applied to the series of quartz veins extending southeasterly along the flank of the Sierra Nevada through Amador, Calaveras, Tuolumne and Mariposa counties, a distance of about seventy miles. The richest mines of the state are now operating along this great series of quartz veins.

Quartz mining presents problems very unlike those of placer mining. In the first place while the veins are frequently to be traced from surface outcroppings, they usually extend far below the surface. To follow them requires expensive operations calling for scientific training and elaborate machinery. Shafts must be sunk or tunnels driven into the mountain sides; hoisting machinery must be used to bring the ore to the surface. Drainage, light, ventilation and the various details for personal safety must also be provided. Thus modern mining is very different from the early methods of the placer miner.

Furthermore the quartz ore is in rock form with other elements closely mixed with the gold. How to separate and secure the gold is still a task. In the early days the miners learned from their Spanish-speaking neighbors primitive methods of operation. The favorite method of the Sonorans and South Americans was to crush the ore by means of an *arrastre* or a "Chile mill." In the former the quartz was thrown in a circular basin of considerable size. To a pivot in the center was attached a long pole to which a mule was hitched. To the pole heavy boulders were fastened by chains. These boulders grinding the quartz rock reduced it to fine sand or powder which could then be washed out by the usual method of pan or rocker. The Chile mill was similar in principle except that a circular millstone was placed in a perpendicular position and when rotated ground the ore into small particles.

Modern methods have eliminated these appliances and in their place are to be found the stamp mills which crush the ore under the successive blows of the stamps or hammers. The remainder of the process is but a variation of the earlier method of separating the gold by making use of its great specific gravity and its affinity for mercury.

In another way the development of quartz mining caused a change in mining methods. This was in reference to the filing upon and holding claims. Placer gold, having been originally deposited in a horizontal position by water action, could be located and the claims defined in relation to the surface. But quartz or lode mines were different, for while the vein might appear upon the surface at a given point the vein itself might extend below the surface at such an angle that surface claims would be of little value. To the miners the vein of gold-bearing quartz was the only thing of material value, therefore, we find them at an early date defining their claims in terms of this quartz vein rather than earth's surface.

A method of mining which has been in use during more recent years is the gold dredge, with which the auriferous sand and gravel of the Great Valley are washed out. The idea of the gold dredge is not itself new, for a progressive New York manufacturer had built such a machine in the early days of the mining excitement and had shipped it around the Horn to California. By it the rich sands lying on the bottom of the Feather and Yuba rivers were to be scraped up and the gold extracted with speed. It was not found practical, for the river was not deep enough to float such a machine and the gold was so imbedded in the heavy rocks and boulders at the bottom of the stream that the dredger could not dislodge it.

Modern methods and equipment have seemed to over-come many of these earlier difficulties with the result that dredges are now worked with profit. For long ages the ancient rivers poured their waters into the gulf that washed the sides of the Sierra Nevada, until the gulf became a great valley with rich alluvial soil. In more than one way does this soil contain wealth: in the minerals that lie in and beneath it upon the bed-rock, and in the fertility of the soil itself. Unfortunately, the great gold dredges are concerned only with the mineral, and the fertile fields which with care could produce food for a large population are left devastated by the greedy monsters.

Chapter VIII

CHAPTER VIII
Miners' Ways

THE POPULAR conception of the man of Gold Days is that of an old gray-haired, long-whiskered man with pick, shovel, pan and burro. To be sure, that is the 'Forty-niner as we see him now in parades and when on display. In 1849, however, he was a typical American youth. Four fifths of these men, we are told, were between the ages of eighteen and thirty-five.

A process of elimination had excluded the old and infirm, the very rich and the very poor. The long, hard trip across the plains effectively checked the enthusiasm of all but the hardy frontiersman, and while the relatively easier route by sea induced many less able men to make the journey from the Atlantic Coast, they either became adapted to the severe life in the mines or drifted back to the cities. In the mines, then, were to be found the best examples of the American youth of the period.

On the other hand, it must be remembered that these youths had been suddenly thrown into a social atmosphere totally unlike that to which they had been accustomed. In the Sierra Nevada there were no laws, not even the usual inhibitions of social refinement, to restrain desires. Although by far the greater number were young men from normal American homes, the prospects for great gain lured to the Land of Gold many less desirable men, some entirely vicious in their purposes and ways of living.

Because of the very strenuous labor required to dig and work over the gold-bearing gravel or dirt it was but natural that many should seek relaxation, even in ways that more established society might not approve. Saloons were common and were often almost the first institutions to be set up in a new mining camp. Associated with the drinking saloon was the gambling hall. The Sonorans and other Spanish-speaking miners were as a rule inveterate gamblers. Among those who had come to California by the water routes from the Atlantic states were many worthless adventurers who sought to gain wealth without the cost of hard labor. To these, gambling and the sale of liquors offered the desired opportunity.

A notable characteristic of life in California during the Gold Days was the democracy among all classes of men. Physical labor was the one requisite for the production of wealth. Men from all ranks and previous stations had to labor with their hands and all were therefore on an equal plane regardless of birth or intellectual attainments. Labor became dignified and honorable, and the man who did not labor was looked upon as a parasite. Delano relates that:

"It was a common thing to see a statesman, a lawyer, a physician, a merchant, or clergyman, engaged in driving oxen and mules, cooking for his mess, at work for wages by the day, making hay, hauling wood, or filling menial offices. Yet false pride had evaporated, and if they were making money at such avocations, they had little care for appearances. I have often seen the scholar and the scientific man, the ex-judge, the ex-member of Congress, or the would-be exquisite at home, bending over the wash-tub, practicing the homely art of the washerwoman; or, sitting on the ground with a needle, awkwardly enough repairing the huge rents in his pantaloons; or, sewing on buttons *a la tailor*, and good-humoredly responding to a jest, indicative of his present employment—thus:

"'Well, Judge, what is on the docket, today?'

"'Humph! a trial on an action for *rents*—the parties prick anew.'

"'Any rebutting testimony in the case?'

"'Yes, a great deal of *re-button* evidence is to be brought in, and a *strong thread* will uphold the suit.'"

This democracy was not without its unfavorable results, for there were many men of inferior grade who took advantage of it to claim for themselves places of which they were unworthy.

Because of this condition of society it was not easy to judge a man's real worth from his outward appearance. In those days when labor was hard, clothing scarce and expensive, and tonsorial parlors unknown, a raggedly dressed, bearded man might be found to be a most refined, highly educated gentleman. Mrs. Bates records an incident of 1851. A man tired and travel-worn, with face covered with a shaggy beard, soiled clothes, came into the hotel barroom. Seeking the proprietor of the place he gave into his keeping a leather bag containing several thousand dollars' worth of gold dust and thereupon sought a chair in which to rest. Nearby was a piano which immediately caught his eyes. As he looked long and interestedly at the piano, attention of the others was drawn toward him and many smiled, believing that either in his simplicity he was fascinated with the marvelous new instrument or probably his mind was weakening. But it was not long before they changed to an attitude of wonder and admiration, for after running his fingers over a scale or two he struck up "Home, Sweet Home" and followed that with music which fascinated all the listeners. Then he also began to sing to his own accompaniment and there soon gathered around him a large company of admiring listeners. Presently he remembered his surroundings and noticed the audience around him. Seizing his greasy hat he made a hasty escape, and did not reappear until he was dressed in a new suit of clothes and so completely changed in appearance that he would scarcely have been known, had it not been for his willingness once again to delight his fellow-guests with his music.

One of the most marked characteristics of the early miners was their kindness to their fellows. There are, of course, many examples of roughness and some cruelty among the men, but as a rule the heart of the 'Forty-niner was kind, especially toward the man who was down and out. Charles N. Shinn, in his *Mining Camps*, relates the incident of a boy of about sixteen years of age who, having apparently suffered bad luck, wandered into a camp where some thirty miners were busy on their claims. He found a seat on the stream bank and was watching their operations when one of the men, seeing the dejected looking youth, spoke up, "Boys, I'll work an hour for that chap yonder if you will." The others took up the challenge and at the end of the hour they turned over to the boy about $100 in gold dust. They then made up a list of tools and instructed him: "Now go and buy these tools and come back and go to work. We'll have a good claim picked out for you and you will then have to paddle for yourself."

Among the many contemporaneous accounts we read of the experience of Sherlock Bristol who, with several others, arrived at Goodyear's Bar on the Yuba River after a hard tramp across the plains and over the mountains. They were at the diggings at last, but both they and their clothing were worn out, their food supply exhausted and, worst of all, the men were dead broke. Bristol made his way through the darkness to what proved to be a store newly opened in a tent. The prices were fabulous but the two proprietors were doing a great deal of business.

Bristol approached the owner of the place and explained briefly that he was one of seven men who had just arrived in the mines. They needed supplies and clothing as well as ten dollars in cash to pay for freighting over the mountains. "Do you know anyone here?" he was asked. "Not a soul!" was the reply. Taking a pencil and paper the shopkeeper listed down the supplies needed and began to fill it. He then gave him the ten dollars, and turned to wait on the next customer. That Bristol had been successful seemed to his companions incredible. Later, when he paid the bill he inquired why the storekeeper trusted him so readily, whereupon he was told that when any man made known his needs in such a straightforward way the storekeeper was satisfied with his honesty.

The miner, like the Spanish Californians of the earlier days, if compelled to borrow money, borrowed it upon his honor. As a usual thing the money was returned when promised, but if the lender became impatient the borrower was apt to feel injured. Amusing incidents are told of the way in which debts were cancelled. One man who had loaned another six ounces pressed the importance of immediate repayment. To this the borrower replied: "Just you wait ten minutes and time it." During this time he hastened out to his claim, washed out a panful of dirt and returned with more than the required amount. Another account tells of a miner who was dunned for payment at night. The creditor was asked to sit and wait while the debtor grabbed a lantern, hastened to his claim, washed out enough gold which he put into a bag and flung into the face of the impatient creditor.

Gold is found where it is. The men of Gold Days experienced a great deal of uncertainty regarding the location of claims which would yield the riches they desired.

To be sure this uncertainty, which had in it a chance of great gain, partook of the nature of a lottery and had all the exhilaration and disappointment of a game. It was the hope of making a lucky strike that carried the miner on in spite of all the toil and hardship.

A story is told of Fletcher, a lanky, sallow-faced Texan who appeared during the Gold Days at Murphy's Camp. He claimed to have invented a goldometer, an instrument whereby he could detect with unfailing accuracy the presence of gold and likewise could trace the course of the rich vein of treasure. To prove his confidence he offered to wager $100 in gold that he could, by use of this instrument, pick out within ten minutes the exact location of a bag of gold hidden away in an acre of ground. None was ready to take his bet, but if he could actually locate gold as he claimed, there was reason enough why they should venture a little to test his machine.

Now the idea of searching for gold by the aid of unseen forces was not entirely new, and who could say but that this might be the way to success and riches? Was not the whole thing largely a game with Luck? Many of the miners during the earlier days practised their own favorite kind of necromancy; magnets, pointers and various kinds of indicators were used from time to time, the favorite method being similar to the divining rod used by some for locating underground water. This consisted of the forks of a hazel bush cut to have a short pointed body with long arms. This was held by the ends of the arms and carried by the fortune seeker in a horizontal position with the point projecting to the front. If properly handled, said the believing ones, the point would invariably dip so as to indicate the location of gold-bearing rocks, the degree of dip being directly in proportion to the richness of the deposit. Perhaps the stranger had the power and skill to make this instrument perform!

The Texan was given a chance to display the workings of his invention. This instrument was much as we have described and was equipped with a wooden pointer mounted on metal. Taking his goldometer in hand he went through a series of preliminary incantations and then, as if the light were beginning to dawn, he hastened in an irregular course over the hill and across a ravine, as if following a quartz ledge. A crowd of eager miners seized picks and shovels and began to work upon the newly revealed ledge. For some reason the surface dirt proved both deep and difficult, but they worked with a will until they had dug twenty-five feet and still no signs of the gold ledge. Possibly the man was a swindler! But the inventor protested his honesty; given a chance he could prove it. Thereupon he selected one of their number; placed him upon an empty whisky keg and caused him to speak from the other world. It was then revealed that the gold lay still deeper but that ten feet more would surely reveal its untold wealth. These ten feet required much labor, for accumulated water was added to the rock and dirt to be removed. Before the ten feet had been excavated the Texan and his goldometer had permanently left Murphy's Camp!

An incident which is not devoid of its humorous element is recorded by Frank Marryat, a visitor to the gold region, in his *Mountains and Molehills*. In the southern mines near Carson Creek a miner, who was very much respected by his companions, died. It was decided to give him a real funeral.

"A miner of the neighborhood, who had the reputation of having been a prominent and powerful preacher in the eastern states, was called upon to officiate; and he consented to do so. After assembling and taking 'drinks all around,' the party proceeded with becoming gravity to the grave, which had been dug at a distance of about a hundred yards from the camp. When the spot was reached and the body lowered, the minister commenced an extempore prayer, while the crowd reverently fell upon their knees. For a while all went well; but the prayer was unnecessarily long and at last some of the congregation began, in an abstracted way, to finger the loose earth that had been thrown up from the grave. It proved to be thick with gold, and an excitement was immediately apparent in the kneeling crowd. Upon this the preacher stopped and inquiringly asked, 'Boys, what's that?' took a view of the ground for himself and, as he did so, shouted, 'Gold! Gold!—and the richest kind of diggings. The congregation is dismissed!' The dead miner was taken from his auriferous grave, to be buried elsewhere, while the funeral party with the minister at their head lost no time in prospecting and staking out the new diggings."

Many other experiences are related that are associated with the lack of knowledge regarding the exact location of gold. Some of these are amusing; others tragic.

A tragic experience took place in connection with the quartz mines of Nevada County. On Massachusetts Hill near Grass Valley a quartz vein had been discovered. This led to the organization of the Mount Hope Mining Company with Michael Brennan as superintendent and probably chief owner in the company. Brennan, with his wife and three children, soon came to occupy a position of importance in the business and social life of the new town. Mr. Brennan's enthusiasm was rewarded, for the company was soon able to pay a large dividend. With increased confidence, the shaft was driven deeper and the mine equipped with the best of machinery. The deeper mine did not, however, reach the gold sought. Brennan consumed his own resources and borrowed all available money and yet failed to strike the lode. Face to face with failure, he decided to end all. One Sunday morning neighbors were horrified to find the whole family, including the wife and children, dead. Prussic acid had brought the end. In his preparation for this deed, Brennan had made his fate more sure by laying out a loaded gun ready cocked near his side. A letter told of his despondency at being unable to keep faith with his company and creditors. Horrible as this story is, it appears the more tragic when we learn that a few years later when work was resumed at the bottom of the Brennan shaft, it was necessary to drive the shaft only a few feet further in order to strike the richest of gold-bearing quartz veins, which during a period of years produced many millions of dollars to the new owners.

It not infrequently happened that gold was found to underlie the very towns themselves. Such was the case at Placerville. During the fall of 1849 the citizens of that town agreed to allow for each building an area free from being undermined. This was set forth as fifteen feet in front and six feet on the sides and rear of the buildings. This did not, however, prevent the purchase of buildings for the sake of tearing them down. The desire for gold was so strong that this did happen in many cases. The *San Francisco Courier* of August 21, 1850, relates that $2,000 was offered for the mining rights in the area beneath a tent. J. D. Borthwick, who visited Placerville about that time, describes the situation as he found it:

"I then had occasion to return to Hangtown. On my arrival there, I went as usual to the cabin of my friend, the doctor, which I found in a pretty mess. The ground on which some of the houses were built had turned out exceedingly rich; and thinking that he might be as lucky as his neighbors, the doctor had got a party of six miners to work the inside of his cabin on half shares. He was to have half the gold taken out, as the rights of property in any sort of house or habitation in the mines extend to the mineral wealth below it. In his cabin were two large holes, six feet square and about seven deep; in each of these were three miners, picking and shovelling, or washing the dirt in rockers with the water pumped out of the holes. When one place had been worked out, the dirt was all shovelled back into the hole, and another one commenced alongside of it. They took about a fortnight in this way to work all the floor of the cabin, and found it very rich."

When we come to consider the daily life of the miner we find that there was much more labor than romance. His claim far up the mountain side or down in a narrow cañon did not permit the usual conveniences of home life. The following picture of a miner's camp will give some idea of the life as seen by a visitor to the mines during the busiest period of the Gold Days:

"It was late when I arrived, and the party of miners had just stopped work for the day. Some were taking off their wet boots, or washing their faces in the river; others were lighting their pipes or cutting up tobacco; and the rest were collected around the fire, making bets as to the quantity of gold which was being dried in an old frying-pan. This was the result of their day's work, and weighed four or five pounds.

"The banks of the river were so rough and precipitous that, for want of any level space on which to camp, they had been obliged to raise a platform of stone and gravel. On this stood a tent about twenty feet long, which was strewed inside with blankets, boots, hats, old newspapers, and such articles. In front of the tent was a long rough table, on each side of which a young pine tree, with two or three legs stuck into it here and there, did duty as a bench, some of the bark having been chipped off the top side, by way of making it an easy seat. At the foot of the rocks, close to the table, an immense fire was blazing, presided over by a darky, who was busy preparing supper;

for where so many men messed together, it was economy to have a professional cook, though his wages were frequently higher than those paid to a miner. A quarter of beef hung from the limb of a tree; and stowed away, in beautiful confusion, among the nooks and crannies of the rocks, were sacks, casks, and boxes containing various articles of provisions.

"Within a few feet of us, and above the level of the camp, the river rushed past in its wooden bed, spinning round, as it went, a large water-wheel by means of which a constant stream of water was pumped up from the diggings and carried off in the flume. The company consisted of eight members. They were all New Yorkers, and had been brought up to professional and mercantile pursuits. The rest of the party were their hired men, who, however, were upon a perfect social equality with their employers.

"When it was time to turn in, I was shown a space on the gravelly floor of the tent, about six feet by one and a half, where I might stretch out and dream that I dwelt in marble halls. About a dozen men slept in the tent, the others lying outside on the rocks."

Because of the strenuous nature of the miner's labor during the week he was ready to observe Sunday. The usual duties were laid aside, but it must not be inferred that all spent the day in religious worship.

The forenoon was usually one of rest and quiet. Some spent their time in reading or writing to their friends or loved ones at home. When opportunity was offered many attended religious services but these occasions were extremely rare. To others Sunday offered merely a change in labor. The laundry of the week always awaited the miner's attention. The sluice boxes might well be cleaned to ascertain the success of the week's operations. One writer observed many signs in shops and boarding-houses reading, "All Bills Paid Up Here on Sunday."

After a morning spent in simple duties the miner was ready for more strenuous recreation in the afternoon. Need of the week's supplies gave excuse for a trip to a near-by town, or the miner might make his way there merely for amusement and recreation. As a result the afternoon was apt to become noisy, and as the day progressed the excitement increased. The gambling places found Sunday a day of rich harvest. William Taylor, the pioneer minister, records that on one bright Sunday morning in the mines he had a fair congregation to hear him preach and had every reason to expect a much larger crowd in the afternoon, when to his surprise he had no congregation at all—by that time they had all become intoxicated. So common was this state of affairs that one writer in describing the day's experiences says that the men of the camp were all "affectionately drunk in the forenoon, fighting drunk in the afternoon and dead drunk at night."

It is probable that tnere was more drinking and gambling in California during the Gold Days than in any other part of the world, yet, paradoxical as it may seem, there were but very few habitual drunkards. Bayard Taylor records that in his excursions through the gold fields in 1849 he found only one drunkard. There was, however, a large amount of "treating" and on occasions "sprees" and whisky "busts." "Dame Shirley," the wife of a physician at Indian Bar on the North Fork of Feather River, refers to a Christmas spree which lasted for three days. Since she lived at the hotel which was also the place of dispensing of liquors, she did not sleep during this entire period. Many of the respected men of the place joined in the carousals, and even those who desired otherwise were required by a mock vigilance committee to join in and "treat the crowd."

Because of this great demand for liquors there was no business more flourishing than that of the barkeeper, and no mining camp was without its saloon. Furthermore there was no liquor too costly for the California miners. The inevitable result was that within a short time there were many men in California who had made wrecks of their lives. What fortunes they had dug out of the mountains and rivers had been expended for whisky. Delirium tremens became so common in certain of the mining camps that some professed to believe that it was caused by the climate of California, whereas it was the strenuous life of hard labor coupled with excessive drinking that led naturally to physical and mental breakdown.

The life of the miner was far from being one continuous round of pleasure. Even on a paying claim the labor was difficult and exacting and demanded men of physical strength and endurance. Often was the miner required to stand day after day with chilly mountain water up to his waist while the hot summer sun beat down between the narrow walls of a river cañon upon his head. Delano declared that the "labor was quite equal to that of digging canals and wells, and the quantity of gold looked small for the large amount of dirt required to be handled." This extremely hard labor, improper food and frequent over-indulgence in stimulating liquors naturally brought on sickness.

"We found that sickness prevailed to an alarming extent," relates William Kelly, "particularly land scurvy, owing to the constant use of salt and greasy provisions without vegetables. In many instances it assumed a fearfully loathsome shape, swelling the limbs to an enormous size, changing the skin to a deep purple hue, contracting the muscles and main tendons of the legs and arms, so that those members were rigid and useless; enlarging the gums immensely and imparting to them a gangrenous appearance, not only disgusting to look at, but highly offensive in smell. There were also rheumatism simple and acute, sciatica, fever and ague, and several cases of pulmonary ailments, which generally ended fatally; all owing, I suppose, to the severity of the season, and especially to sleeping in damp clothes on the cold wet ground.

"The California ague," he states elsewhere, "is said to be the very worst type of that fearful malady; and its victims being, for the most part, unprovided with the means and appliances to mitigate its attacks, suffer proportionately. Living in cold tents, sleeping on the damp earth, working very generally knee-deep in water, rarely provided with changes of clothing, and using unwholesome diet, they become an easy prey to its ravages."

James L. Tyson, a physician by profession, visited the diggings in 1850 and described health conditions as he saw them. He also gave some words of advice to prospective gold miners:

"At the bottom of steep rocky glens or ravines, through which a small stream flows with banks so high and precipitous that you can not walk over them, except on the little dusty paths worn in their sides, and up to his knees in muddy water, with which his clothes are well be-dabbled, plying a pickax or shovel, or rocking a washer, behold the gold-seeker! The sun pours his scorching rays upon his devoted head. Sometimes he will work, day after day and week after week, in a stooping posture, at as severe toil and great exposure as man ever felt or knew, and scarcely get a return for his labor . . . .

"If I could convey to the reader an adequate conception of what a gold-seeker in California has to endure, it would scarcely be credited. Quarrying, the digging of canals, cellars, and wells, or all combined, are not capable of comparison with the intense hard labor, and almost un-bearable privations he is compelled to undergo. None but a laboring man is fit for the business. He must have been inured to the most trying hardships from his earliest infancy, and have a constitution and frame of iron, to en-dure it for any length of time; sickness in some form often overtaking even the most robust, after a few weeks' toil. Many had been here since the preceding fall, and were no better off than on the day of their arrival. The majority leave with broken health and spirits, the consequence of exposure and privations to which they had been unac-customed, and the utter prostration of all their brilliant hopes . . . .

"Do not work in the heat of the day. You can accom-plish *more* by working *two hours* in the early morning and the same length of time late in the afternoon, and your health will not be so liable to suffer from the unaccus-tomed toil and exposure. This relaxation from the stoop-ing posture of the miner is indispensable, not only to pre-serve bodily vigor, but as a protection from disease. It also affords time for domestic duties in the preparation of food, etc., a most important branch of California life, as on the quality of this in a great degree depends, not only the comfort and health, but the life of the miner. Obtain a receipt for making good, not sour bread. The exclusive use of dried and salted meats is highly prejudicial. It fires the blood, and prepares the system for disease, which will soon result if its use be persisted in. Some terrible cases of scurvy I witnessed from this cause, and much of the sickness at the mines results from inattention to this mat-ter. Stewed fruits, pickles, and acidulous drinks, should be freely used, if your reliance is on salt provisions. In most of the severe cases of disease, and in many of the deaths which have occurred at the mines, a scorbutic habit prevailed along with the existing complaint. As this bad condition of the system can be so readily avoided, it was strange to me that it should be so prevalent. Men are apt to forget health and everything in the pursuit of gold. The use of a vegetable diet and fresh meat occasionally, would be a protection from this scourge, but as such luxuries, except the latter at long intervals, could heretofore rarely be obtained in the mining districts, it becomes necessary to guard against it by the means suggested. Cleanliness should never be neglected. Frequent bathing will be found of essential benefit.

"With due regard to the foregoing hints, health will rarely suffer. Should sickness in ever so mild a form occur, abandon labor at once, and gain a higher locality, if in the cañons of the river. Consult a physician, many of whom are in the neighborhood of the mines, and keep quiet. Above all, avoid the low, marshy, febrile districts, on the shores of the Sacramento and San Joaquin rivers.

"It may be said that some have paid little regard to health, and adopted no precautions for its preservation, either on the journey to California, or during a residence at the mines, and have yet returned unscathed. Such instances are rare exceptions. The majority, who work at the mines, rarely leave with their accustomed health, while much fatal sickness has occurred there. I never saw so many broken-down constitutions as during my brief stay in California. And this was generally owing to ignorance of, or inattention to, such matters as I have presented.

"The writer never enjoyed better health than while in the vicinity of the mines of California. It is true that he was not subjected to the same influences as the miner, but others under similar circumstances sickened, and sometimes died. His exemption from disease, is mainly attributable to care in diet, and avoidance of such other influence, as prudence and a regard for the laws of health require, and which the miner could as readily adopt as any other."

The life of a miner was strenuous and while the returns at times were large, more often they were far too small. This heavy labor, uncertain compensation, and absence of the steadying influences of refined society created abnormal conditions. These have been set forth by many writers in such a way as to depict the 'Forty-niner falsely. A careful study of the facts shows the greater number of them were young men full of hope and energy, responding either to the high and worthy motive, or the low and debasing impulses in a manner not uncommon to the normal American youth.

Chapter IX

CHAPTER IX

Vox Populi in the Diggings

LAWLESSNESS AND disorder have been given a prominent place by some writers in their picture of life in the Gold Days, yet to one who gives the subject any study worthy of consideration the outstanding character-istic is rather that there was so much order and business-like activity under such extraordinary condi-tions. One hundred thousand men from all quarters of the globe suddenly finding themselves thrown together in a new land, without established government, and all intent upon the rapid acquisition of wealth—was ever the stage better set for a lawless and blood-thirsty drama?

That order and stability to even a moderate degree were to be found in the gold mines of 'forty-nine and 'fifty was due to the extraordinary capacity of the Anglo-American for self-government, and to the nature of the men who comprised the mining society. In California, for the first time, Americans were able to demonstrate their ability to set up a new government in accordance with their own ideals. Heretofore the westward movement of the Ameri-can frontiersman had but crowded the border a little fur-ther westward, taking with him the institutions to which he had become accustomed in his former homes. Upon the shores of the Pacific there was to spring into being a new community, which while predominantly American was nevertheless made up of diverse elements. The result was to give opportunity for the expression of American self-government in a manner never before experienced.

When gold was discovered in California, there was no Federal law relating to mining upon the public domain except the provision contained in the general preemption act of 1841 that excluded from preemption "all lands on which are situated any known salines or mines." Even under the later preemption acts relating definitely to California, provision was made that "settlers" could not take up mining lands. This absence of legislation was doubtless due to the fact that the government had previously had experience only with mineral lands that contained the baser metals. For these the policy was to reserve the mineral lands to be leased to miners. The leasing system had not proved satisfactory because the cost of collection was too great for the amount collected.

This defect in the Federal mining law had already been noted by government officials. President Polk in his message of December, 1845, referred to it as radically defective. He recommended the abolition of the leasing system and suggested that mineral lands be offered for sale. Subsequent acts of Congress had provided for the sale of lands containing lead, copper and other base metals. The discovery of gold in California brought out forcibly the inadequacy of the Federal law. The treaty with Mexico had given the United States a vast area, the greater part of which was public domain. Upon this public land gold had already been discovered and thousands of eager miners were soon busy seeking their fortunes in the mineral store of Uncle Sam. The Secretary of the Interior, Thomas Ewing, in December of 1849 reported:

"Thus it appears that the deposits of gold wherever found in the territory are the property of the United

States. No existing law puts it in the power of the Executive to regulate these mines or protect them from intrusion. Hence in addition to our own citizens, thousands of persons of all nations and languages, flock in and gather gold, which they carry away to enrich themselves, leaving the lands the less in value, by that which they have abstracted, and they render for it no remuneration, direct or indirect, to the government or the people of the United States. Our laws, so strict in the preservation of public property that they punish our own citizens for cutting timber upon public lands ought not to permit strangers, who are not, and who never intend to become citizens, to enter on these lands at pleasure, and take from them the gold which constitutes nearly all their value. Some legal provision is necessary for the protection and disposition of these mines."

Governor Richard B. Mason had attempted to deal with the situation as best he could with his limited authority. In a proclamation of February 12, 1848, before his knowledge of Marshall's discovery, he had declared that: "From and after this date the Mexican laws and customs now prevailing in California relative to the denouncement of mines are hereby abolished."

The result of this was to prevent any from acquiring private ownership over mineral lands based upon right of discovery as allowed on Mexican law. This, however, did not provide a solution to the problem of the government's relation to the gold-seeker. When Mason visited the diggings during the summer of 1848 he saw the need of action but was unable to suggest or recommend any definite plan. Until Congress made some definite provision he chose not to interfere with the operations unless conditions required it. In his own words:

"The entire gold district, with a few exceptions of grants made some years ago by the Mexican authorities, is on land belonging to the United States. It was a matter of serious reflection with me how I could secure to the government certain rents or fees for the privilege of procuring this gold; but upon considering the large extent of the country, the character of the people engaged and the small scattered force at my command, I am resolved not to interfere but permit all to work freely, unless broils and crimes call for interference.

"I would suggest that the United States surveyors, with high salaries, bound to serve specified periods be sent out; a Superintendent to be appointed at Sutter's Fort, with power to grant licenses to work a spot of ground, say one hundred yards square for one year at a rent of from $100 to $1,000, at his discretion. The surveyor would survey the ground, and place the renter in possession."

Mason also advised the sale of the land at public auction to the highest bidder, the amount sold to include not more than forty acres to each bidder.

President Taylor in his message of 1849 seems to have given this idea consideration, for he recommended that instead of retaining the mineral lands under permanent government control, they should be divided into small lots and sold, under such restrictions as to quantity and time as "will insure the best price and guard most effectively against combinations of capitalists to obtain monopolies." In this he was following closely the suggestion of Secretary of the Interior Ewing who had recommended as follows:

"The gold which is found in the alluvium in California is continuous over a great extent of country, and it may be wrought upon any lot having surface earth and access to water. The district may be, therefore, divided into small lots, with a narrow front on the margin of the streams, and extending back in the form of a parallelogram. Where gold is found in the rocks in situ, the lots to embrace it should be larger, and laid off according to the Spanish method with regard to dip and strike. But so various are the conditions under which the precious metal may be found by a careful geological exploration, that the mode of laying off the ground cannot be safely anticipated, but must be left to the direction, on the spot, of a skilful engineer, whose services will be indispensable."

In accordance with these suggestions there was introduced in the Senate, by its committee on public lands, a bill dividing the mineral lands into small lots to be offered for sale at public auction at a price not less than $1.25 per acre. Senator Benton, who was the guardian of the rights of the frontiersman, was unalterably opposed to any plan whereby the government should try to secure revenue from the mineral lands. The proposed act was not adopted.

Inasmuch as Congress had failed to pass any legislation upon this subject, the military officials in charge of the government of California were required to adopt a policy of *laissez faire*. The miners in so far as there was not disorder and bloodshed were allowed to continue their operation in the diggings.

Dr. Mary Floyd Williams calls attention to the critical condition of affairs in the mines at this juncture. Legally all were trespassers upon the public lands and had no right to work the mines. There were no laws to guide, restrain or protect them and little or no interference was to be feared or expected from Federal officials.

"The popular imagination has been delighted by many pictures of the California miner of 1848 and 1849, with his uncouth virtues and his picturesque vices, his courage, his rough kindness, his swift and unsparing justice, and his simple standards of manliness and intregrity. But the crucial moment of his adventurous life has been passed over with a light touch, possibly because he met it lightly and without melodrama. It was the moment when the

[169]

secret strike of a prospector became public property. He
had traveled far, perhaps quite alone, perhaps as a member of some little company; he had carried on his own
back tools and food and rifle across country still impassable for a pack animal; he had spent days in barren,
heart-breaking toil, and nights at the mercy of murderous
Indians, and at last he had 'struck it rich!' But before
his dream of fortune might be realized there came others
who had spied on his movements, followed his trail, and
overtaken him in time to divide the fruits of his suffering,
his patience, and his skill. Such an incident was described
by E. G. Buffum, who found a rich ravine and hoped to
make a fortune from the location. Within twenty-four
hours he was traced, and the gulch was overrun with
other miners. About $10,000 was taken in a few days, of
which the discoverer realized only about $1,000. This
was the danger point in California life—excited men in a
remote mountain gorge, with gold uncovered at their feet
and loaded weapons in their hands. And this was the
salvation of that life: they put their guns aside, sat down
and talked things over, estimated the richness of the
placer, and apportioned it fairly between them."

Since the lure of abundant wealth had brought men of
all kinds and races together it would appear natural that
human cupidity should here have a chance to express itself without restraint and that spoils would go to the
man with the strong arm and a finger quick on the trigger.

It was under these circumstances that the adventurers
of the Gold Days, of their own initiative, instituted neighborhood and district laws for the purpose of defining for a
brief time their rights as temporary owners of the mining
claims, thus to avoid the collisions that would inevitably
arise through conflicting rights and demands. On every
bar, gulch or ford where gold was found such laws were
adopted as the majority of the miners saw fit to enact.

These were not always set down in written documents, for frequently in the early days they were formed through mere verbal understanding.

One of the first things done in the founding of a new camp was to enact a set of rules regarding the holding of mining claims. To draw up such a set of laws was not a new idea to most of the men. In many cases groups of men had associated themselves together in companies before leaving the eastern states, whether to sail around the Horn or to make the great trip across the plains. Although very few, if any, of these associations had been able to weather the unforeseen conditions that later arose, yet in the gold fields existence of those rules and the ease with which their members were able to abolish or modify them indicate an aptitude for government characteristic of a people which had for generations been accustomed to self-government.

When the news of the gold discovery reached the New England Coast many companies of men banded themselves together to share the expense of chartering vessels to carry them on the quest of the Golden Fleece. The questions of chief concern dealt with the distribution of costs and profits. In some cases the rules of the association provided only that each should bear his share of the cost of the expedition, in others it was provided that the company was not only to divide the cost but that the members were also to pool their earnings, distributing to each, share per share. These companies or associations as a usual thing had their presidents and other necessary officers who assumed their respective responsibilities in connection with the details of the long journey. All matters of concern were subject to popular vote: upon arrival at the gold region they decided their choice of camp site, selection of cook and other relevant matters. Since these associations were originated amid the more settled society of the eastern states and the journey was usually undertaken in vessels flying the flag of the United States, it was not considered necessary that by-laws be adopted dealing specifically with the conduct of the individual members. Upon reaching the gold fields conditions were so different from what had been anticipated before leaving home, that most of these companies were soon disbanded. There were, nevertheless, elements of unity in the groups that came to the fore, time and again, as those men individually or in groups gathered in mining communities on the slopes of the Sierra, and whenever necessity demanded it they were ready to act and even fight for the common good at any time.

For those who crossed the plains, the usual plan of organization was somewhat different. The initial expense was not so large; consequently the form of organization, if any was required, was less elaborate. On the other hand, the need of defense and mutual assistance in the long journey across the plains made it customary for parties before starting west to group themselves into a sort of semi-military organization, under a captain of their own choosing and under laws and regulations of their own making. Under the stress of the long journey amid unforeseen conditions most of the larger associations broke up before crossing the Rocky Mountains. Smaller groups were found more satisfactory when traveling under inexperienced leaders.

With these preliminary experiences before reaching the diggings, the miners were by no means unprepared to take matters into hand and draw up and adopt laws and regulations suitable for the new conditions.

The principle which formed the basis for all the regulations of the mining camps was, that all men are equal and that each should have an equal opportunity so long as he did not encroach upon the rights of others. If a small group of prospectors discovered a paying placer mine, they voted to divide the area, giving to each an allotted share. If a larger number should later be attracted to the same digging a new vote might be taken and claims re-assigned.

This orderly assignment of claims upon the idea of the rule of the majority and fairness to all, shows that these men, in spite of their eagerness to make their fortunes, were capable of recognizing the fundamental principles which are the basis for law. This was not easily done. It is related that a determined miner in Nevada County was not in accord with the idea of miners' regulations and claimed all the area as far as his rifle could reach. Fortunately such cases were few and the general spirit of the miner was in favor of more equitable action.

An excellent picture of one of these miners' meetings is given us by an Englishman who visited California during the Gold Period. He writes:

"The miners met in front of the store to the number of about two hundred; a very respectable-looking old chap was called to the chair; but for want of that article of furniture he mounted an empty pork-barrel, which gave him a commanding position; another man was appointed secretary, who placed his writing materials on some empty boxes piled up alongside of the chair. The chairman then, addressing the crowd, told them the object for which the meeting had been called, and said he would be happy to hear any gentleman who had any remarks to offer; whereupon some one proposed an amendment of the law relating to a certain description of claim, arguing the point in a very neat speech. He was duly seconded, and there was some slight opposition and discussion; but when the chairman declared it carried by the ayes, no one called for a division, so the secretary wrote it all down, and it became law.

"Two or three other acts were passed, and when the business was concluded, a vote of thanks to the chairman was passed for his able conduct on the top of the pork-barrel. The meeting was then declared to be dissolved, and accordingly dribbled into the store, where the legislators, in small detachments, pledged each other in cocktails as fast as the storekeeper could mix them. While the legislature was in session, however, everything was conducted with the utmost formality, for Americans of all classes are particularly *au fait* at the ordinary routine of public meetings."

Just when the first of these mining districts was created has not been determined, but it was probably during the summer and fall of 1848 or the spring of 1849. J. T. Brooks, writing of his experiences as early as 1848, remarked that it was "curious how soon a set of regulations sprung into existence, which everybody seemed to abide by." We have noted how many of those sets of regulations probably originated with the organizers of companies before they had left the shores of New England, or had started across the plains, but it is probable that the earliest to be put into effect in the mines were the work of the discharged soldiers of Colonel J. D. Stevenson's regiment who hurried to the mines when mustered out in the early fall of 1848. One authority credits Colonel Stevenson himself with being the author of those which were adopted by the miners above Mokelumne Hill; others give this credit to the men of Jackass Gulch. Both of these were presumably adopted in the fall of 1848. J. H. Carson makes the statement that he first saw men measuring off claims at Wood's Creek near Sonora in the spring of 1849; and Steele, another writer, says the first was at Park's Bar on Yuba River in April, 1849. These various conflicting accounts give strength to the opinion that probably the need for regulations was so universally

recognized that at various places they were adopted more or less spontaneously without regard to precedent. We do know that by the spring of 1849 these laws were already common throughout the mining region and were humorously referred to by at least one writer of the times as the "lex diggerorum."

Practically all the districts soon adopted the practice of keeping written records, for all claims were recorded; yet the many fires which swept the mining camps destroyed all of the earlier records save a very few. At a later period the public archives were made depositories for these mining records and since then more of them have survived. The following extract from the records gives some idea of the method used in the organization of a mining district:

"A convention of Quartz Miners convened pursuant to a public call in the town of Quartzburg, County of Mariposa on the 25th of June, 1851. The meeting being called to order, on motion, Colonel Thorn was unanimously chosen president of the meeting, and J. T. Temple, Secretary. On motion a committee of seven was appointed to draft a preamble, and resolutions for the consideration of the meeting. The chair appointed the following gentlemen as the committee—Colonel Kyle, Major Barney, Major Gaines, Judge Lansing, Messrs. Thurmond, Jr., F. Johnson and J. T. Temple.

"The committee after retiring for some time made the following report:

"Whereas the committee deems the protection of the Quartz Mining interest in the County of Mariposa essential to the peace of said county, and whereas certain definite and fixed rules are requisite to the protection of said interest and maintenance of the peace and harmony of the county; therefore, resolved:

"That all quartz being now owned and occupied in the

[177]

County of Mariposa or which may hereafter be discovered or claimed, shall be governed by the following rules . . . .

J. F. TEMPLE, *Secretary*.
THOMAS THORN, *President*."

The regulations made at the camps were for the purpose of keeping harmony within the community. For any group to work together congenially and efficiently there must be certain rules set up to guide the action of the individual and to protect the mutual interests of the group.

The ownership of the land was not involved in the questions of these mining laws for, as pointed out by the commissioners of the General Land Office, "The ravines and river bars were valueless for settlement or homemaking, but were splendid stakes to hold for a few short seasons, and gamble with nature for wealth or ruin." The main purpose for these men was to determine upon rules and regulations fixing the size and boundaries of mining claims, specifying how they should be marked and what was necessary to perfect and hold a title to the claim.

"To establish one's claim to a piece of ground," says a miner of the Gold Days, "all that was requisite was to leave upon it a pick or shovel, or other mining tool. The extent of ground allowed to each individual varied in different diggings from ten to thirty feet square, and was fixed by the miners themselves, who also made their own laws, defining the rights and duties of those holding claims; and any dispute on such subjects was settled by calling together a few of the neighboring miners, who would enforce the due observance of the laws of the diggings."

While the regulations varied from place to place, there was, nevertheless, a striking similarity between them.

Major H. W. Halleck pointed out that in accordance with their usual practice, "The miners of California have generally adopted . . . the main principles of the mining laws of Spain and Mexico, by which the right of property in mines is made to depend upon discovery and development; that is, discovery is made the source of title and development or working, the condition of the continuance of that title."

Accordingly, the discoverer of new diggings was generally, although not invariably, awarded first choice and a double share in the claims. Another rule more or less general provided that two claims could not be held by one person except by purchase, or as a reward for dis- covery. If, when the season permitted a claim to be worked, a man let his claim lie unworked a certain num- ber of days (the number varying from five to fifteen), he forfeited his right to hold it and anyone not having a claim might take it. Tools were left on the claim to indicate the temporary absence of the owner and were sufficient to hold the claim for a short period. It was therefore a serious offense to remove tools from the claim of another. In the public archives of Siskiyou County an interesting example is to be found where a human touch was incorporated into the miners' law. One of the sections of the code of Little Humbug Creek expressly states: "Resolved, That no person's claim shall be jump- able on Little Humbug while he is sick or in any way dis- abled from labor, or while he is absent from his claim attending upon sick friends."

The earliest regulations were made to apply to claims of surface or placer gold which were located along the river beds. It was soon discovered, however, that the gold came from auriferous quartz veins in the bed-rock. To provide regulations to cover this class of claims re- quired a distinct change from the earlier rules. The common sense of the miner was again called into play with the result that provision was made that, regardless of the direction of the vein, a claim should consist of a specified section of the quartz ledge together with certain surface rights necessary for successful operation. In comment upon this point Justice Morrow in his *Introduction to California Jurisprudence* observes:

"To the law of mines the American miners of early California offered a notable contribution. In advance of any enactments by Legislature or Congress, their common sense which had proved strong enough to govern with wisdom the ownership of placer mines rose to meet the question of lode claims, and decreed that ownership should attach to the thing of value, namely, the thin, sheet-like veins of gold-bearing quartz, and that a claim should consist of a certain horizontal block of the vein, however it might run, but extending indefinitely downward, with a strip of surface, on or embracing the vein's outcrop, for the placing of necessary machinery and buildings. Under this theory, the lode was the property, and the surface became a mere easement. This early California theory of a mining claim is the obvious foundation for the Federal legislation and present system of public disposition and private ownership of the mineral lands west of the Missouri River. Contrasted with this is the mode of disposition of mineral-bearing lands east of the Missouri River, where the common law has been the one rule, and where the surface tract has always carried with it all minerals vertically below it. The Mexican system also was, in the matter of lode claims, the direct antithesis of the California system, the former recognizing vertical planes through the exterior boundaries and the latter recognizing the extralateral right."

It is of interest to note that these local laws were adopted voluntarily by the men in the mines without any external influence or pressure and that by means of them the community was governed through an expression of the will of the majority. It is further noteworthy that these laws, thus voluntarily adopted by the rough appearing miners in their crude miners' assemblies, not only provided their own local government for the period but also constituted practically the sole legal basis for their mining operations from the time of the gold discovery in 1848 until the passage of the general Lode Mining Law of 1866, and furthermore that in the adoption of this mining code the various regulations in use by the early miners played a very significant part.

"These miners' rules and regulations which seemed to suit the interest of the miners so well," writes Dr. Joseph Ellison, "were the outgrowth of necessity and experience, built upon the foundation of the European and Mexican mining laws, and adjusted to the needs of the new environment. By 1860 there grew up a miner's code on equitable principles, democratic in character . . . . The promulgation of the rules and the settlement of disputes were also handled in a typical frontier democratic fashion. The rules were generally framed and amended at a public mass meeting, conducted in an informal manner."

As early as 1851 the legislature of California expressly provided through formal legislation that in all actions respecting mining claims, "Proof must be admitted of the customs, usages or regulations established and in force at the bar, or diggings, embracing such claim; and such customs, usages or regulations, when not in conflict with the laws of this state, must govern the decision of the action."

Likewise when Congress at last determined to adopt a mining code it turned for guidance to the mining district regulations adopted by the men of the Sierra Nevada. In urging the passage of the mining act of 1866 the chairman of the Committee on Mines and Mining paid tribute to the wisdom of these men in his report as follows:

"It will be readily seen how essential it is that this great system, established by the people in their primary capacities and evidencing by the highest possible testimony the peculiar genius of the American people for founding an empire and order shall be preserved and affirmed. Popular sovereignty is here displayed in one of its grandest aspects, and simply wants us not to destroy but to put upon it the stamp of national power and unquestioned authority."

The Federal lode law as finally adopted gave legislative approval to these miners' laws and regulations and provided a way whereby one might acquire legal title to lands bearing veins of the precious metals. It provided that a miner who had or should thereafter occupy and improve a mine according to local laws might receive a patent upon paying the price of five dollars per acre. The act in part read thus:

"The mineral lands of the public domain, both surveyed and unsurveyed, are hereby declared to be free and open to exploration and occupation by all citizens of the United States, and those who have declared their intention to become citizens, subject to such regulations as may be prescribed by law, and subject also to the local customs or rules of miners in the several mining districts, so far as the same may not be in conflict with the laws of the United States."

Justice Morrow thus comments on the legislation of the miners in their primary assemblies along the slopes of the Sierra Nevada, pointing out that they in their democracy were working out and administering laws well adapted to meet the needs of the time:

"With the object of encouraging the active miner and checkmating those who wished merely to speculate on the industry of others, the local laws or regulations of the mining camps contained many provisions which afforded the basis of acts of Congress. The main object of these regulations was to fix the boundaries and the size of the claims, the manner in which they were to be marked, the amount of work which must be done to secure the title, and the circumstances under which the claim was to be considered abandoned and open to occupation by new claimants.

"The act of Congress of 1866, and later acts respecting the subject of mining, embody many a provision that was first enacted in some rough and crude miners' meeting in a Sierran camp.

"This act marked a new era in the land policy of the government, and banished the specters of governmental licenses, leases, taxes on industry, royalties and confiscation which deterred mining as an industry in countries less liberal and fair than America has always been in its relations to that hardy body of men who seek among the hills for the treasure that is wholly theirs for the finding. On May 28, 1866, Senator Conness, chairman of the Committee on Mines and Mining in the United States Senate, in reporting back to that body, said: 'In the absence of legislation and statute law, the local courts, beginning with California, recognize those "rules and regulations," the central idea of which was priority of possession, and have given to the country rules of decision, so equitable as to be commanding in their national justice, and to have secured universal approbation. The California reports will compare favorably, in this respect, with history of jurisprudence in any part of the world.'"

Chapter X

CHAPTER X

Judge Lynch and the Miners' Jury

N THE PREVIOUS chapter we have considered the manner in which the miners, in spite of the absence of any legal authority, handled the question of mining claims. The problem of the proper relationship between men was not so easily adjusted. During the summer and fall of 1848 disorders were rare, and from various accounts it would appear that the miners were more honest than the usual run of frontiersmen. Governor Mason commented upon the good behavior of the men in the mining district.

Unfortunately this condition could not last. The first miners were the older residents of California who were working alongside of friends and neighbors from the valley settlements. But as the news of the discovery spread there began a migration to the gold fields that included all classes of society. Dr. Mary Floyd Williams notes this change in the nature of the population of 1849:

"The typical pioneer was no longer in the ascendant. Men came from every section of the land, and from every walk of life. Puritans and drunkards, clergymen and convicts, honest and dishonest, rich and poor—they strode side by side across the plains, crowded the decks of steamers, and worked shoulder to shoulder in the diggings. A little later came all the world, and the people of Europe and Asia and Africa brought to California every social inheritance entailed upon humanity since the dawn of history."

The newspapers of the late fall of 1849 reported vessels in the San Francisco harbor flying the flags of more than a score of foreign countries, including the flags of England, France, Spain, Portugal, Italy, Hamburg, Bremen, Belgium, New Granada, Holland, Sweden, Oldenburg, Chili, Peru, Russia, Mexico, Equador, Hanover, Norway, Hawaii, and Tahiti. Not only was there an influx of foreigners unacquainted with American ideals, but many of the lowest elements of society were swept hither in the flood of gold-seeking humanity. J. H. Carson, who wrote of the honesty and good behavior of the mining population during 1848, had a different report a few months later. "This honesty was not to be found in the crowds that daily thickened around us in Forty-nine. Hordes of pick-pockets, robbers, thieves, and swindlers were mixed with men who had come with honest intentions . . . . Murders, thefts and heavy robberies soon became the order of the day."

The problem was one fraught with difficulty because of the lack of any governmental machinery capable of coping with a dangerous criminal class, for, as pointed out by Mr. Bancroft: "During the autumn of 1848 there were no such things along the Sierra Drainage as government, law, law-courts, statutes, constitution, legislatures, judges, sheriffs, tax-collectors or other officers of the law."

The reason for this chaotic condition was that the gold discovery and consequent rush to the California diggings had followed so closely upon the acquisition of the Mexican cession that Congress, still puzzled over the problem of slavery, had had no time to provide adequate legislation. The Mexican law not only was inadequate but also repugnant to the Anglo-American settlers who now composed the greater part of the population. Even when efforts were made to put these laws into effect such attempts were only partly successful due to lack of knowledge of Mexican jurisprudence. Under these circumstances the only law that seemed effective was that based upon the individual sense of what was inherently just.

Fortunately the experience of the Anglo-Saxon had trained him in self-government, for here was an even more severe test than that relating to his mining claim. Experience with rough elements in unsettled communities had taught the frontiersman the effectiveness of direct action. Many of the 'Forty-niners, while crossing the plains, had found it necessary to resort to such measures to protect their company against the unscrupulous whose regard for others was only in direct proportion to their ability to defend their rights.

It is essential that we understand these conditions before attempting to pass judgment upon the actions of the hardy men of the Sierra Nevada. While lynch law is a name frequently applied to the miners' courts, yet we must not confuse these courts with the attempts of armed mobs to administer their own brand of justice in a summary manner through irresponsible and irregular tribunals in places where regular courts exist, and in opposition to them. Unfortunately there were cases where the mob spirit did influence the trial and execution of an accused man and in the whole method the conviction of the defendant was dangerously easy. Yet when judged with true knowledge of the conditions it is to be seen that instead of being a retrograde movement, tending toward anarchy and lawlessness, these miners' tribunals were the means employed to protect society and to establish an orderly method of social control in the place of individual and personal vengeance.

"One would ask," writes Marryat, in his *Mountains and Molehills*, "how it is that Murderer's Bar, despite its name, is a peaceable village, where each man's wealth, in the shape of ten feet square of soil, is virtuously respected by his neighbor; it is not because there is enough for all, for every paying claim has long ago been appropriated, and the next comer must go further on. There is a justice of the peace (up to his arms in the river just at present), and there is a constable (who has been 'prospecting' a bag of earth from the hill, and been rewarded with a gold flake of the value of three cents); these two, one would suppose could scarcely control two or three hundred men, with rude passions and quick tempers, each of whom, as you observe, carries his revolver even while at work. But these armed, rough-looking fellows themselves elected their judge and constable, and stand, ever ready, as 'specials' to support them.

"If a man wanted a pickax or a shovel, and thought to help himself to one of those that lie about at all times at Murderer's Bar, he would find it inconvenient if discovered; for, as there is no extenuating clause of hunger or misery in the diggings, theft is held to be a great crime; in all probability the offender would be whipped at the tree; and this brings us again to the perplexing subject of Lynch law as relating to the miners . . . .

"Still it is a question, taken from first to last, that one may split straws on, when we see how peacefully Murderer's Bar progresses, not under the *execution*, but under the *fear* of Lynch law. In most mining villages public indignation has been confined to ordering men to 'leave the camp' in twenty-four hours or otherwise take the consequences; and after being thus warned, the nefarious digger invariably 'slopes.'"

"The mining population have been allowed to constitute their own laws relative to the appointment of 'claims,'
and it is astonishing how well this system works. Had
the Legislature, in ignorance of the miners' wants, interfered and decided that a man should have so much, and
no more, of the soil to work on, all would have been
anarchy and confusion.

"Whereas now, every 'digging' has its fixed rules and
by-laws, and all disputes are submitted to a jury of the
resident miners; except in those instances where twenty
men or so are met by twenty men, and in these cases
there is first a grand demonstration with firearms, and
eventually an appeal to the district court. The by-laws
of each district are recorded in the Recorder's Office of
the county, and these laws are stringent although self-
constituted; ill-defined at first, and varying as they did,
they were conflicting and troublesome, but though they
have been jumbled as it were, in a bag, they have come
out like Mr. Crockett, 'right side up.'

"I have had my claim in the digging more than once,
of ten feet square; if a man 'jumped' it, and encroached
on my boundaries, and I didn't knock him on the head
with a pickax, being a Christian, I appealed to the 'crowd,'
and my claim being carefully measured from my stake
and found to be correct, the 'jumper' would be ordered to
confine himself to his own territory, which of course he
would do with many oaths."

Because of the growing complexities of mining society
it became necessary to develop a more definite kind of
civil government with powers to regulate individual
conduct as well. The people of Jacksonville were among
those who first saw the desirability of such a set of regulations and laws. In response to a call, a group of
twenty or thirty miners met at the store of Colonel

Jackson on January 30, 1850, and proceeded to adopt the following laws for the Jacksonville District:

"Art. I. The officers of this district shall consist of an alcalde and sheriff, to be elected in the usual manner by the people, and continue in office at the pleasure of the electors.

"Art. II. In case of the absence or disability of the sheriff, the alcalde shall have power to appoint a deputy.

"Art. III. Civil cases may be tried by the alcalde if the parties desire it; otherwise they shall be tried by a jury.

"Art. IV. All criminal cases shall be tried by a jury of eight American citizens, unless the accused shall desire a jury of twelve persons, who shall be regularly summoned by the sheriff and sworn by the alcalde, and shall try the case according to the evidence.

"Art. V. In the administration of law both civil and criminal, the rule of practice shall conform as near as possible to that of the United States, but the forms and customs of no particular State shall be required or adopted.

"Art. VI. Each individual locating a lot for the purpose of mining shall be entitled to twelve feet of ground in width running back to the hill or mountain and forward to the center of the river or creek, or across a gulch or ravine (except in cases hereinafter provided for), lots commencing in all cases at low water mark and running at right angles with the stream where they are located.

"Art. VII. In cases where lots are located according to Art. VI and the parties holding them are prevented by the water from working the same, they may be represented by a pick, shovel or bar, until in a condition to be worked; but should the tools be stolen or removed, it shall not dispossess those who located it provided he or they can prove that they were left as required; and said location shall not remain unworked longer than one week, if in condition to be worked; otherwise it shall be considered as abandoned by those who located it. (Except in cases of sickness.)

"Art. VIII. No man, or party of men, shall be permitted to hold two locations, in a condition to be worked at the same time.

"Art. IX. No party shall be permitted to throw dirt, stones or other obstructions upon located ground adjoining them.

"Art. X. Should a company of men desire to turn the course of a river or stream they may do so (provided it does not interfere with those working below them) and hold and work all the ground so drained, but lots located within said ground shall be permitted to be worked by their owners, so far as they could have been worked without the turning of the river or stream; and this shall not be construed to affect the rights and privileges heretofore guaranteed, or prevent redress by suit at law.

"Art. XI. No person coming direct from a foreign country shall be permitted to locate or work any lot within the jurisdiction of this encampment.

"Art. XII. Any person who shall steal a mule, or other animal of draught or burden or shall enter a house or tent and steal therefrom gold dust, money, provisions, goods or other articles amounting to $100 or over in value, shall upon conviction thereof, be considered guilty of felony and suffer death by hanging. Any aider or abetter therein shall in like manner be punished.

"Art. XIII. Should any person wilfully, maliciously and premeditatedly take the life of another, on conviction of the murder, he shall suffer death by hanging.

"Art. XIV. Any person convicted of stealing tools, clothing or other articles of less value than $100, shall be punished and disgraced by having his head and eyebrows close shaved and shall leave the encampment within twenty-four hours.

"Art. XV. The fee of the alcalde for issuing a writ or search-warrant, taking an attestation, giving a certificate or any other instrument of writing shall be $5.00; for each witness he may swear $2.00, and one ounce of gold dust for each and every case tried before him. The fee of the sheriff in each case shall be one ounce of gold dust, and a like sum for each succeeding day employed in the same case. The fee of the jury shall be half an ounce in each case. A witness shall be entitled to $4.00 in each case.

"Art. XVI. Whenever a criminal convict is unable to pay the costs of the case, the alcalde, sheriff, jurors and witnesses, shall render their services free of remuneration.

"Art. XVII. In case of the death of a resident of this encampment, the alcalde shall take charge of his effects and dispose of them for the benefit of his relatives or friends, unless the deceased otherwise desire it.

"Art. XVIII. All former acts and laws are hereby repealed and made null and void, except where they conflict with claims guaranteed under said laws."

These laws have been quoted in full because they give such an excellent idea of the plan of government the miners had in mind as well as the wide range of matters considered. For it will be seen that not only does this plan partake of the nature of a constitution and by-laws for a mining company but it actually provides for civil officers and defines crimes and punishments and does not hesitate even to specify the death penalty.

Not all of the mining camps followed the plan of government as outlined in the laws for the Jacksonville district. The plan here given placed the government in the hands of an alcalde, assisted by the sheriff, a peculiar combination of Spanish and Anglo-Saxon institutions.

In other places a standing committee or commission was named with power to act. Rough and Ready, in Nevada County, was an example of this type of government. There a committee of citizens was placed in control of the government. From their decision there was no appeal except to the citizenship itself. This committee performed almost all the functions of government, from laying out the town and miners' claims to hearing disputes and trying cases of men accused of crime.

In probably the greater number of the camps the miners resorted to the more primitive method of general assemblage. Here at a general miners' meeting all were heard and action would be taken as the needs of each case might determine. The meetings were democratic in both form and spirit as every man was given an opportunity to be heard on any issue.

Both in the making of their laws and in passing judgment in disputes, the miners were concerned neither with form nor technicalities. They took the most direct method to determine the issues involved and to arrive at a just decision. Time from their work meant loss of profits and, after all, results were more important than form. Borthwick gives an interesting picture of a civil suit before a miner's court.

"When the jury had squatted themselves all together in an exalted position on a heap of stones and dirt, one of the plaintiffs, as spokesman for his party, made a very pithy speech, calling several witnesses to prove his statements, and cited many of the laws of the diggings in support of his claims. The defendants followed in the same manner, making the most of their case; while the general public, sitting in groups on the different heaps of stones piled up between the holes with which the ground was honeycombed, smoked their pipes and watched the proceedings.

"After the plaintiff and defendant had said all they had to say about it, the jury examined the state of the ground in dispute; they then called some more witnesses to give further information, and having laid their shaggy heads together for a few minutes, they pronounced their decision; which was that the men working on the race should be allowed six days to work out their claim before the water should be turned in upon them.

"Neither party was particularly well pleased with the verdict—a pretty good sign that it was an impartial one; but they had to abide by it, for had there been any resistance on either side, the rest of the miners would have enforced the decision of this august tribunal. From it there was no appeal; a jury of miners was the highest court known, and I must say I never saw a court of justice with so little humbug about it."

As one reads these early records one is impressed with the earnestness of the men. When action was taken by them they meant what they said. An interesting illustration is at hand from the archives of Trinity County where in the fall of 1853 a dispute had arisen between a Dr. Ware and a group of men headed by Mr. McDermott over water rights. The record reads:

"Miner's Meeting, Weaverville, June 7th, 1853.

"The Miners of this district met today en masse in front of the Independence, for the purpose of finally settling the claims to the water of West Weaver, and which heretofore has been conducted to those diggins by two Races known as Dr. Ware's and Fiddler's Races; but is now claimed by the Miners of West Weaver. On motion, Colonel Wm. B. May was appointed President and Wm. Feast, Secretary. Colonel O. H. Allen rose and stated in a concise and short address the object of the meeting, giving the history of the above Races—the cause of their origin and concluded with an exposé of the law on the subject. After some desultory remarks from some few of the Claimants and others, the following preamble and resolutions were adopted by a seventh eighth vote.—

"Whereas, some malicious persons residing on West Weaver, have without cause or provocation, committed a wanton destruction of property in the burning of Dr. Ware's reservoir on West Weaver, and cut and otherwise injured the race known as Dr. Ware's Race, which in part supplies water for the diggins on McKinzie's Gulch and its tributaries, to the serious injury of not only Dr. Ware, but also, the Miners working on said Gulches, and Whereas the several Race Companies of East and West Weaver have endured considerable expense in constructing reservoirs and conducting water from said Creeks to Weaver for mutual benefit, without having interfered with the right of any miner or miners working on Said Creeks at the time and,

"Whereas, it becomes us as Americans and as good citizens to protect one another in our rights and privileges: Therefore, be it Resolved, That We, the Miners of Weaver, assembled en masse, do hereby repudiate and frown upon any and every such spirit of agrarianism, as has so lately manifested itself in the burning of the Reservoir and cutting of Dr. Ware's Race, and will protect all persons in their respective rights and privileges, as guaranteed to them by the constitution of this state as well as that of the United States, Resolved, that the aforesaid Race Companies be entitled, according to their priority of right, to so much of the water of said Creeks as their respective Races will convey, Provided always that a sufficient quantity be allowed to run in the natural beds of said Creeks, for the benefit of miners at present working, or who may hereafter work said beds; and that

[197]

four tom heads shall be deemed sufficient for that purpose,
Resolved, that any individual or company of individuals,
who have dug or may hereafter dig a race or races (not
otherwise mentioned in this our act) for the conveyance
of water not in use at the time, from any gulch or Creek,
in this district, shall be protected in and to said water,
so long as he or they shall keep said race or races in
proper repair, provided, that such water be used for
mining purposes, Resolved that We will assist Dr. Ware
in the repair of his race, and do hereby constitute a committee of the whole, and pledge ourselves to see that the
provisions of this meeting be complied with. On motion
it was resolved, that the President appoint at his leisure
six persons to act as directors of said Committee; on
motion the proceedings were ordered to be published in
the Shasta Courier, when the Meeting adjourned sine
die. By order

Wm. Feast, Sec'y   W. B. May, President."

It is, of course, one thing to make laws and sometimes
another thing to see that these laws are enforced. To the
men of the Gold Days there was no such distinction, as is
shown by the account of this second meeting:

"A Miners Meeting at Weaverville, Trinity Cty., Cal.,
Pursuant to Notice a meeting of Miners was held on
Tuesday, the 9th day of August [1853] at Johnson's old
house on Sidney Flat. Mr. Cameron was appointed
Chairman and called the meeting to order. On motion,
R. T. Miller was appointed Secretary, the object of the
meeting was to investigate the existing difficulties between Dr. Ware, and a mob of miners on West Weaver
who without any apparent cause and in violation of all
laws of the country and of honor have destroyed his
property with that of other individuals, and as we are
creditably informed are now holding water by force of

arms that is justly the property of Ware and others. Dr. Ware explained the object of the meeting in a few pertinent remarks. He said that McDermot told him on yesterday that unless he gave up one half of the water in the Creek aforesaid that he McDermott would take a body of men and take the water by force of arms and hold the same until he and his men were whiped off the ground his party as above mentioned have taken possession of the water and are holding it by force of arms, in this dilemma Dr. Ware calls upon his fellow miners to assist him in defending his rights, agreeable to the old Miners laws, they said that this was a serious affair but that they were willing to defend the old and established miners laws and the rights. Mr. Miller then moved that a Committee of five be appointed to investigate the nature of the grievance and examine the law on the subject and report to an adjurn meeting at one o'clock. Motion carried unanimously. Messrs. Brown Gordon Caton Pencost & Cameron appointed said Committee, meeting adjurned to one o'clock. Pursuant to adjurnment meeting met at one o'clock were called to order by the Chairman, Mr. Cameron. Committee reported as follows having thouroughly investigated the laws and customs of the miners of Weaver — We fully concur in the opinion that Dr. Ware is fully entitled to all the water in West Weaver except four tom heads which is allowed for the bed of the stream also that the burning of his reservoir and the destruction of his dam and other property & the taking of his water from his race by force of arms are malicious acts & Should not be submitted to by those who are in favor of law and order. On motion the report was received and the committee discharged, on motion it was resolved that we assist Dr. Ware in turning the water into his race and that we sustain him to the last extremity in keeping it in the race. On motion meeting then adjurned for the purpose of carrying this resolution into effect." Here the record ceases, leaving one to imagine the method used to enforce the resolution adopted.

Because of the lack of jails and prisons the methods of punishment were quite different from those employed in the settled areas. When a man was judged guilty of a serious crime it was considered important that the camp be rid of the criminal since it was impossible to incarcerate him. Immediate execution was the most effective way of dealing with such cases. When the offense was less serious or if it was thought the guilty man might reform, other methods of punishment were resorted to. Whippings were the most commonly used. Thirty-nine lashes well laid on the bare back was the common sentence, but a hundred or more were not unknown. We also read of cases where the culprit was branded upon the cheek with a letter "R" and had his head and eyebrows closely shaved before being driven from camp. In one case at hand, a man's ears were also clipped as a mark of disgrace. Corporal punishment was then not considered in the same light that it now is and whippings and more severe punishments were meted out in many of the states.

Placerville had the doubtful honor of being the first mining camp to resort to the miners' court for the punishment of serious offenses. In January, 1849, five men were caught in an attempted robbery. What to do with the culprits was a serious problem. Having neither jail, sheriff nor judge, their choice lay between turning the miscreants loose to prey upon other camps or to resort to such punishment as they could mete out. It was decided to hold a trial and judge and jury were immediately selected. The men were found guilty and sentenced to thirty-nine lashes each. This was relatively light punishment and would have passed unnoticed had not addi-

tional charges been preferred against three of the men for attempted murder and attempted robbery on the Stanislaus a few months previous. Since this was a much graver charge the whole camp, some two hundred men, served as jurors and having heard the evidence agreed that they should be hanged. In spite of the opposition of Lieutenant E. G. Buffum, this sentence was carried out forthwith by hanging them to the limbs of a tree standing in town. Because of this exhibition of frontier justice the name of "Hangtown" has ever since clung to the town.

Soon after this an affair occurred at Ford's Bar on the Middle Fork of the American River. In a drunken row, two men started a fight which soon became general. Finally a huge miner named Graham decided it had gone far enough, and seizing a musket, afterward reported as empty, he mounted a barrel and threatened to shoot the first man that started the fight anew. He appeared to mean what he said and peace was restored for a time. During the lull in the storm the men of the bar decided to take steps to prevent any recurrence of this affair and to wipe off from Ford's Bar the reputation it had gained. Graham was named alcalde and a large Missourian was made sheriff. The next day the new government was put to the test. A man who assaulted another with a knife was brought before a jury, found guilty, fined the cost of the court and required to leave the camp within twenty-four hours.

The influx of a very large disorderly element in 1849 was expected to cause a rapid increase in crimes. It is therefore with interest that we read in the statement of General Bennet Riley, who visited the mining district during the summer of 1849, a very favorable report of order throughout the whole area. He says the miners in each small community had chosen their alcaldes and sheriffs and were sustaining their official acts with loyalty and energy. Likewise General P. F. Smith, commander of the Pacific Division of the Army, reports: "I doubt whether any part of the United States has presented a community in which there have been so few crimes and even disorders committed. The public records of any of our large cities will present more of these in one day than have taken place in the whole of California since my arrival."

The miners' court was frequently organized for a particular occasion but it was based upon the fundamental principle of justice both to the individual and to society. It is probable that there were times when the ends of justice were not met, but the same may be said of more formal courts of justice. That they were effective in the restraining of the lawless element is admitted by the critics of California life during the Gold Days. Not all critics of the present day are willing to make similar admission for our courts.

One case may be related which is often cited as a miscarriage of justice, in which a woman was the victim. This is considered by most writers as an unfortunate affair in which justice was hindered by racial passion. Downieville was a thriving mining camp where stern punishment awaited the evil-doer. During the excitement of a Fourth of July celebration an intoxicated miner burst open the door of a house occupied by a beautiful young Mexican woman named Juanita. Some said the entrance was accidental, others that it was a climax of a series of unwelcome advances made to the woman who was living faithfully with a Mexican who may or may not have been her husband. The miner returned the next day, some say to apologize, but his advance was unwelcome and his excuses not accepted. The young woman, in keeping with the characteristics of her race, had a quick passion. A dispute between the two parties ended in the stabbing of the miner. The woman contended that he had taken occasion to add further insult and that she had acted in defense of her self-respect.

The dead miner had many friends and they proceeded to act. An improvised court was called. There was no doubt of the killing which the woman acknowledged while protesting her action in self-defense. But the angry passions of the men were not allayed. In spite of the pleadings even of Stephen J. Field, later of the United States Supreme Court, it was decided that she must pay the penalty as a murderess.

Mounting an elevation beneath the gallows she spoke calmly to her executioners declaring that if the law of the Americans declared she must die she would do so without regret or apology. She then adjusted the rope with her own hands and with a brave "Adios Señores!" swung lightly from the scaffold. Before the week had passed Downieville came to feel a sense of shame for the deed and the judge and jury were strongly denounced for the part they had taken.

This sad affair might be matched with other similar accounts, but they are not numerous, for the purpose of the miners was to maintain the law rather than to punish their individual enemies.

During the summer of 1850, in the southern mines, two Chilean miners were tried in an alcalde's court and convicted of crime by a jury of six upon evidence which was very largely circumstantial. The American miners who had gathered to witness the execution were not satisfied with the judgment. The evidence was not conclusive and the jury had consisted of only six men. These men should have a fair trial. A miners' court was organized, a full jury was selected, an attorney was appointed to represent the defendants, with the result that they were acquitted and set free.

There are furthermore many cases to show that the miners did intercede to see that justice was done to one accused of crime. May S. Corcoran has written of the experiences of her father, later Judge John M. Corcoran, then a young miner in Hornitos, Mariposa County. On one warm summer afternoon a little Chinaman came rushing into his place. Already had the fellow felt the hangman's noose, and had even been brought to the point of confessing to the theft of nuggets, gold-dust and re-volvers from the miners of the neighborhood. Hasten-ing to the young lawyer he appealed to him for help in the cause of justice. His frank manner indicated to the young American that he was a victim of persecution; of his innocence there could be no doubt.

Hastening before the threatening miners Corcoran pleaded for the accused Chinese. Would they only per-mit him to speak for himself! An Italian then came for-ward and related how the men had lost numerous articles from their stores and tents and how on last night they had kept watch and had caught the Chinaman as he was slipping out of his cabin with a punk in his hand. A search of his person had given them no evidence against him but they firmly believed him guilty, and had taken action which had led to his confession.

Although there seemed no uncertainty among the men as to the Chinaman's being involved in the thefts, he was given a chance to explain. He then related how a short time before, his young wife, whom he had stolen in China, and whom he dearly loved, had died. He had quietly buried her in an old sluice box up the cañon. Every night he went up to her grave to put a punk upon it to keep away the devils. He was going out to do this last night when caught by the white men. Here his eyes filled with tears and he was no longer able to talk.

This was sufficient to satisfy a burly Irishman of the Celestial's innocence, and others, including the aggrieved Italian, joined in, all thankful and happy that they had been spared from shedding innocent blood. The young lawyer and his client made their way together from the scene of the near tragedy. As they reached the home of the Chinese boy, the young lawyer could not but express to his companion his sincere sympathy for the loss of his young wife, whereupon the Chinese brightened up and replied: "No die! Wait, I give you something! You like one revolver, two revolvers, dozen revolvers? I give you all."

In wonderment the lawyer asked, "Where did you get them?"

"In stores, blankets, tin cans, from Greaser, Dagoes, Micks, Gringoes, Dutchman allee same fools. Hide here. Now make you rich, for you one good man, Lawyer Juan."

The truth then dawned upon the young lawyer. Full of rage he declared that while as his attorney he could not turn his client over for quick justice, he would order him out of the country immediately and that if he returned he would be one to assist in his hanging. Whereupon the Chinese youth accompanied by his girl wife slid away down the cañon and the young lawyer was left to reflect upon the ways of justice!

"There was sometimes a grain of grim humor in the American alcaldes," is the statement of Governor Burnett in his *Recollections*, "which was well illustrated in the following incident that appears to have taken place in one of the northern mining camps. In the autumn of 1849 a tall, handsome young fellow, dressed in a suit of fine broadcloth and mounted on a splendid horse, stole a purse of gold dust from the cabin of an honest miner and disappeared. As soon as the fact became known the loser and several of his friends went in pursuit of the thief. It being ascertained that he had taken the main road that led around a high mountain, his pursuers cut across by a trail, which was much shorter than the road, and overhauling the young man took him before the alcalde. That officer, after patiently listening to the testimony, quietly said to the prisoner, 'The Court thinks it right that you should return that purse of gold to its owner.' To this the culprit readily assented and handed it over. The alcalde next remarked, 'The Court thinks you ought to pay the costs of the proceedings.' To this also the culprit made no objection, evidently thinking he was very fortunate to get off so easily, and inquired the amount. Being informed the costs were two ounces of gold dust, he cheerfully produced and paid that sum. 'And now,' continued the alcalde, with a twinkle in his eye, 'there is another part of the sentence of this Court that has not yet been mentioned; and that is, that you receive thirty-nine lashes on your bare back, well laid on.' The wheels of justice moved much quicker in those days than in these; and long before nightfall that young man had occasion to be sorry.''

On a Sunday in March, 1851, in a quarrel between two drunken men, one of them killed the other, who was his partner. He attempted to escape but was caught, tried and condemned to be hanged at four o'clock that afternoon. This man took the affair very coolly and admitted that he deserved to die. He had had no reason to kill his partner who had been his best friend. He ate a hearty dinner, talked with the men as usual and when the time came, mounted the platform without hesitation. After the rope was fixed, he was given an opportunity to speak. He warned all against the evils of intemperance,

which had been the cause of his rash act. He would like
to have a chance to write to his wife but he judged there
was not sufficient time. Since the program before him
was one that must be followed he judged he might as well
be about it. With that he leaped high in the air and
came down with a jerk that brought his career to an end.

Mrs. Eliza Farnham records another like incident:

"A gentleman told me that news was one day acciden-
tally brought to the locality, where he was mining, that
a man who had committed a robbery in a neighboring
camp, or diggings, some two miles away, had been ar-
rested, and was to be hanged. It created no excitement;
drew nobody from their employment; but, being himself
somewhat curious in such things, he walked over to the
spot, and found several miners gathered near some trees,
talking very quietly in little groups. Not knowing anyone, and wishing to have the criminal pointed out to
him, he inquired of a person who was standing a little
apart, which was the man they were about to hang; to
which he replied, without the slightest change of countenance: 'I believe it's me, sir!' Half an hour after, he
was suspended from a bough of a tree, and the little
community dispersed to their respective suppers, without
the smallest demonstration.

"There have been a great many such administrations of
popular justice (?), and I believe that their righteousness
has rarely been questioned. These people's courts have,
at least, been far more efficient and prompt in the desperate conditions of society than the duly authorized ju-
diciary of the state. Juries have been empaneled on the
spot; witnesses examined; and proof made, in almost all
cases, stronger than would be required in the legal tribunals; and, if the accused were found guilty, his doom
was pronounced, and swiftly executed, in a cool, al-
together unique manner; and the people, in an hour or

two, fell quietly back upon their picks, pans, and toms, as if nothing had happened out of the daily routine of their lives."

In passing judgment upon the justice of the numerous courts with this tendency to swift action, it should be borne constantly in mind that as a usual thing those who served as judge and jury were men of the immediate neighborhood and that the reputation and character of the accused was pretty well established before the case came up, and moreover, in the greater number of cases the culprit was taken red-handed in the act. Since the guilt was in many cases perfectly evident before the trial was begun, the only action necessary was to determine what sentence would most suit the offense.

Notwithstanding many undesirable features which found place in such a system of government, the miners' codes and courts of justice were the chief agencies that prevented absolute anarchy in the early mining camps. Bayard Taylor, who has so accurately described the life in the mines during the Gold Days, records his observation as follows:

"From all I saw and heard, while at the Mokelumne Diggings, I judged there was as much order and security as could be attained without a civil organization. The inhabitants had elected one of their own number Alcalde, before whom all culprits were tried by a jury selected for that purpose. Several thefts had occurred, and the offending parties been severely punished, after a fair trial. Some had been whipped and cropped, or maimed in some other way, and one or two of them hung. Two or three who had stolen largely had been shot down by the injured party, the general feeling among the miners justifying such a course when no other seemed available. We met near Livermore's Ranch, on the way to Stockton, a man whose head had been shaved and his ears cut off, after receiving one hundred lashes, for stealing ninety-eight pounds of gold. It may conflict with popular ideas of morality, but nevertheless, this extreme course appeared to have produced good results. In fact, in a country without not only bolts and bars, but any effective system of law and government, this Spartan severity of discipline seemed the only security against the most frightful disorder. The result was that, except some petty acts of larceny, thefts were rare."

Perhaps we find in the words of the Reverend William Taylor the soundest justification for the miners' courts:

"Wicked as were the mass of California miners, they displayed some good qualities . . . . 'Judge Lynch' transacted a great deal of business in California in those days. However much may be said in condemnation of his court, this could be said in favor of the denizens of California, that riots and promiscuous shooting into the masses, killing innocent with guilty, such as has been enacted in some of our Eastern cities was never known in California. In the administration of California lynch law, the thunderbolt of public fury always fell on the head of the guilty, who by the enormity and palpable character of his crime, excited it, and not till his guilt was proved to the satisfaction of the masses comprising the court." Here indeed was the American capacity for self-government most clearly illustrated.

Chapter XI

CHAPTER XI
Paper Towns and Easy Money

WHILE HITHERTO attention had been devoted largely to the mining area, the fact must not be overlooked that the gold excitement had also been working great changes in those parts of the state less immediately connected with the process of mining. The development of the great metropolis upon the bay will be considered later, but at this time we may well turn our attention to the growth of the many towns tributary to the gold area. In those places, as elsewhere, there was to be witnessed a high degree of the spirit of venture and speculation that was so noticeable in the mining camps.

In an earlier chapter we have noticed the beginnings of some of the interior towns. Charles M. Weber's attempt to promote the town of Tuleburg in 1847 was not marked with success. After the gold discovery he tried his luck in the diggings and then thought once again of this infant town. A re-christening gave it the name of "Stockton," and Stockton soon became a rapidly growing youngster. The location of Stockton was strategic in relation to the southern mines. The San Joaquin River offered ready access to Stockton from the bay region, while the river channel further up was not deep enough to accommodate vessels conveniently. This, therefore, fixed Stockton as the chief depot for supplies for the mines in what later came to be Amador, Calaveras, Tuolumne and Mariposa counties.

"A view of Stockton was something to be remembered," says Bayard Taylor of his visit here in 1849. "There, in the heart of California, where the last winter stood a solitary ranch in the midst of tule marshes, I found a canvas town of a thousand inhabitants, and a port with twenty-five vessels at anchor! The mingled noises of labor around—the click of hammers and the grating of saws—the shouts of mule drivers—the jingling of spurs—the jar and jostle of wares in the tents—almost cheated me into the belief that it was some old commercial mart, familiar with such sounds for years past. Four months, only, had sufficed to make the place what it was; and in that time a wholesale firm established there (one out of a dozen) had done business to the amount of $100,000. The same party had just purchased a lot eighty by one hundred feet, on the principal street, for $6,000, and the cost of erecting a common one-story clapboard house on it was $15,000."

Notwithstanding the lead achieved by Stockton there were rivals that beset her way. By this time New Hope, the embryo town of Samuel Brannan's Mormon colonists, had disappeared. Brigham Young had ordered the Saints to assemble at Salt Lake, and this together with the gold discovery was sufficient to put an end to the newly projected town. But on the other hand San Joaquin City had been laid out in the same vicinity. Its location was on the western bank of the river of that name and nearly opposite the mouth of the Stanislaus. Along the Tuolumne River also were Adamsville, Empire City and La Grange, all of which for a brief period enjoyed the honor of being county seats. Besides these,

Crescent City also struggled for an existence although it never became a county seat.

Although Stockton was able to maintain a recognizable lead over these rival towns in her vicinity, there were others nearer the bay that for a while disputed her supremacy. Among the latter we find the short-lived New York-of-the-Pacific and Benicia. The former was a paper town laid out by speculators on the south side of Suisun Bay at the mouth of the San Joaquin River. This projected city was founded as a commercial rival to the city of like name on the Atlantic by members of the regiment of New York Volunteers who arrived in California during the Mexican War. E. G. Buffum, a visitor to the gold region in 1849, describes for us New York-of-the-Pacific as he saw it. From his enthusiastic description one is inclined to wonder if Buffum was also one of the promoters, or if he had merely yielded to the temptation to speculate in its town lots:

"The town is seated on a broad and well-watered plain, covered with many groves of magnificent oaks, extending from the waters of the bay and the river San Joaquin to the hills some three miles back. So gradual is the slope that it seems a perfect level, viewed from the river's bank; but standing at the base of the hills looking toward the water, the slope will be found to be perfect and regular to the water's edge, where it terminates upon a fine sand-beach, from five to ten feet above the level of the highest tide. New York is beautifully laid out, with large reserves for churches, a university, and other public edifices, and is perhaps one of the most healthy points in the country, being free from ague and fever and the prevailing fevers usual on fresh-water rivers below and between the mining region and San Francisco. But the great advantage which New York-of-the-Pacific possesses over other places above San Francisco is that it is

[217]

at the head of ship navigation, as two regular surveys, published by distinguished military and naval officers of Suisun Bay have demonstrated. Ships of the largest class can sail direct from the ocean to New York, where they will find a safe and convenient harbour, and where at this time are lying a number of merchant ships from different parts of the Union, directly alongside the bank upon which they have discharged their cargoes."

Notwithstanding the fact that at the fall election of 1849 this embryo metropolis cast more votes for governor than did the town of Los Angeles, the dreams of the founders of New York-of-the-Pacific did not materialize. Its location and even its name are remembered by only a few antiquarians interested in the Days of Gold. The eclipse of New York-of-the-Pacific was as sudden as its rise—one might say it was contemporaneous with its rise. A writer of the early 'fifties philosophizes in this manner:

"We entered Suisun Bay, on the shores of which a city was attempted—New York by name—but failed. There is something to admire in the audacity of speculators who, finding themselves possessed of a few acres of swamp, wave their wands and order a city to appear. The working human tide of California ebbed and flowed past New York with great regularity, but all commands to arrest it, and direct it from its natural course were futile as regarded that city, which really presented no advantages that I could see."

Across the Suisun Bay was a more formidable rival for metropolitan honors. This was Robert Semple's town of Benicia. The site of this town had been selected by Semple in 1846 and a town had immediately been projected. The name first taken was "Francesca," under which name its promoters waged such an aggressive campaign that the rising town of Yerba Buena on the shores of San Francisco Bay began to realize that the publicity value of the name of San Francisco Bay was being capitalized by "Francesca" on Suisun Bay rather than by "Yerba Buena" on San Francisco Bay. It was because of this keen competition between the two towns that Alcalde Hyde issued a decree on January 7, 1847, changing the name of the latter town from "Yerba Buena" to "San Francisco." This shift forced Semple to make a change also, resulting in "Francesca" becoming "Benicia."

The advantages of Benicia above the older town of San Francisco were emphatically proclaimed by Semple and his associates. More practical methods were also used to boost the new town, for it is recorded that the promoters paid settlers a bonus of $1,000 each for moving bag and baggage to Benicia from the neighboring town of Sonoma. With the rise of San Francisco some of Semple's associates began to lose their deep devotion for Benicia, but not so Semple himself. When he heard that Thomas O. Larkin, one of these men, was actually erecting a row of buildings in San Francisco, it is said that Semple practically gave away his San Francisco lots in order to show his contempt for such poor business judgment as Larkin displayed. For a while this spirit won recognition for Benicia. Upon the arrival of General Persifor F. Smith the Pacific headquarters of the United States army were established at Benicia, this being a prestige which its promoters were sure it justly deserved.

"It is conjectured that at a future day Benicia will rank second to San Francisco," wrote William Shaw in 1851, "as it is a matter of considerable importance to discharge goods near to where there is a market for them, and Benicia being more accessible from the provinces of the interior, shippers will naturally prefer chartering vessels to that port. The site is also well adapted for an extensive city; it has been surveyed and marked out into various lots and streets, and numerous buildings have been already erected. Benicia is also used as the naval and military depot of Upper California; the barracks, magazines, and government storehouse are situated on a high promontory, a short distance from the contemplated city."

Benicia's star was in the ascendency. The Pacific Mail Steamship Company selected Benicia for its docks and the largest of ocean vessels found berth there. Why should not Benicia become the leading city in the state? There could be found nothing to justify any other than an affirmative answer. When, therefore, General M. G. Vallejo was found to be unable to erect a fully equipped capital city on the banks of Napa River, Benicia's success in pressing her advantages upon the state legislators found expression in an act effective February 11, 1853, whereby Benicia became the "permanent capital" of California. For a period of thirteen months Benicia enjoyed this exalted honor, but was finally "robbed" of it by the "politicians" of Sacramento. Marryat, who wrote in 1855, thus describes Benicia as it appeared to him at that time:

"In two hours we arrived at Benicia, and the steamer ran alongside of an old hulk connected by a gangway with the shore . . . . Benicia is a city in embryo; there is ample room for building, for in every direction extend undulating hills, covered with wild oats, but unobstructed by timber, of which none can be found within many miles. But the natural advantages of this spot have not been embraced by the public, for one reason, that the opposite town of Martinez is more fortunately planted among groves of trees; and for another, that no one requires a town in this particular part of the world. So Benicia is a failure just now; and instead of raising an imposing front, in evidence of man's progress, it hides its diminished little head among the few huts that stand in commemoration of its failure. I pitched my tent at a short distance from the beach, and, as I afterward discovered on reference to the 'plan of Benicia,' on the exact spot that had been selected as the site of the 'Public Botanical Gardens' of that flourishing city . . . ."

Sacramento Valley also had its quota of ambitious young towns. Journeying up the river below Sacramento itself the traveler in 1849 would pass the sites of Onisbo, opposite the mouth of Steamboat Slough, Webster, on the east bank about ten miles below the mouth of the American River, and Washington on the western bank opposite the Sacramento embarcadero. Even more promising than these was Suttersville about three miles down-river from Sacramento. This was located on a slight elevation overlooking the river and was but about three miles from Sutter's Fort. Sutter himself believed this to be the best site for a town along the river and a settlement had already begun here before the gold discovery. That Suttersville had the idea that a great future lay before it seemed to be the opinion of many who visited it in the early Gold Days.

"The city of Sutter," says a writer of 1849, "is beautifully located on the eastern bank of the Sacramento River, adjoining Sacramento City, and is perhaps the most eligible site for a commercial town in all Northern California. It is situated on the highest and healthiest ground on the whole river, the banks at this point not being subject to the annual overflow. The largest class of steamboats and all vessels navigating the Sacramento River, can lie and discharge their cargoes directly at its banks . . . . Excellent roads diverge from this point to the rich placers of the North, Middle and South forks, Bear River, Yuba and Feather rivers, and also to the mines of the

San Joaquin. It is surrounded on all sides by a fine agricultural and well-wooded country, and will soon be the depot for the great northern mines."

Sacramento itself had a very decided advantage over its rivals. Near at hand was Sutter's Fort, the one spot most known in all the mining region. Not many months had passed after the gold discovery before people began to crowd in upon the low lands near the mouth of the American River. Shops sprang up, and before anyone realized the fact a town had come into being. Taking its name from the adjacent river it became known as "Sacramento City," the "city" being an important part of the name of many of the struggling towns. Alonzo Delano first visited Sacramento in September, 1849, at which time he says it "contained a floating population of about five thousand people. It was first laid out in the spring of 1849, on the east bank of the Sacramento River, here less than one eighth of a mile wide, and is about a mile and a half west of Sutter's Fort. Lots were originally sold for $200 each, but within a year sales were made as high as $30,000. There were not a dozen wood or frame buildings in the whole city, but they were chiefly made of canvas, stretched over light supporters; or were simply tents, arranged along the streets. The stores, like the dwellings, were of cloth, and property and merchandise of all kinds lay exposed, night and day by the wayside, and such a thing as a robbery was scarcely known. This in fact was the case throughout the country, and is worthy of notice on account of the great and extraordinary change which occurred. There were a vast number of taverns and eating houses, and the only public building was a theatre. All these were made of canvas."

Describing the place later Delano says:

"Sacramento City had become a city indeed. Substantial wooden buildings had taken the place of the cloth tents and frail tenements of the previous November, and, although it had been recently submerged by an unprecedented flood, which occasioned a great destruction of property, and which ruined hundreds of its citizens, it exhibited a scene of busy life and enterprise, peculiarly characteristic of the Anglo-Saxon race by whom it was peopled. An immense business was doing with miners in furnishing supplies; the river was lined with ships, the streets were thronged with drays, teams, and busy pedestrians; the stores were large, and well filled with merchandise; and even Aladdin could not have been more surprised at the power of his wonderful lamp, than I was at the mighty change which less than twelve months had wrought, since the first cloth tent had now grown into a large and flourishing city."

At the November election in 1849, Sacramento cast nearly 1,700 votes, which showed it to have the largest voting population of any place outside of San Francisco. The census of 1850 credits the place with a population of 20,000. By 1854, it had achieved the distinction of securing permanently the capital of the new state.

Across the American River north from Sacramento the 'Forty-niner came to the town of Boston. Buffum, who writes of his visit to the region in 1849, has these words of praise for the youthful town:

"The city of Boston is located on the northern bank of the American Fork, at its junction with the Sacramento River, about one hundred yards above the old *Embarcadero*, the site upon which Sacramento City now stands. It extends upon the banks of both rivers for several miles, and is destined to become a flourishing town. The banks of the Sacramento at this point are not subject to overflow, being more than twelve feet in many places above high-water mark. The town is situated upon a broad and well-watered plain, covered with many groves of magnificent oaks, and the largest class of steamers, and all vessels navigating the Sacramento River can lie and discharge directly at its banks.

"Boston has been surveyed by J. Halls, Esq., and Lieut. Ringgold, U. S. N., and is laid out in squares of two hundred and forty feet by three hundred and twenty feet, subdivided each into eight building lots eighty feet by one hundred and twenty feet, with large public squares, and reservations for school-houses, churches, and public buildings. One of the peculiar advantages of Boston is that, being located on the northern bank of the American Fork, it is not necessary in proceeding to the gold mines to cross that river, which is exceedingly high and rapid at some seasons of the year. The direct and most travelled road proceeds from this point to the rich placers of the Yuba, Feather River, Bear Creek, and the North, Middle and South forks of the American. The soil is of the richest description, the surrounding scenery highly picturesque, and the plains in the immediate vicinity are covered with wild game of every variety which California affords . . . . Lots are selling rapidly at from $200 to $1,000 each, and before many months the city of Boston on the golden banks of the Rio Sacramento will rival its New England namesake in business and importance."

After leaving Boston the next town was a second Washington City about twelve miles further up the river, then came Springfield and Vernon. The latter was at the mouth of Feather River opposite the rival town of Fremont, which lay on the west side of the Sacramento.

"Vernon," says Buffum, "is situated on the east bank of Feather River at the point of its confluence with the Sacramento, one of the most eligible positions for a town in the whole northern region of California. The banks of the river are high and not subject to overflow, and this point is said to be at the head of ship navigation on the

Sacramento. The ground is a gentle slope, surrounded by a beautiful country. From the town of Vernon, good and well travelled roads diverge to the rich mineral regions of the North and Middle Forks, Bear Creek, Yuba and Feather rivers, rendering the distance much less than by any other route. The town is growing rapidly, and promises to become a great depot for the trade of the above-mentioned mines."

Along the Feather River there were many towns seeking an opportunity to demonstrate their importance. At the old ranch of Nicolaus Altgeier was the town of Nicolaus, which proudly claimed for itself a position at the head of navigation. One wonders from reading the enthusiastic accounts sent out by the promoters of these various towns whether navigation may not have been a hydra-headed being. In a broadside issued by the proprietors of town lots in August, 1850, we read that:

"The advantages of this town are now too manifest to be any longer denied and doubted . . . . The close proximity of Nicolaus to the rich placers on the Feather and Yuba rivers, Deer, Dry and Bear creeks, and the Forks of the American, ensures its continuance *as the depot for the supplies for all the northern mines . . . .*

"To the merchant, the speculator, the trader, the mechanic and the miner, we unhesitatingly assert that Nicolaus presented greater advantages than any other place in California."

Between Nicolaus and the Yuba River lay the towns of Oro, just below the mouth of Bear River; Plumas City at the mouth of Reed's Creek; El Dorado City, just across from Sutter's Hock Farm; and Eliza, a few miles further north. Delano writing in 1853 describes his experiences when he came down from the mines in the latter part of 1849:

[225]

"Being unable to continue mining and have a care over my cattle at the same time, I drove them to Marysville and sold them. And here I met with a surprise. When I forded the Yuba, in September previous, there stood then but two low adobe houses, known as Nye's Ranch, but early in the following winter a town had been laid out, which, in this space of time had grown to over a thousand inhabitants, with a large number of hotels, stores, groceries, bakeries, and (what soon became a marked feature in California) gambling-houses. Steamboats were daily arriving and departing, which seemed strange, for it had been a matter of doubt the previous fall as to Feather River being navigable for craft larger than whale boats. On this river, a mile from Marysville, Yuba City had sprung into existence, with a population of five hundred inhabitants; and two miles below, the town of Eliza had been laid out, and buildings were rapidly going up. The two latter places, however, were eventually swallowed up by the rapid growth of Marysville, which has become a beautiful city, while the others, at the moment of writing this, have dwindled into nothing, and are nearly deserted. Speculation in towns and lots was rife; and on every hand was heard, 'Lots for sale,' 'New towns laid out,' which looked as well on paper as if they were already peopled. There seemed to be a speculative mania spreading over the land, and scores of new towns were heard of which were never known, only through the puffs of newspapers, the stakes which marked the size of lots, and the nicely drawn plat of the surveyor."

Finding himself "strapped," Delano decided to try his luck in Marysville. Since he had some ability as an artist he set up a stand and for three weeks did a thriving business sketching the heads of the long-bearded miners at an ounce a head. This netted him the sum of four hundred dollars. He then explains that the fever of speculation in town lots was too much for him, so, "Wishing to make money a little faster, I played the speculator, purchased paper town lots, and—lost nearly half of my earnings in the operation! It was, however, at this period that one of the most interesting events of my California life began. The rage for town speculations was still rife, when a friend proposed that we should make a claim twenty miles above Marysville, on Feather River, lay out a town, and get rich by selling the lots. We proceeded accordingly, made our claim, laid off the lots, and in a few days I was installed the patroon of our new village, with a fine stock of goods, cheap enough, if customers could only be coaxed to that really beautiful, but isolated spot. But that was a difficulty not easily overcome. My friend, by adverse circumstances, was finally compelled to give up the speculation, and I called my town an addition to one which my nearest and only neighbor, Captain Yates, had laid out."

Just above Marysville upon the Yuba River was the town of Linda, whose span of life was very short; then up the Feather River came Columbia on the west bank and nearly opposite it stood Oakland, while Featherton was laid out on the east bank just below the mouth of Honcut Creek. Up that smaller stream about two miles on what had formerly been Charlie's Ranch was located Veazie City.

Where the Feather River issued from the mountains was located Bidwell's Bar, which because of its early establishment and mineral wealth became for a time the county seat of Butte County. Other towns sprang up in which agriculture shared with gold in contributing to their development. Among those were Ophir, soon to become Oroville, and her neighbors and rival towns Lynchburg, Oregon City and Hamilton. The last-named, located on the west side of the river, was for a time the seat of justice of the county.

Up the main Sacramento River were also many rising cities, some connected with the mining interests, others centers for agricultural development: Colusa, Butte City, Placer City and Monroeville. All of these with the exception of Butte City were located upon the western bank of the river. Lassen's trading post was located at Deer Creek and above it came Tehama and Red Bluffs. The latter, located at a point where the river had cut into a reddish-colored bank, has grown to a city of importance but has long since changed its name to Red Bluff. It held a position of importance because at this point navigation of the river ceased for most freight-bearing craft, and goods for the Trinity mines were transferred from the boats to wagon-teams. In the same vicinity, but at present without positive location, was Trinidad City, a place not to be confused with the town on the bay of that name. The newspapers of 1850 carried glowing advertisements of this new town which was located, as were so many others, "at the head of navigation."

Just below Red Bluffs was the site of the town of Laodicea. The scriptural counterpart of this last-named town does not bear an enviable record for inasmuch as it was "lukewarm" the Lord threatened to "spue it out of His mouth." It is probable that the promoters of the modern town did not have the warm enthusiasm needed to develop a city and so it sank into oblivion much as did that ancient city.

On Clear Creek at the foot of the Trinity Mountains was located Shasta City. This was both a mining town and a transfer point of freight from the great freight wagons to mule trains, for the journey over the mountains could not be made by wagon trains. This town, now one of California's ghost cities, was for over three decades the county seat of its district, which at one time included all of California to the north and east.

The development of the Trinity-Klamath mines created a need for easier access to this area, resulting in
the discovery of Humboldt Bay by the Josiah Gregg
party during the winter of 1849-50. A rush to the
new region followed. The occupation of Trinidad and
Humboldt bays during March and April, 1850, resulted
immediately in the appropriation of eligible sites for towns
which could act as depots for the mines in the interior.
In this manner Trinidad, Bucksport, Humboldt City,
Uniontown and Eureka came into existence within a
period of a few days.

A study of the documents indicates that the promoters
of these towns were as jealous of their rights as if they
were proprietors of mining claims. Trinidad, the first of
the north coast towns, was laid out by a number of individual proprietors, but the other towns were initiated
by well organized companies, whose aim was to secure
control of the lands on Humboldt Bay suitable for
town sites. Thus Uniontown (subsequently Arcata) was
founded by the Union Company, Humboldt City by the
Laura Virginia Association, and Eureka by the Mendocino
Exploring Company. These companies were especially
interested in town-site speculation. According to the
articles of agreement of the Laura Virginia Association:
"When any important discoveries were made the members
accompanying the expedition were to select and take possession of such lands and locations as they should deem
most eligible for commercial or agricultural purposes.
Each locator was to hold his claim for the joint benefit
of all the members, until, by a subsequent allotment, he
should have his interest defined in severalty, with due
regard to rights and shares in town sites as well as in the
exterior lands. A certain proportion (one sixteenth) of
the whole was reserved as a contingent, chargeable with
such extraordinary expenses as the making of trails and

bridges . . . . and all matters of a public nature in which the benefit of the community was distinguished from that of the individual." The methods followed by the companies were not always laudable and it is probably fortunate that they did not long continue.

Trinidad was located upon the bay discovered by the Spanish in 1775. Trails opened to the diggings made it possible for the new town to bid for freight to the mines, and speculation in town lots was rife. The records show that during the first few months one of the promoters of Trinidad obtained approximately $30,000 from the sale of town lots in that place. The mining excitement of Gold Bluffs caused a veritable boom in town lots and by February of 1851 Trinidad had a population variously estimated from 1,500 to 3,000 people and it successfully aspired to become the county seat of the newly created Klamath County. Unfortunately for Trinidad the Gold Bluff mines did not come up to expectation, and with the collapse of that boom the chances for Trinidad to become a great city were gone. In 1854 the county seat was removed elsewhere and Trinidad lapsed into "comparative insignificance,"—to use the expression of a contemporary writer.

Humboldt City was laid out in May, 1850, as a city of great dimensions if one may judge by a map still on file in the Humboldt County archives. Its water front extended (on paper) for three or four miles along Humboldt Bay, and the town was capable of unlimited expansion into the interior. It is of interest to note the methods of operation of these promoters of new towns in Gold Days. One of the promoters with headquarters in San Francisco was busy with the program of having the Pacific Mail Steamers stop at Humboldt City on the way to and from Oregon. He writes that the *Columbia* under Captain Le Roy is to stop on the next trip in order to examine the port and he advises: "It will be politic to make him directly interested in the place, by giving him individually, such an interest as shall enlist him for us—I should say at least a half a share. His report to Captain Knight will be very important." It may be of interest that the donation was made and that for a time the steamer made regular visits to Humboldt City. But in spite of the efforts of its founders the city did not thrive and a visitor during the fall of 1851 speaks of it as already "nearly deserted."

Bucksport was another Humboldt Bay town that struggled against fate. It was marked out as a town covering eighty square blocks. In 1852 it became the site of a military establishment and aspired the next year to become the capital of the county. Failure to secure this honor, however, caused the town to drop back in the race for supremacy.

For many years the leading town on Humboldt Bay was Union (Arcata). Laid out at the northern end of the bay by the strong Union Company it held a position that its rivals had difficulty in matching. Trails were early cut through the dense redwoods to both the Trinity and Klamath mines and Union became an important depot for the importation of supplies. As the result of this success, when Humboldt County was created in 1853 Union was named as its county seat, a distinction it maintained until 1858 when the honor was given by the legislature to its rival, Eureka.

Eureka was the latest of the towns to be established in the spring of 1850, and for a time it lagged behind the others, but it had very enthusiastic and strong boosters. Trails to the Trinity mines came out on the bay at Eureka, which held a favorable position, being not too far from the entrance to the harbor. Eureka's supremacy was not definitely established, however, until she had won the county seat in 1858.

The story of the county seat election furnishes a good picture of the rivalry between these early towns and their methods of operation, not all of which would be considered ethical by present-day standards. As stated earlier, the county seat of Humboldt County had been fixed at Union. This was not to the liking of either Eureka or Bucksport, and an election was consequently called to settle the issue in October, 1854. The two towns that hoped to gain an advantage by a change worked very hard and did not leave a stone unturned. William Roberts, the largest land-holder in Bucksport, made a public offer, now on file in the county archives, of a block of land to the county for a county building and one lot to each voter in the county who could establish "by his oath . . . that he had voted for Bucksport as the county-seat." In spite of this tempting offer Bucksport won third place in the contest. Another remarkable thing about this election was that Eureka polled so many votes; in fact it would appear that every man, woman and child of the place must have cast a ballot. In spite of her large vote Eureka failed to secure a majority of the ballots and the county seat remained at Union. A new election was immediately called for the next month. It was evident that this would be a duel of ballots be-tween the two rivals, Eureka and Union, and neither proposed to give in without a fight. Evidence of this battle is still to be seen in the archives of Humboldt County. During the four weeks between the elections the Eureka voters increased from 469 to 1,804. The poll list, still available, gave the names of all these "voters" sworn to by the judge and tellers of the election. We are told that the Eureka boosters were very confident of success and produced their ballot and poll list with a feeling of great pride. In spite of this masterly cleverness of Eureka the knowing people of Union held their nerve. There still remained to be counted the returns from Angel's Ranch.

Since in the preceding election twenty-five votes had been all that precinct could muster, Eureka had given it but little thought. When, however, the returns were brought in from Angel's Ranch, the poll list was longer than was to be expected; in fact, it was on a long roll with a double column of names on both sides of the paper. The results, fully attested by the proper election officials, showed that Angel's Ranch went solidly for its neighbor Union to the number of 2,136 votes. Thus was Eureka "robbed" of the fruits of victory. Those who know tell us that the names upon the Angel's Ranch poll list were in fact copied from the list of passengers arriving at San Francisco on the Panama steamers. Although the county seat could not be won by local elections there remained an effective way. Eureka sent one of her worthy citizens to the state legislature and a statute was passed and duly signed by the governor placing the county seat where in the eyes of the Eureka boosters it should always have been. Thus was Eureka's supremacy established.

County seat disputes have made and unmade both towns and counties. Klamath County is an example of the latter. In the northwestern corner of the state Crescent City grew up during the middle 'fifties and aspired to greatness. It was located with a fair degree of convenience to Happy Camp and the upper Klamath River mines. Since the county seat at Trinidad was at the very southwestern corner of Klamath County, it was removed with good reason to Crescent City, where it remained for a brief period. Although the county seat was now in the extreme northwest corner of the county, its removal by vote of the people to Orleans Bar in the mining region itself was a blow to the pride of Crescent City. That city knew that it deserved to be a county seat and it set about to secure this end by creating a new county at the expense of Klamath. The legislature was agreeable to the desires of

Crescent City, and as a result Del Norte County came into being, and Crescent City became once again the capital city of its county.

Attention has been directed thus far in this chapter to those towns that were located just outside of the mining area. These played an important part in the gold period, for it was from them that supplies were obtained for the mining camps. The fact, however, must not be overlooked that along the slopes of the Sierra Nevada and in the mountains of the northwest there were growing up towns which for a time assumed considerable magnitude as mining centers and whose existence was to be more or less permanent. Inaccessibility and lack of land for the location of a town did not effectively prevent the growth of a mining center if only gold was to be found there. Eliza Farnham, who has left many interesting pictures of life in the gold region, describes a visit to a typical mining camp. It was located, as were so many, at the bottom of a deep cañon.

"The great height and steepness of these border-hills on many of the streams, make one of the grandest features of California scenery. Some of them are two, three, and four miles high, and they rise at angles varying from 45° to 60°. You scramble down them, in the best way you can. Sometimes you feel as if your horse were about to turn a summerset, but you push back as forcibly as possible, by way of helping him to preserve the center of gravity, and with an occasional halt and then a rush—a detour to the right and another to the left—a fearful looking forward, and an anxious glance backward, you finally reach the bottom, and, drawing a free breath, once more look about you, and ascertain that, deep down as you are, there have been plenty before you; that Mary Avery keeps a boarding-house for miners on your right; and that Patrick Doyle has the best of liquors and wines for your refreshment in his shanty or tent, on your left; that John Smith, honest man, is a carpenter and no swindler, as he has so often been represented to be in the wicked world you have left up yonder; that he is ready to furnish the busy community about him, indiscriminately, with 'rockers, long toms, or coffins,' as their condition or convenience may require; that the National, or the United States, or the American hotel is kept in that rough one-story hut, which, as you pass, discloses dismal rents in its cotton walls and ceilings, and allures the thirsty wayfarer by a display of a bar, bristling with bottles—and that at the El Dorado or Pavilion are billiards and bowling, and also, of course, the more spicy and earnest games in which men are wont to try their chances for fortune or ruin.

"Twice, or maybe thrice, as your horse loiters through the dusty street, you see a little garden spot, wherein a few cabbages, laden with dust, plead silently for water, and half a dozen rows of choked potatoes remonstrate against their hard lot. At the door of this shanty, you, perhaps, see a child, which looks much like the plants; for its mother cannot keep it clean, and she, perhaps, sits within, or maybe by her husband's rocker in the bared bed of the river, working it while he shovels the earth. If it be at midday, the sun pours his light and heat into this gorge so fiercely that you scorch beneath his rays, and envy the men working in the cool stream or upon the damp ground.

"The heat will soon drive them to the shade for a couple of hours and then all will be still for the time, save the gurgling of water and the hum of voices occasionally raised above the drowsy noontide tone. Between two and three o'clock the miners straggle out again, the shoveling recommences, lazily at first, by two or three, who are soon joined by a score or two, and the familiar sounds

[235]

return. The traders and publicans stand at their doors or lounge upon a bench just within; your horse is brought round looking sleepy and tired, you mount, ride through the stream, and push him up the opposite hill with a deal of toil and dust, and when you have gained the dry and sunny plain, wish you could again feel around you, if only for a moment, the dampness and coolness of the 'Bar.'"

It is not possible here to give in detail the story of the development of the towns of the mining area, but it is important to note the beginnings from which much later development has come. During the early gold period practically every one of the present county seats of the mountain counties came into existence and assumed its position of leadership. From such beginnings we have Quincy, Oroville, Downieville, Nevada City, Marysville, Auburn, Placerville, Jackson, San Andreas, Sonora, and Mariposa along the flank of the Sierra Nevada, and Weaverville and Yreka in the northwestern mines.

It will be seen that the men who came to California during the 'fifties were not averse to finding ways of securing wealth outside of the diggings themselves, and speculation in town sites was a favorite method. Furthermore, up-to-date realtors would find many helpful suggestions should they be permitted to examine fully the records of the boosters of the paper towns of Gold Days.

In considering the towns and mining camps of early California the reader has doubtless been impressed by the uniqueness of the nomenclature. Native Indians and silver-tongued Spaniards have contributed generously to California's place names, but probably none are more fascinating than the names bestowed by the men of the mines. The bestowal of a name upon an individual or a town has usually been looked upon as a matter of much concern and doubtless it was so considered by the early miners, but they solved the problem with an originality that is at least refreshing. The repetition of the names of national heroes such as Madison, Monroe, Washington and Jackson, of which each eastern state has its share and which preserved a dignity at the cost of considerable monotony, did not appeal strongly to the virile men of the Sierra Nevada; besides, the supply of such names was not inexhaustible. A short analysis of the place names given may therefore be of interest.

While we find that the names of great statesmen and of older eastern places were used, their proportion to the whole number was not large. Washington, Boston, New York-of-the-Pacific, Baltimore, Concord, and Bunker Hill appear; but along with these, there are places named for contemporaries such as Frémont, Carson Creek, Angel's Camp, Goodyear's Bar, Weaverville, Downieville, Knight's Ferry, Foster's Bar and Shaw's Flat.

Physical features and the natural life furnished the cue for the naming of many places, as seen in Dry Creek, Aqueduct City, Volcano Diggings, Sawpit Flats, Salmon Falls, Bridgeville, Red Bluffs, Big Canyon, Emerald Lake and Slippery Ford; also Grizzly Flat, Coon Hollow, Wild Cat Bar, Coyote Hill, Skunk Gulch, Rat Trap Slide, Rattlesnake Bar and Centipede Hollow. Whether these names may be characterized as being beautiful is subject to diverse opinion, but many of them are plainly suggestive. Somewhat more aesthetic are Plum Valley, Cherry Creek, Wild Rose Creek, Willow Springs and Strawberry Valley.

Very often we can discern that the name was bestowed because of the interest in some individual, or racial group, or because of attachment to some other home. Thus we find Susanville, Sarahville, Marysville, Elizabethtown (Bettysburg), Katesville, Eliza, Johnsville, Georgetown, and Yankee Jim's. The race or nationality of the earliest inhabitants may have given names to Irish Creek, Italian Bar, French Corral, German Bar, Dutch

Flat, Kanaka Bar, Malay Camp, Chinese Camp and Nig-
ger Hill. One can almost picture the various groups of
men that moved westward and gave such names to their
new location as follows: Missouri Bar, Iowa Hill, Wisconsin Hill, Illinoistown, Michigan Bluffs, Tennessee
Creek, Kentucky Flat, Minnesota Flat, Cape Cod Bar,
Vermont Bar, Georgia Slide, Alabama Bar, Dixie Valley
and Mississippi Bar.

Probably none of the names of 'Forty-nine appeal more
to the romantic sense than the rough nomenclature that
grew out of the life of the times. It is difficult to see how
many of these names came to be adopted unless it is
remembered that often the name was applied by men of a
neighboring settlement and was so characteristic that it
clung to the place in spite of all efforts on the part of those
who might have taken the place of the local chamber of
commerce. Thus we read of Whisky Slide, Port Wine,
Brandy Gulch, Poker Flat, Loafers' Retreat, Lazy Hollow,
and Lousy Level. The moralizer will hasten to point out
the result of such a life as was to be seen in Swell Head
Diggings, Hungry Camp, Poorman Creek, Poverty Hill
and Ragtown. Closely associated also were such names
as Mad River, Squabbletown, Gouge Eye, Cut-Eye-
Foster's Bar, Murderers' Bar, Hangtown, Devil's Elbow,
and Helltown.

Having thus descended into the very depths, we are
much relieved to be able to turn to the other side of the
picture and find such places as Fair Play, Lucky Creek,
You Bet, Git-up-and-Git, Industry Bar and Civil Usage;
as well as the more proper Piety Hill, Happy Valley,
Christian Hill, Methodist Creek, Gospel Gulch, Mt.
Zion, Paradise Ravine, and even New Jerusalem.

That many of the pioneers of the gold district were
men of education and culture is deducible from the names
given by them, for some show familiarity with the Scrip-

tures and the classics. Such names are Alpha, Omega, Troy, Hector, Mt. Sanhedrin, Rubicon Creek, Eureka, Damascus, Pisgah, Havilah, Ophir, Cathay Valley, Auburn, Ben Hur, Minerva Bar, Faith, Hope and Charity valleys.

Thus it is seen that the Gold Days were not only a period of fervid mining activity but also one of the laying of foundations. Excessive enthusiasm, developed by the chances to amass fortunes, led to over-speculation and abnormal development in many towns. Many places did not develop beyond the stage of paper towns while others flourished for a brief season and still remain as ghost cities. It is by neither of these that we are to judge fairly the trend of the times, for during this same period there were also being established and developed those cities and communities which were to contribute permanently to the development of the great commonwealth.

Chapter XII

CHAPTER XII

San Francisco, the Mushroom City

WHILE THESE developments were taking place in the mining district and the adjacent region, San Francisco was making rapid strides and was fast outstripping in population the other towns of California. Speculation in town lots was keen, for it now appeared certain that San Francisco was to be the metropolis of the Pacific Coast. By the beginning of 1848, it had become a town of eight hundred inhabitants.

The American immigration following the raising of the American flag created a demand for real estate unknown before. Under the Mexican régime, the granting of town lots had been restricted to one lot per person. This lot the owner agreed to fence and build upon, and for it was asked to pay the nominal fee of twelve and a half dollars. After the conquest the American alcaldes had continued to grant lots under the same method, but while the price was satisfactory to American purchasers, the idea of restricting them to one lot each was not to their liking. Yankee ingenuity soon conceived the idea of having others acquire lots to be deeded over to the speculator. Up to the time of the raising of the American flag in July, 1846, there had been a total of only one hundred and twelve lots granted in Yerba Buena, but during the succeeding months before the treaty was signed, five hundred and seventy-six lots had been sold by American alcaldes and the town was beginning to assume an air of importance rivaling even the older settlements of the province.

As previously noted, the gold discovery had, by the middle of May, 1848, caused the streets of San Francisco to be deserted and practically all business to be suspended. To the casual observer it appeared quite evident that the discovery of gold had been a distinct blow to the progress of San Francisco.

But while the immediate effect of the gold discovery had been to depopulate the town, its permanent result was far different. The knowledge of that discovery found the whole world in a receptive mood, and soon hundreds of vessels turned their prows toward the Golden Gate and thousands of emigrants set forth on the great trek overland. During the fall of 1848 and early weeks of 1849 vessels from Pacific ports reached San Francisco bringing gold-seekers, but the great immigration came during the summer and fall of 1849.

On February 28 the steamship *California*, the first of the Pacific Mail Steamers, arrived bringing General Persifor F. Smith and about four hundred passengers. About a month later came the *Oregon* with some three hundred and fifty passengers including Colonel J. W. Geary, the newly appointed postmaster for San Francisco. Vessel then followed vessel, a few at first, then more and more until the approach to the Golden Gate was white with the flying sails of the Argonauts of 'Forty-nine. By the middle of the year, Bancroft asserts, upwards of six hundred vessels had entered the bay to be followed during the coming months by even a greater number. The number of persons arriving by vessel was estimated at approximately 40,000. The majority of these hastened to the gold fields, but

many merchants, craftsmen and others remained in the rapidly growing city. The result was that the population of San Francisco grew to 2,000 in February, had reached six thousand by August, and upon the coming of winter, when returning miners swelled these figures, it boasted not less than 20,000.

The appearance of San Francisco in 1849 was not one to inspire awe or admiration in the new arrival. William Taylor, who reached San Francisco in the fall of that year, describes the town as he saw it in these words:

"When we reached the summit of the hill above Clark's Point, we stopped and took a view of the city of tents. Not a brick house in the place, and but few wooden ones, and not a wharf or pier in the harbor. But for a few old adobe houses, it would have been easy to imagine that the whole city was pitched the evening before for the accommodation of a vast caravan for the night; for the city now contained a population of about twenty thousand, and I felt oppressed with the fear that under the influence of the gold attraction of the mountains, those tents might all be struck some morning, and the city suddenly leave its moorings for parts unknown."

Bayard Taylor likewise describes his first impression of the San Francisco of August, 1849:

"Hundreds of tents and houses appeared, scattered all over the heights, and along the shore for more than a mile. A furious wind was blowing down through a gap in the hills, filling the streets with clouds of dust. On every side stood buildings of all kinds, begun or half-finished, and the greater part of them were mere canvas sheds, open in front, and covered with all kinds of signs, in all languages. Great quantities of goods were piled up in the open air, for want of a place to store them. The streets were full of people, hurrying to and fro, and of as diverse and bizarre a character as the houses."

[247]

As these quotations point out it was largely a canvas city stretched out as a crescent around the shores of Yerba Buena Cove. Its northern tip was at Clark's Point near the foot of Telegraph Hill, while its southern portion reached to Rincon Point. The peculiar topography of the site forced the new arrivals either to spread out along the shores of the cove or to ascend the sand hills rising abruptly from the bay.

Under the early American administration the tide lands along the shores of the cove had been the object of much interest and General Kearny was induced to grant to the town the title to the "beach and water lots" excepting only those reserved by the government for its own use. During the summer of 1847, these had been surveyed by Jasper O'Farrell and sold at prices ranging from $600 for beach lots, to $50 for lots covered by high water.

The demands of the new conditions now also called for adequate wharves and docks, a thing not needed in the Mexican days. During 1847, W. S. Clark had built a wharf at the Embarcadero, later known as Clark's Point, and in October, 1848, the brig *Belfast* docked there—the first vessel of size to land at San Francisco without the aid of a lighter. During the spring of 1849, a joint stock company began the construction of Central or Long Wharf which that year was built eight hundred feet into the bay and the next year extended to a total length of two thousand feet, with a width of thirty-five feet. The Pacific Mail Steamship Company's steamers were able to dock alongside this wharf which soon became a promenade for the people of the city. Other wharfs and piers soon followed until practically every street had its extension into the waters of the bay.

As these wharves extended into the bay many hulls of vessels were anchored alongside and came into use for land purposes. During the last nine months of 1849, no less than seven hundred vessels entered San Francisco Harbor. Many of these lay at anchor in Yerba Buena Cove. Dr. James L. Tyson tells of the impression these vessels made upon him when first he saw them:

"The question which was very forcibly suggested to the mind at first view was, what commercial inducement could such a mean and insignificant-looking place as this present, to bring together such a forest of masts as the harbor disclosed? We soon learned that every vessel, which had arrived since the first discovery of gold in the country, was quickly deserted by its crew, and left to idly swing at its cable's length; however anxious the captains or owners might be to depart, it was impossible to man a ship with a sufficient number to work her to the nearest port. The wages for even a common laborer in the town were higher per day than a sailor was accustomed to receive monthly."

Many of these ships had come laden with valuable cargoes but their sailors had deserted immediately, leaving the owners to land their goods and man their vessels as best they could. At great expense goods were landed on shore, but even then there was no one to remove them to shelter, nor were there storage buildings. The result was that a great quantity of goods lay exposed to the weather and blocked the way. While goods sold at high prices, there were no hands to assist in removing and delivering the articles, for even later, when men returned from the mines, they either had acquired sufficient wealth to be independent of manual tasks or they were weakened by sickness, and dispirited. It had therefore become the plan to utilize these otherwise worthless vessels as storage ships and even as shops and lodging houses.

The extension of the wharves naturally gave additional value to these numerous dismantled vessels which either floated at anchor alongside the wharves or rested upon foundations of piles. It was estimated in 1850 that one thousand persons lived over the water in these vessels or in buildings resting upon piles. The most famous of the vessels was the *Niantic*, which had brought to California two hundred and fifty gold-seekers. This ship found a resting place along the Clay Street Wharf at what later became Sansome Street. One block further down Clay Street was the *General Harrison*, while the *Apollo* was moored at Sacramento Street near Battery, and became famous as a lodging-house and drinking-saloon. The fire of May 4, 1851, swept over this area and destroyed all of these vessels and with the exception of the *Niantic* they were largely forgotten. Upon the resting place of that ship the Niantic Hotel was later built, and even later a building known as the Niantic Block. At the close of October, 1851, reports state that of the four hundred and fifty-one vessels in the bay, one hundred and forty-eight were used as "store-ships."

In the rapid development of the town but little attention could be given to anything that did not require immediate action. The result was that the streets of San Francisco during the winter of 1849-50 were anything other than what proper city streets should be. In the rush to the diggings and back again to the bay, the mushroom city had sprung into being. Tents appeared over night along so-called streets, rude shacks took their places beside tents. Little attention was given to the form or durability of these early buildings and no consideration at all to the streets between them.

The winter of 1849 was one of unusually heavy rainfall. The mountain streams and rivers increased until they overflowed their banks. Miners hastened back to the cities to spend their idle time and accumulated wealth. The streets of Sacramento soon became canals from flood water and those of San Francisco became quagmires.

Upham, a visitor of the period, relates that: "It was no uncommon occurrence to see at the same time a mule stalled in the mud of the street with only his head above the mud, and an unfortunate pedestrian, who had slipped off the plank sidewalk, being fished out by a companion."

General W. T. Sherman, in his *Memoirs*, in recalling his days in San Francisco, says: "I have seen mules stumble in the streets and drown in the liquid mud. Montgomery Street had been filled up with brush and clay, and we always dreaded to ride on horseback along it because the mud was so deep that a horse's legs would become entangled in the brush below and the rider was likely to be thrown and drowned in the mud."

Other authorities bear record that along this street between Clay and Sacramento at least two horses sank so deeply into the mud that all efforts to rescue them were futile. Pedestrians also had to pick their way with extreme care. Three men who had over-indulged in strong liquors lost their way and were drowned in the mire between Jackson and Washington streets. Efforts were made to remedy this by temporary expedients. The throwing of brush and clay soil only made matters worse and on one of the main street corners a wag posted the timely warning:

"This street is impassable;
Not even jackassable."

It was, of course, imperative that the streets be kept traversible to some degree. To fill this need the San Franciscan found material close at hand. Goods had been shipped for the gold fields for which the miner had no earthly need and even useful goods at times accumulated to such an extent that their value was nil, so that they in reality became a liability because of lack of storage room. Why not use this superfluous material for the building of sidewalks? Acting upon this sensible suggestion, there was constructed about seventy-five yards of sidewalk along Montgomery Street between Clay and Jackson streets. Cook stoves made a good foundation, but large boxes of tobacco, Chilean flour, barrels of spoiled beef, gold-washing machines, rolls of sheet-lead, and tons of wire sieves all helped to make up this unique pathway for the San Franciscans of Gold Days. To be sure, these walks were neither of uniform grade nor width and a side-step might be disastrous. Lanterns were therefore indis-pensable for safe evening travel. William Shaw in writing of his experiences furnishes us with this picture:

"In the roadways of the principal streets, the mud was in some places four feet deep; they were full of holes, and to form a footing, empty cases and casks were sunk in the slough; but it taxed the agility of the pedestrian in leap-ing from one to the other. Incredible as it may seem, I have found a foothold across streets and pathways on Mexican beef, bags of flour and bales of other damaged goods, devoted to that purpose. The roads having been worn and loosened during the summer, continual rains from the hills made them a flood of mire; and at some crossings, the soundings varied from two to five feet. In one street a boat floated down the torrent of mud, much to the amusement of the spectators; mules and carts fre-quently foundered, and were with great difficulty dragged out. It is reported that a man's hat having been seen floating above a notorious quagmire in Pacific Street, on raising it, the head of the wearer was seen underneath; when extricated from this 'Serbonian bog,' he begged that the horse which was underneath him, might like-wise be rescued, but his steed was too deep down to be got at."

The experiences of the winter of 1849-50 showed very clearly that something had to be done to remedy these conditions. As soon as the weather permitted, work was begun upon street improvement. In the absence of better material, sand was used for grading and even in many cases for street building; but for the more frequently used streets the abundance of lumber gave rise to the suggestion that the streets be paved with planks such as were used for the construction of wharves. In this manner plans were made for permanent street improvement. Sewers were laid, the streets graded and covered with heavy planking. When marshy land required it, piles were driven deep into the ground and the street carried over it as a bridge. The expense of these improvements during 1850 was about $500,000, two thirds of which was borne by the owners of the adjoining property.

In addition to these street improvements undertaken by the city itself, the board of aldermen was induced to accept a plan suggested by Colonel Charles L. Wilson, whereby he agreed to construct a plank toll-road to Mission Dolores, two and a quarter miles across the sand hills from the plaza. From the earliest days the mission had been the center of a considerable settlement and in addition was on the direct route down the peninsula toward San José. Because of the sandy soil the road or trail was difficult to travel with wheeled vehicles and as a consequence the hauling of a load of hay from the mission to the plaza cost from fifteen to twenty dollars. After much delay, Wilson acquired the franchise and constructed the road, about seven hundred feet of which was built upon piling across a quagmire. The road met a great need and within a few months its proprietors had recovered their total expenditures from the tolls collected.

The growth of San Francisco during the first two years of the gold era was unprecedented. The increased population required the rapid construction of buildings wherein to house the people as well as care for the increased business. Before the discovery a few adobe houses and some frame buildings had sufficed; later some brick buildings were added. The business houses were nearly all clustered around Portsmouth Square and along Montgomery Street between Broadway and California, while the dwelling places stood but a short distance further from the bay shore. As the population increased the sand hills became covered with tents and shanties. Bayard Taylor, after a short absence from the city during the fall of 1849, thus describes its appearance upon his return:

"When I had climbed the last sand-hill, riding in towards San Francisco, and the town and harbor and crowded shipping again opened to the view, I could scarcely realize the change that had taken place during my absence of three weeks. The town had not only greatly extended its limits, but seemed actually to have doubled its number of dwellings since I left. High up on the hill, where I had seen only sand and chaparral, stood clusters of houses; streets which had been merely laid out, were hemmed in with buildings and thronged with people; new ware-houses had sprung up on the water side, and new piers were creeping out toward the shipping; the forest of masts had greatly thickened; and the noise, motion and bustle of business and labor on all sides were incessant.

"Verily, the place was in itself a marvel. To say that it was daily enlarged by some twenty to thirty houses may not sound very remarkable after all the stories that have been told; yet this, for a country which imported both lumber and houses, and where labor was then $10 a day is an extraordinary growth. The rapidity with which a ready-made house is put up and inhabited strikes the stranger in San Francisco as little short of magic. He walks over an open lot in his before-breakfast stroll—the next morning, a house complete, with a family inside blocks up his way. He goes down to the bay and looks out on

the shipping—two or three days afterward a row of store-houses, staring him in the face, intercepts the view."

The undue haste with which the city was built up led to many of its later misfortunes; not the least of these was the series of disastrous fires which swept the city during the early years of its existence. The first of the fires occurred on December 24, 1849. The town had enjoyed a night of revelry, when at six o'clock in the morning the cry of "Fire!" was heard from the vicinity of Denison's Exchange, a saloon in the midst of the gambling district. Although the weather was calm, the fire spread with great rapidity among the inflammable buildings. The heat was so intense that the block was soon destroyed and buildings near at hand were threatened and would have been consumed had they not been torn down. The loss amounted to $1,250,000. Fifty buildings were destroyed including the Eldorado, Parker House, Denison's Exchange and other noted resorts.

The ashes had scarcely cooled before new buildings were hastily erected upon the area covered by the fire and soon all traces of the blaze were wiped out. But these buildings were of no more substantial material than their predecessors and therefore served as excellent fuel for the second fire, which broke out May 4, 1850. This, too, began in a drinking and gambling-saloon, the United States Exchange. The fire spread rapidly and soon had swept three whole blocks including the one burned in the former fire. This time three hundred houses and property valued at over $4,000,000 were destroyed. The first fire had fallen heaviest upon the gamblers but the second took toll of the merchants. The attitude of many of the idle spectators led to the belief that it may have had an incendiary origin. The city council felt justified in offering a reward of $5,000 for information leading to the arrest and conviction of any who had been found guilty of starting it.

Although several arrests were made, no convictions were secured.

Before six weeks had elapsed, and while the rebuilding of the burned area was still in progress, the fire alarm sounded at 8 o'clock on the morning of June 14. The origin of the third fire was from a defective stove pipe in a bakery on Kearny Street, a block south of the point where the former fires began. A brisk wind fanned the flames and within a short time four blocks had been burned over. The loss was about three hundred houses and a total value of from three to four million dollars.

The frequency of these fires and the difficulty of combatting them made it very evident that San Francisco must take vigorous action to require more substantial construction and also to provide facilities for fighting fires. Several brick buildings, especially on Montgomery Street, were now erected, but lumber was still the more common building material. Three months had scarcely passed before a fire broke out in the Philadelphia House, a saloon on Jackson Street, one block north of the Plaza. There was no wind but the houses here were dry frame buildings and were quickly consumed. Four city blocks were swept clean, but because of the nature of the buildings the loss was lower than from the former fires—estimates placing it at from $500,000 to $1,000,000. Although these fires had been very destructive, their damage was small compared with that of the Fifth Great Fire on May 4, 1851. This fire broke out about midnight on May 3, in a building on Clay Street opposite the Plaza. A strong northwest wind caused it to sweep toward the bay, taking all before it. The plank streets furnished excellent fuel for the fire, especially where they were built upon piers; the open space below served as a ventilator to carry the conflagration from one part of town to another. Nothing seemed to stop the fire which so lighted up the heavens that the glow was visible for a hundred miles around. After a period of ten hours the fire subsided, but not until what had the day before been a great city, was reduced to a few outlying buildings about a mass of smoldering ruins. Twenty-two city blocks had been consumed including from one thousand to two thousand buildings, the total property loss being estimated at approximately $12,-000,000. Although this loss exceeded the combined destruction of all former fires, the stricken city was not permitted to recover without further disturbance by the fire fiend, for on June 22, came what is known as the Sixth Great Fire. Beginning in a house on Pacific Street, near Powell, a western wind carried it down toward the bay. Before it was done, from four to five hundred homes had been consumed and property valued at nearly three million dollars destroyed.

These six disastrous fires left a permanent impression upon San Francisco. The rapid growth of the city in 1849 and 1850 had been based less upon any general feeling of confidence in the ultimate future of the place than because of the opportunity for immediate gain. Not many of the eager gold-seekers at that time thought of California as a place to establish a permanent residence—they would acquire a fortune as soon as possible and then return to their eastern homes. With this view of matters, there was little to induce men to invest beyond what was reasonably certain to bring immediate returns, for the cost of building materials and labor was excessive. But as time went on the promises of success in California became more assuring, immigration continued and the expansion of the city went steadily on. Many fires had swept away the early buildings and had in an effective way taught that only buildings of permanent construction could be expected to withstand the flames.

Quick to recuperate, the men of early San Francisco

scarcely waited for the embers to cease smouldering before plans were made for rebuilding on a better scale. Fire limits were determined and buildings of a combustible nature rigidly excluded. Solid brick walls, double iron shutters and doors were now to be seen in place of the pine and redwood frame buildings. No longer content with building materials readily at hand, search was made and material brought from points far distant, even granite from China, lava from the Sandwich Islands and burned brick from the eastern states. With structures thus erected, the appearance of the city was likewise changed and it began to take on a semblance of permanence that was not to be found in 1849.

In order to combat future conflagrations, volunteer fire departments were organized and soon became very important factors, not only in preventing the great losses due to fire, but also for their prominence as social and political organizations. The various companies were housed in substantial buildings equipped with elegant furniture and good libraries. To be a volunteer fireman was a great honor and every man of ambition sought membership in one of the many fire companies.

The early fires had likewise taught clearly the need for an abundant water supply. The first plan was to sink wells and dig cisterns at the street intersections. As time went on these were provided at nearly every principal street crossing and were to be kept filled by pumping water from the bay. These precautionary measures at last were successful and San Francisco was saved from any great devastation from fire until 1906, when the great catastrophe disrupted her water system and left her once again the victim of the fire demon.

In other ways San Francisco was going through a metamorphosis from a village to a city. Attention has already been called to the location of the early town along the shores of Yerba Buena Cove, and how as shipping increased wharves were gradually pushed out into the bay to facilitate the expanding commerce. The demand for building sites had at an early date called attention to the value of the beach and water lots. As the demand increased, their value became still greater and the city gradually moved out onto this area. The lots were first used by resting the buildings on piles, but later were filled in with earth. The first lot to be thus filled in was owned by Captain Joseph L. Folsom and was on California Street, west of Sansome. The cost was high, but the value of the lot was so enhanced that others soon hastened to follow Folsom's example.

The topography of San Francisco determined this line of development. The hills rising so abruptly from the shore did not invite expansion as much as did the possibility of filling in the tide lands; on the other hand the loose sandy soil of the surrounding hills suggested the feasibility of using them to reclaim the mud flats in the bay. Borthwick, a visitor to San Francisco during this period, thus describes the process of reducing the hills:

"The soil was so sandy that the hills were easily cut down, and for this purpose a contrivance was used called a *Steam Paddy*, which did immense execution. It was worked by steam, and was somewhat on the principle of a dredging-machine, but with only one large bucket, which cut down about two tons of earth at a time and emptied itself into a truck, placed alongside. From the spot where the Paddy was thus walking into the hills a railway was laid, extending to the shore, and trains of cars were continually rattling down across the streets, taking the earth to fill up those parts of the city which were as yet under water."

This leveling of hills and filling in of the bay, was, however, not without its disadvantages. The sewer system which had been installed at an earlier date was based upon the idea of the shore line being fixed, and the buildings that had been constructed were also on the grade of the streets as they had previously been determined. These matters therefore had to be readjusted. The writer just quoted makes the following observation in relation to this condition:

"Some of the streets in the upper part of the city presented a very singular appearance. The houses had been built before the grade of the different streets had been fixed by the corporation, and there were places where the streets, having been cut down through the hills to their proper level, were nothing more than wide trenches, with a perpendicular bank on either side, perhaps forty or fifty feet high, and on the brink of these stood the houses, to which access was gained by ladders and temporary wooden stairs, the unfortunate proprietor being obliged to go to the expense of grading his own lot, and so bringing himself down to the level with the rest of the world. In other places, where the street crossed a deep hollow, it formed a high embankment, with a row of houses at the foot of it, some nearly buried, and others already raised to the level of the street, resting on a sort of scaffolding, while the foundation was being filled in under them . . . .

"Two or three years later, in '54, when an alteration was made in the grade of some of the streets, large brick and stone houses were raised several feet, by means of a most ingenious application of hydraulic pressure. Excavations were made, and under the foundation walls of the houses were inserted a number of cylinders about two feet in height, so that the building rested entirely on the heads of the pistons. The cylinders were all connected by pipes with a force-pump, worked by a couple of men, who in this way could pump up a five-story brick building three or four inches in the course of the day. As the house grew up, props were inserted in case of accidents; and when it had been raised as far as the length of the pistons would allow, the whole apparatus was readjusted, and the operation was repeated till the required height was obtained. I went to witness the process when it was being applied to a large corner brick building, five stories high, with about sixty feet frontage each way. The flagged sidewalk was being raised along with it; but there was no interruption of the business going on in the premises, or anything whatever to indicate to the passer-by that the ground was growing under his feet. On going down under the house, one saw that the building was detached from the surrounding ground, and rested on a number of cylinders; but the only appearance of work being done was by two men quietly working a pump amid a ramification of small iron pipes. The apparatus had of course to be of an immense strength to withstand the pressure to which it was subjected, and the utmost nicety was required in its adjustment, to avoid straining and cracking the walls; but numbers of large buildings were raised most successfully in this way without receiving the slightest injury."

Thus during the Gold Days, San Francisco passed from a mere village to a thriving city. In the early period her development was rapid and appeared to lack elements of permanence but soon in spite of seemingly overwhelming disasters there emerged the great city by the Golden Gate. Not the least among the elements which brought about this transformation had been the destructive fires. While these disasters had eliminated the faint of heart, men of vision, courage and strength only set about anew the task of build-

ing for a greater and more permanent city. It was therefore very appropriate that the city council should adopt as
the seal for the city the image of a phoenix rising from the
flames in front of the Golden Gate. "Nil desperandum" was
the motto one man placed in large letters upon his
house after it had repeatedly been destroyed,
and this in fact was to become the
working principle of the new
city by the Golden Gate.

Chapter XIII

CHAPTER XIII

Life at High Pitch

A WILD BULL dashing through the streets is not the modern conception of decorum in a city. The San Franciscan of 1849, however, was not to be surprised at such an occurrence if we accept a vivid description from the pen of Bayard Taylor:

"The groups in the plaza suddenly scatter; the city surveyor jerks his pole out of the ground and leaps on a pile of boards; the venders of cakes and sweetmeats follow his example, and the place is cleared just as a wild bull which has been racing down Kearny Street makes his appearance. Two vaqueros, shouting and swinging their lariats, follow at a hot gallop; the dust flies as they dash across the plaza. One of them in mid-career, hurls his lariat in the air . . . . The bull is 'brought up' with such force as to throw him off his legs. He lies stunned a moment, and then, rising heavily, makes another charge. But by this time the second vaquero had thrown a lariat around one of his hind legs, and thus checked on both sides, he is dragged off to slaughter. The plaza is refilled as quickly as it was emptied, and the course of business is resumed."

San Francisco, during the Gold Days, was laying the foundation of the city that was to be. In the previous chapter consideration was given almost exclusively to the material development of San Francisco during this period. A city, however, is something more than streets, buildings, wharves, and ships. It is made up also of that intangible something which in a man is known as personality. San Francisco, the youthful city, was developing during the Gold Days that spirit which was to characterize it during the decades to follow. Boisterous, pleasure loving, independent in action, undaunted by disaster—all these traits of the later city became evident even during its earlier years and were moulded into the character of the city by the conditions encountered. In this chapter it is proposed to consider those elements which helped to make up the economic and social life of the city, to create the spirit of San Francisco.

Most of the other cities of the West had developed slowly and the characteristics of their inhabitants tended to follow more or less the traits of some dominant nationality or people—Yankee, Southern, French or Spanish they were, as the origin of the greater mass of people might be. In the case of San Francisco, however, growth of population had been so rapid that all traits of nationality were lost in the great cosmopolitan mass.

"It would be difficult to describe my sensations after the first day's ramble in San Francisco," says William Shaw. "I had witnessed so many startling sights, that had I not been well assured of their reality, I might have imagined them phantasies of the brain: buildings were springing up 'as at the stroke of an enchanter's wand'; valuable merchandise was strewn about in every direction; men of every costume and colour—Down-Easters with sharp-set faces, sallow Southerners, gaunt Western Squatters, vivacious Frenchmen, sedate Germans, sturdy English Colonists, Californians and Chilians, Mexicans, Kanakas and Celestials, hurried to and fro, pursuing their various avocations; and business to an incalculable amount seemed to be transacted. Looking at the rude sign-boards inscribed in various languages, glancing at the chaos of articles exposed for sale, and listening to the various dialects spoken, the city seemed a complete Babel."

Contemporaries thus describe early San Francisco. It appeared that there was no method in anything. On the street and in the shops people "bustled and jostled each other, bawled, railed and fought, cursed and swore, sweated and labored lustily and somehow the work was done"—this is the description of another writer. To add to the confusion, the ordinary orders of society were very much upset. Professional men sought employment as cooks, draymen or bootblacks; merchants became laborers, auctioneers or butchers; while on the other hand laborers became merchant princes. All classes sought profit in keeping lodging houses, hotels and saloons, and partook of the wild spirit of speculation in goods and real estate. Everybody was extremely busy and knew what he wanted to accomplish. Goods would disappear from the wharves and streets as if by magic and other goods take their places. Vacant lots of one day would be covered the next day by half a dozen tents and canvas houses.

"A better idea of San Francisco, in the beginning of September, 1849," says Bayard Taylor, "cannot be given than by the description of a single day. Supposing the visitor to have been long enough in the place to sleep on a hard plank and in spite of the attacks of innumerable fleas, he will be awakened at daylight by the noises of building, with which the hills are all alive . . . . The wooden buildings unlock their doors, the canvas houses and tents throw back their front curtains; the lighters on the water are warped out from ship to ship; carts and porters are busy along the beach; and only the gaming-tables, thronged all night by the votaries of chance, are idle and deserted . . . .

"As early as half-past six the bells begin to sound to breakfast, and for an hour thenceforth, their incessant clang and the braying of immense gongs drown all the hammers that are busy on a hundred roofs . . . . By nine o'clock the town is in the full flow of business. The streets running down to the water, and Montgomery Street which fronts the Bay, are crowded with people, all in hurried motion."

"The crowd in the streets is now wholly alive. Men dart hither and thither, as if possessed with a never-resting spirit. You speak to an acquaintance—a merchant, perhaps. He utters a few hurried words of greeting, while his eyes send keen glances on all sides of you; suddenly he catches sight of somebody in the crowd; he is off, and in the next five minutes has brought up half a cargo, sold a town lot at treble the sum he gave, and taken a share in some new and imposing speculation. It is impossible to witness this excess and dissipation of business, without feeling something of its influence. The very air is pregnant with the magnetism of bold, spirited, unwearied action, and he who but ventures into the outer circle of the whirlpool, is spinning, ere he has time for thought, in its dizzy vortex."

"In the course of a month, or a year, in San Francisco," says Borthwick, "there was more hard work done, more speculative schemes were conceived and executed, more money was made and lost, there was more buying and selling, more sudden changes of fortune, more eating and drinking, more smoking, swearing, gambling, and tobacco-chewing, more crime and profligacy, and, at the same time, more solid advancement made by the people, as a body, in wealth, prosperity, and the refinements of civilization, than could be shown in an equal space of time by any community of the same size on the face of the earth.

"The every-day jog-trot of ordinary human existence was not a fast enough pace for Californians in their impetuous pursuit of wealth. The longest period of time ever thought of was a month. Money was loaned, and houses were rented, by the month; interest and rent being invariably payable monthly and in advance. All engagements were made by the month, during which period the changes and contingencies were so great that no one was willing to commit himself for a longer term. In the space of a month the whole city might be swept off by fire, and a totally new one might be flourishing in its place. So great was the constant fluctuation in the prices of goods, and so rash and speculative was the usual style of business, that no great idea of stability could be attached to anything, and the ever-varying aspect of the streets, as the houses were being constantly pulled down, and rebuilt, was emblematic of the equally varying fortunes of the inhabitants."

Bayard Taylor says that many of the passengers aboard his vessel began to speculate at the moment of landing. One ingenious Yankee had brought out 1,500 copies of the *New York Tribune* which he sold within two hours at the rate of one dollar apiece. Within a short time many of these enterprising men had made large sums of money. One had added $20,000 to his fortune by handling town lots; another shipped $1,000 worth of lumber from New York. Probably no better idea can be had of business conditions in San Francisco in the fall of 1849 than from the business report of a reputable San Francisco house to its Boston clients. Because of its strictly business character, there would be no reason for the slightest conscious exaggeration. It reads:

"We arrived here on the 18th [of August, 1849] prepared

to find an extraordinary state of things and confess that reality exc'ds our expectations. A speculation is going on here in real estate wilder than anything that we have known. Lots of land which sold for $1,500 six months since have been sold lately for $15,000 & $20,000 . . . . We see nothing to warrant such a state of things except the enormous rates of rents. In some instances a man can pay these enormous rates erect a building & let rooms enough to pay the whole rent in one year.

"Gamblers infest the place, & by the enormous rates which they are able to pay $1,800 a month in some inst. establish the rents. Almost the entire population is involved in this mania so that money is very scarce & brings enormous rates. From 4c & 20c per m. is freely paid by houses in high standing both here & at home. How long it may continue you can tell as well as we can, but it seems to us that there must be a wind up before long.

"This state of things has embarrassed us somewhat in getting a place suitable to do our business in, but we have refused to purchase real Estate preferring to pay high rates for short leases believing that these prices must come down. The market is generally overstocked. Lumber, however, is in demand at $300 a 350 pr M. & Houses sell at $1,500 upwards. A better class of houses two stories high twenty-five by forty with green blinds &c if to many are not coming will sell well. Zinc and Iron houses ought to do well. Of course there is no such thing as Insurance here & if a fire should take place during the high winds which prevail daily the whole place would be swept.

"We find a much better population than we expected, there is better security for property here than in N. Y. The sts. in the eve. or Sunday are as quiet as a New England village doors are left unlocked at night & large amts. of gold are left unguarded in counting rooms remote from dwellings & goods unwatched on the Beach. Immense quantities of goods are suffering for want of storage & must be ruined when the rainy season comes on as it will be impossible to get storage for them & we fear our friends will receive some Flemish accts."

One cause of the great spirit of speculation was the lack of knowledge regarding market conditions. California was far removed from the eastern supply houses; transportation was by means of slow-sailing ocean vessels, and no telegraph or quick mail service made it possible for merchants to forecast market conditions. The result was that the market was controlled by the simple workings of the law of supply and demand. Since this might vary with the arrival of the next ship's cargo, it was very largely a game of chance. Consequently there was no scale of profits and the item of cost had little to do with the selling price. Two persons might buy the same kind of article at two places on the same day and find very great difference in price. This condition gave a great opportunity to the auctioneers who for many years were among the leading factors in handling all incoming commodities, for practically all goods were sold immediately upon their arrival at whatever price the market would bring. Many were the bargains knocked down by the hammer of the auctioneer. The retail merchants gave their attention largely to "auction watching" in order to provide their wares, but not infrequently a purchaser had a problem to dispose of his commodity in case the market were glutted. One contemporary gives an account of a vessel which arrived bringing a large consignment of white shirts and collars. Before the ship had reached the Golden Gate a merchant from a small boat had boarded the ship and begun negotiations with the master for his cargo. "Biled shirts" were not an article in great demand by the men of the Gold Days; this point was made clear and thus helped to prepare the way for a satisfactory purchase price. The local merchant having thus acquired at a reasonable rate the entire lot of shirts and collars found it necessary to create a demand for his goods. His Yankee ingenuity soon worked out a plan to accomplish this and arrangements were announced not long thereafter for a grand ball at which the leading women of the city would be present. This last feature insured its success, and all went well. Shortly before the date for this great social event, announcements stated that no man would be admitted to the ball unless dressed in a white shirt and linen collar. The one merchant in town who had a supply of these articles did a thriving business and his supply was quickly exhausted.

Incidentally it may be noted here that laundry prices were very high, with the consequence that frequently it was really cheaper to buy new apparel than have the old washed. William Kelly complained that even bad washing cost six dollars a dozen, taking big and little pieces together, while new shirts ready to wear cost but ten dollars a dozen, and sox but four dollars. Bayard Taylor gives the price of laundry at eight dollars per dozen and states that as a consequence large quantities of soiled linen were sent to the Antipodes to be purified. A vessel had just arrived from Canton, he states, bringing two hundred and fifty dozen, which had been sent out a few months earlier; another vessel from the Hawaiian Islands brought over one hundred dozen.

It was no uncommon thing, we are told, to find the streets in the vicinity of the Jewish clothing shops thickly strewn with old clothing. Borthwick estimated that there were "always tons of cast-off garments kicking about the streets" for, he explained, "the majority of the population carried their wardrobe on their backs, and when they bought a new article of dress, the old one which it replaced was pitched into the street."

This apparently unstable economic condition impressed nearly every writer who described early San Francisco, but in spite of all, the city continued to prosper. A writer to the *New York Post* may or may not have exaggerated his experiences when he wrote:

"The people of San Francisco are mad—stark mad . . . . A dozen times or more, during the past few weeks, I have been taken by the arm by some of the *millionaires*—so they call themselves, I call them madmen—of San Francisco, looking wondrously dirty and out at the elbows for men of such magnificent pretentions. They have dragged me through the mud and filth almost up to my middle from one pine box to another, called mansion, hotel, bank or store as may please the imagination and have told me, with a sincerity that would have done credit to the Bedlamite, that these splendid structures were theirs and they the proprietors, were worth from two to three hundred thousand dollars a year each . . . . There must be nearly 2,000 houses besides the tents . . . . and what do you suppose to be the rental, the yearly value—of this card-house city? Not less they said than $12,000,000 and this with a population of about 12,000. New York, with its 500,000 inhabitants does not have a rental of much more than this, if as much."

In fact it was this rental value that determined the price of real estate and made possible the great profit. The rental value in turn was dependent upon the profits merchants and gamblers were able to make through their location upon a particular site. Mayor Geary in his first message to the city council in 1850 stated that real estate within a short time had increased in value in many instances as much as a thousand-fold, and even at that high rate would produce in rents the largest average income on record.

[275]

Without doubt the great driving force dominating the life of San Francisco was the desire to amass riches; next, and probably in close association with it, came the craving for amusement and recreation. The same feverish excitement characterized both.

When one considers the strenuous life of the 'Forty-niner, the wild spirit of speculation in the commercial world about him, the large element of luck upon which his fortune depended, the absence of the social inhibitions that a more refined society would afford, one cannot be surprised to find that these men were often enthusiastic devotees of the Goddess of Chance. Gambling flourished as nothing else did. In view of the later prevalence of this vice, it is of interest to note that in January, 1848, the town council passed stringent resolutions regarding gambling, laying heavy fines upon persons engaged in gambling and authorizing the town officers "to seize for the benefit of the town, all the money found on a gambling table where cards are played." The sentiment of the town soon changed and the act was repealed when, in 1849, because of the need of municipal funds, the alcalde recommended the laying of a license tax upon the gambling resorts. This action gave the gambling fraternity the political and social status they desired.

For a picture of the night life in San Francisco we have nothing better than that penned for us by Bayard Taylor: "The appearance of San Francisco at night, from the water, is unlike anything I ever beheld. The houses are mostly canvas, which is made transparent by the lamps within, and transforms them, in the darkness, to dwellings of solid light. Seated on the slopes of its three hills, the tents pitched among the chaparral to the very summits, it gleams like an amphitheatre of fire. Here and there shine out brilliant points, from the decoy-lamps of the gaming-houses; and through the indistinct murmur of

the streets comes by fits the sound of music from the hot and crowded precincts. The picture has in it something unreal and fantastic; it impresses one like the cities of the magic lantern, which a motion of the hand can build or annihilate.

"The only objects left for us to visit are the gaming-tables, whose day has just fairly dawned. We need not wander far in search of one. Denison's exchange, the Parker House and Eldorado stand side by side; across the way are the Verandah and Aguila de Oro; higher up the plaza the St. Charles and Bella Union; while dozens of second-rate establishments are scattered through the less frequented streets. The greatest crowd is about the Eldorado; we find it difficult to effect an entrance. There are about eight tables in the room, all of which are thronged; copper-hued Kanakas, Mexicans rolled in their serapes and Peruvians thrust through their ponchos, stand shoulder to shoulder with the brown and bearded American miners. The stakes are generally small, though when the better gets into a 'streak of luck,' as it is called, they are allowed to double until all is lost or the bank breaks. Along the end of the room is a spacious bar, supplied with all kinds of bad liquors, and in a sort of gallery, suspended under the ceiling, a female violinist tasks her strength of muscle to minister to the excitement of the play.

"The Verandah, opposite, is smaller, but boasts an equal attraction in a musician who has a set of Pandean pipes fastened at his chin, a drum on his back, which he beats with sticks at his elbows, and cymbals in his hands. The piles of coin on the monte tables clink merrily to his playing, and the throng of spectators, jammed together in a sweltering mass, walk up to the bar between the tunes and drink out of sympathy with his dry and breathless throat. At the Aguila de Oro there is a full band of Ethiopian serenaders, and at the other hells, violins,

[279]

guitars or wheezy accordions, as the case may be. The atmosphere of these places is rank with tobacco-smoke, and filled with a feverish, stifling heat, which communicates an unhealthy glow to the faces of the players."

In considering the prevalence of gambling it should be noted that these resorts did not exist merely because there was such a strong demand for them, for as a matter of fact the gamblers spent vast sums of money to make their places alluring to the men of the city and thus built up a business which otherwise would not have been so universally recognized. Society in San Francisco lacked many of the finer things that make for a man's happiness. Many a youth and older man as well was lonely and homesick. Wages and profits were high, gold dust was plentiful, but to the man of the Gold Days, family and the usual social ties were lacking. His lodging quarters were crowded and uncomfortable; there was no place where one could find social enjoyment except in the commercialized places of pleasure, which were almost entirely gambling and drinking saloons. The cunning proprietors of these dens did not hesitate to make their places as alluring as money could provide.

"Every device likely to beguile the stranger is resorted to, regardless of cost," says a contemporary, "gamblers being well aware that the force of example is apt to induce those who only entered as casual spectators to stake money. From the twanging of guitars and scraping of violins, to clashing of cymbals and banging of drums, musical sounds of all kinds attract the ear of the passer-by; in the Aguila D'Oro, a band of Ethiopian Serenaders beat their banjoes, rattled their 'Bones,' and shouted their melodies. But the most successful decoy has been the introduction of women; in some gaming-houses fascinating belles, theatrically dressed, take their stand at roulette tables, purposely to allure men to play; and, there being a scarcity of the fair sex in this country, these syrens too often prove irresistible."

These gambling saloons glittered at night like fairy palaces and the lively music attracted the passers-by. All classes were swept into the whirlpool of passion. "The heated brain was never allowed to get cool while a bit of coin or dust was left." The authors of the *Annals of San Francisco* thus dwell upon the prevalence of gambling in the early city:

"Gambling was a peculiar feature of San Francisco at this time. It was *the* amusement—*the* grand occupation of many classes—apparently the life and soul of the place. There were hundreds of gambling saloons in the town. The barroom of every hotel and public house presented its tables to attract the idle, the eager and covetous. Monte, faro, roulette, rondo, rouge et noir and vingt-un, were the games chiefly played. In the larger saloons beautiful and well-dressed women dealt out the cards or turned the roulette wheel, while lascivious pictures hung on the walls. A band of music and numberless blazing lamps gave animation and a feeling of joyous rapture to the scene.

"The sums staked were occasionally enormous. One evening sixteen thousand dollars' worth of gold dust was laid upon a faro table as a bet. This was lost by the keeper of the table, who counted out the money to the winner without a murmur, and continued his business with a cheerful countenance, and apparently with as good spirits as though he had incurred no more than an ordinary loss. As high as twenty thousand dollars, it is said, have been risked upon the turn of a card. Five thousand, three thousand, and one thousand dollars were repeatedly ventured. The ordinary stakes, however, were by no means so high as these sums—from fifty cents to five dollars being the usual amount; and thus the common day laborer could lay his moderate stake as stylishly as a lord. It was only when the rich gamester was getting desperate, or a half tipsy miner had just come from the diggings with a handsome 'pile,' that the larger sums were put on the cloth. Generally speaking, the keepers of the tables, or 'bankers,' had no objection to these heavy stakes; they knew the game better than the player, and were well aware of all the chances in their favor. But it was scarcely necessary for the professional gambler to encourage particularly large stakes. The combined amount of all the usual small ones was very large; while every two minutes there was a new game formed, and new stakes put down."

It must not be considered that gambling was the only form of amusement furnished the men of the gold period. Theatres, grand balls and bull fights all added to the miner's enjoyment and subtracted from his supply of gold dust. As early as 1848, amateur dramatic performances had been given at Sonoma, Monterey, Santa Barbara and elsewhere, largely under the patronage of the soldiers recently arrived in California. With the gold excitement, professional performers came to the coast. In October of 1849 Rowe's Olympic Circus appeared, followed by the Philadelphia Minstrels, and later the Pacific Minstrels. Early in 1850 there was opened in San Francisco the National Theatre, the first in that city to have its own building. This was followed a few months later by the famous Jenny Lind and still later by the American Theatre. Soon nearly every town of any size had its theatre or hall for public entertainments. The large amount of gold in circulation attracted many actors of national fame such as Stark, Atwater, Kirby, Bingham and others, who were all well received, although the most enthusiastic applause was reserved for women vocalists who sang with sweet voices the stirring songs of the hearthstone.

In places where the enjoyment of theatre performances

could not be had, grand balls were frequently held in order to vary the program of amusement. It might be thought that the scarcity of women would discourage such events, but such was not the case. Long-bearded men with flannel shirts went through all the steps and figures of the dance with apparently as much enthusiasm as if their partners had been of the gentler sex. Since some means had to be devised to overcome this lack it was the common rule, we are told, that every miner who was adorned by a patch upon his nether garments should for the occasion be raised to the class of highly respected femininity.

"The most curious," says Borthwick, "were the masquerades. They were generally given in one of the large gambling-saloons, and in the placards announcing that they were to come off, appeared conspicuously also the intimation of 'No weapons admitted'; 'A strong police will be in attendance.'

"The company was just such as might be seen in any gambling room; and, beyond the presence of half-a-dozen masks in female attire, there was nothing to carry out the idea of a ball or a masquerade at all; but it was worth while to go, if only to watch the company arrive, and to see the practical enforcement of the weapon clause in the announcement. Several doorkeepers were in attendance, to whom each man as he entered delivered up his knife or his pistol, receiving a check for it, just as one does for his cane or umbrella at the door of a picture-gallery. Most men drew a pistol from behind their back, and very often a knife along with it; some carried their bowie-knife down the back of their neck, or in their breast; demure, pious-looking men, in white neckcloths, lifted up the bottom of their waist-coats, and revealed the butt of a revolver; others, after having already disgorged a pistol, pulled up the leg of their trousers, and abstracted a huge bowie-knife from their boot; and there were men, terrible fellows, no doubt, but who were more likely to frighten themselves than any one else, who produced a revolver from each trouser-pocket, and a bowie-knife from their belt. If any man declared that he had no weapon, the statement was so incredible that he had to submit to be searched; an operation which was performed by the doorkeepers, who, I observed, were occasionally rewarded for their diligence by the discovery of a pistol secreted in some unusual part of the dress."

After this reference to the shooting-irons that were considered so indispensable to the men of early San Francisco, it is well to learn Borthwick's opinion that it was a most providential circumstance that the climate of San Francisco was to such a high degree favorable for the cure of gunshot wounds. In general, he adds, they heal very rapidly and many miraculous recoveries had taken place even after the most skilled and experienced surgeons had exhausted their skill upon the patient.

While the staid city men were enjoying the theatrical performance and the more sedate were happy at a stag dance, outside communities found enjoyment at a real show as may be seen from this announcement handed down to us by a contemporary of the period:

"War! War!! War!!!

The Celebrated Bull-killing Bear,
GENERAL SCOTT,
will fight a Bull on Sunday the 15th inst., at 2 P. M.,
at Moquelumne Hill

"The Bear will be chained with a twenty-foot chain in the middle of the arena. The Bull will be perfectly wild, young, of the Spanish breed, and the best that can be found in the country. The Bull's horns will be of their natural length, and '*not sawed off to prevent accidents.*' The Bull will be quite free in the arena, and not hampered in any way whatever."

Although it would seem from early accounts that there was little or no interest in anything but money and pleasure, there were, nevertheless, also to be found those elements which were already at work to bring order out of social and moral chaos. While by far the greater element in the population was made up of unmarried men who were seeking their fortune and not unwilling to take great risks both economically and morally, there were others who brought with them their families, and even a considerable number of men who came for the purpose of ministering to the moral and spiritual improvement of society.

At the time of the gold discovery there was but little active interest in religious matters in California. At that time there were in California about a dozen clergymen of the Roman Catholic faith besides a few lay preachers of the Protestant denominations. Elihu Anthony and A. A. Hecox of Santa Cruz were Methodist local preachers; Walter Colton, a Congregational chaplain; Samuel Brannan, a Mormon elder, and T. M. Leavenworth, an Episcopalian chaplain. During the spring of 1847 the Reverend William Roberts, while on his way to the mission field in Oregon, stopped in San Francisco and organized a Methodist class of six members, together with a Sunday School. This Sunday School continued until disrupted by the gold excitement.

Meanwhile the discovery of the gold made other changes. In the migration from the Hawaiian Islands came the Reverend T. Dwight Hunt, a Congregational minister who soon accepted the position of chaplain for the town of San Francisco. Services were held in the public school on the plaza. The first steamers brought other

[285]

Protestant clergymen including Albert Williams, Sylvester
Woodbridge and J. M. Douglas, Presbyterians; O. C.
Wheeler, Baptist; S. A. Willey, Congregationalist; J. L.
Ver Mehr, Episcopalian. With the advent of these men
various Protestant churches were organized in San Fran-
cisco and the surrounding cities.

Probably none of the pioneer ministers held a larger
place in early California than did the circuit rider, Isaac
Owen, who drove across the plains in 1849 to take up his
work in the mining area, and William Taylor of San
Francisco. The latter devoted himself for a period of
seven years to improving the conditions in the metropolis. Not content to occupy a pulpit on the Sabbath
only, "California Taylor" purchased an abandoned ship
and organized a sailors' "Bethel" along the water front
until burned out by one of the many fires.

The gambling around the plaza persistently called forth
denunciation from Taylor. Because of the moral and social
conditions in San Francisco, his friends were fearful that
the gamblers would resent his attacks and were therefore
very solicitous for his safety when he announced that on
the next Sunday he would preach in the street near the
plaza. At the time appointed, with the support of a few
faithful adherents, Taylor mounted a work bench and
began the service by singing with a strong voice his
favorite hymn, "Hear the Royal Proclamation." The song
had many verses and served to gather a crowd of restless
listeners. Realizing that the critical time had arrived,
Taylor began his talk in a manner which stands out as
an excellent example of tact and forensic skill.

"Gentlemen, if our friends in the Atlantic states, with
the views and feelings they entertained of California
society when I left them, had heard that there was to be
preaching this afternoon on Portsmouth Square, in San
Francisco, they would have predicted disorder, confusion,

and riot; but we who are here believe very differently. One thing is certain, there is no man who loves to see those Stars and Stripes floating on the breeze [pointing to the waving flag of our Union] and who loves the institutions fostered under them; in a word, there is no true American but will observe order under the preaching of God's word anywhere, and maintain it if need be. We shall have order, gentlemen.

"Your favorite rule in arithmetic is the rule of 'loss and gain.' In your tedious voyage around the Horn, or your wearisome journey over the plains, or your hurried passage across the isthmus, and during the few months of your sojourn in California, you have been figuring under this rule; losses and gains have constituted the theme of your thoughts and calculations. Now I wish most respectfully to submit to you a question under your favorite rule. I want you to employ all the mathematical power and skill you can command, and patiently work out the mighty problem. The question may be found in the twenty-sixth verse of the sixteenth chapter of our Lord's Gospel by Saint Matthew. Shall I announce it? 'What is a man profited if he shall gain the whole world, and lose his own soul?' "

During the early 'fifties the influence of the churches became more manifest until nearly every denomination had its congregation and its place of worship, and in addition to the churches there were other religious agencies at work such as the Bible Society, the Pacific Tract Society and the Young Men's Christian Association. After speaking of the various religious organizations in early San Francisco, the authors of the *Annals* conclude:

"We have said enough, we hope, to prove that not all, nor nigh all the citizens of San Francisco are lost to everything but reckless dissipation. No city of equal size— few of ten times its age—can present such a list of men and institutions, who have accomplished so much *real* good, with so little of cant and hypocrisy."

We have already referred to the relative scarcity of women. Good women are essential to a well-ordered society. Unfortunately the condition of the gold rush was not conducive to the migration of the better class of women. Too many of those who did hasten to the gold fields were of a type whose presence did not improve social conditions. In San Francisco, a census taken in the spring of 1848 showed 177 women. It is reported that during the year 1849, when the total immigration was approximately 40,000, there were but 700 women in this number. The census of 1850 indicates that in California there were only seven women in every hundred of the population.

The absence of women of the better type was deplored by all interested in the improvement of the moral life and the permanent development of California. In an attempt to overcome this lack, Mrs. Eliza M. Farnham, the widow of Thomas Jefferson Farnham, in his day an enthusiastic booster for the Far West, conceived the brilliant idea of bringing to California a number of young women. Mrs. Farnham had been the matron of Sing Sing prison, was a woman of broad social vision and was prompted by the highest motives.

Early in February, 1849, Mrs. Farnham made public her plan which would have such beneficial effect upon California society. In her announcement, Mrs. Farnham called attention to the needs in California and stated:

"Among the many privations and deteriorating influences to which the thousands who are flocking thither will be subjected, one of the greatest is the absence of woman, with all her kindly cares and powers, so peculiarly conservative to man under such circumstances.

"It would exceed the limits of this circular to hint at

the benefits that would flow to the growing population of that wonderful region, from the introduction among them of intelligent, virtuous, and efficient women. Of such only it is proposed to make up this company. It is believed that there are hundreds, if not thousands, of such females in our country, who are not bound by any tie that would hold them here, who might, by going thither, have the satisfaction of employing themselves greatly to the benefit and advantage of those who are there, and at the same time of serving their own interest more effectually than by following any employment that offers to them here.

"It is proposed that the company shall consist of persons not under twenty-five years of age, who shall bring from their clergyman, or some authority of the town where they reside, satisfactory testimonials of education, character, capacity, etc., and who can contribute the sum of two hundred and fifty dollars, to defray the expenses of the voyage, make suitable provision for their accommodation after reaching San Francisco, until they shall be able to enter upon some occupation for their support, and create a fund to be held in reserve for the relief of any who may be ill, or otherwise need aid before they are able to provide for themselves."

In the endorsement of her plan, Mrs. Farnham had the support of many men of national fame, among them Horace Greeley, William Cullen Bryant and Henry Ward Beecher.

Through some unfortunate circumstance, Mrs. Farnham's plans were not realized. She had engaged the packet ship *Angelique* to sail about the middle of April, but illness on her part interfered with the preparations and the company numbered only three women. The report of her proposal, however, preceded her to California, and the San Francisco papers gave adequate publicity to the supposed shipload of young women that was soon to arrive at the Golden Gate. The excitement was intense as the time approached when the vessel should arrive. Likewise there was bitter disappointment when the facts became known. According to a contemporary writer: "I verily believe there was more drunkenness, more gambling, more fighting, and more of everything that was bad, that night, than had ever before occurred in San Francisco within any similar space of time."

As time went on more and more men with families came to California and many men already here sent for their wives and children. Homes began to take the place of bachelor quarters and public lodging houses. With this, society became more refined and much of the earlier restlessness and recklessness passed away.

The coming of families and the preparation for their proper care led to many improvements, among them being the organization of an efficient school system.

The people of San Francisco had not been unmindful of the advantages of educational institutions. During April, 1847, J. D. Marston opened a school in a rude building at San Francisco and had an attendance of from twenty to thirty people. Toward the end of 1847 the people saw the need of a proper building and had erected on the plaza a public schoolhouse, the first in California. Here, on April 3rd, 1848, Mr. Thomas Douglas, a graduate of Yale, began "dealing out instruction." The gold excitement resulted in a vacation being declared before the courses of instruction had been more than started, for the amount of the teacher's salary was no attraction when compared with the prospects of the gold fields. According to an account of a contemporary, the pedagogue "locked the school-house, and shouldering his pick and pan, himself started for the 'diggings.'"

While the gold fever of 1848 caused rapid depletion of

the population of San Francisco, this effect was not permanent and schools were again established. This next effort to advance popular education was in April, 1849, when the Reverend Albert Williams opened a private school in the school building on the plaza. This he continued for some months until his duties as pastor of the newly organized Presbyterian Church required all of his time. The work was, however, taken up soon afterward by Mr. J. C. Pelton who had established a private school in the Baptist Church. This school developed into what was probably the first public school in the state when the city council in April, 1850, took it over as a city enterprise.

Soon afterward other schools were started by churches and private parties, the most important being that of Colonel T. J. Nevins, who had come to the coast as agent of the American Tract Society. In June, 1850, Colonel Nevins obtained the use of a building in Happy Valley, near Mission and Second streets. This began as a school supported by voluntary contributions but was taken over by the city and became the Happy Valley School. When the city government became fully established, Colonel Nevins drew up an ordinance for "the establishment, regulation and support of free common schools in the city." On September 25th, 1851, this became a law. A Board of Education was created and soon thereafter they named Colonel Nevins superintendent of schools.

The growth of schools and school attendance was rapid notwithstanding the migratory nature of the early population. In 1854, there were seven public schools with an attendance of 1,574 pupils, besides a number of private schools. The citizens of San Francisco rejoiced at the progress in education.

"The school-bell now echoes through the streets of the busy city, and the astonished stranger meets groups of bright and smiling faces merrily trudging to their daily tasks, and ere long may listen to learned professors expounding to classes of intelligent students, art, literature and science as completely and perfectly as can be heard in the most time-honored institutions of the world."

By the middle of the decade of the 'fifties San Francisco had begun to settle down to a more sedate way of living. Her social institutions were not less developed than those of other more settled communities, and the boisterous days were largely over. Yet this period of the Gold Days had left an indelible imprint upon the character of the city which three quarters of a century have been unable to efface.

Chapter XIV

CHAPTER XIV

The Golden State

WHEN JAMES MARSHALL picked up the flake of gold at Sutter's mill on the 24th of January, 1848, little did he realize the tremendous economic, social and political forces his act was about to set in motion. In the previous chapters many of the economic and social phases of Gold Days have been considered. The story would not however be complete did it not give some consideration also to the great political movements thus initiated. This chapter will, therefore, seek to sketch in a very brief manner some of the most significant of these political phases.

Although the discovery of gold was not the cause of the American occupation of California, that event did so effectually accelerate immigration to the region as to upset all the previous schemes and calculations of the politicians. For several decades the American frontiersmen had been casting longing eyes toward the fertile but unoccupied fields across the Mexican frontier. Texas had been settled and later wrenched from Mexico by American colonists in a conflict which led to wider conquests including the territory of California itself. This process of expansion at the expense of a sister nation was not carried on without strenuous opposition among the American people themselves, especially when it was evident that the chief gains would probably be gathered in by the political faction which was endeavoring to strengthen the slavery cause. The annexation of California could not, therefore, be looked upon as independent of the issue involved in the expansion of slavery. Compromise legislation enacted in 1820 had set up a line which was looked upon as marking the northern limits of slavery. In as much as the Mexican lands lay very largely south of this line it appeared evident that any new territory would result in the strengthening of the slave power. To prevent this, a minority in Congress had waged a bitter fight to carry through a measure declaring that any annexed territory should be closed to slavery. Despite the best efforts of the anti-slavery forces, they were not successful in imposing a legal bar to slavery extension. The intense passion aroused by the struggle and the apparent future significance to the nation as a whole did, however, result in a deadlock when it came to the matter of providing a suitable government for the new territory.

Because of this critical state in national politics the new conditions in California became most significant. At the time of the conquest the population of the newly acquired province, excluding Indians, totaled about 13,000, over one half of whom were of the Spanish race. The desirability of an efficient civil government under the American system was evident, but in view of the conditions in Congress the formation of a state government might, without grave political results, have been postponed until a more convenient season had it not been for the discovery of gold.

Within a year after the knowledge of the gold discovery became general, the number of inhabitants had reached approximately 100,000. An immense population, gathered from the four corners of the earth, had been thrown suddenly into the mountains and cities of California. The spirit of mañana no longer found a home in California. Among these new arrivals the Anglo-American naturally greatly predominated, and, jealous of his political institutions, chafed under the inadequate and inefficient Mexican system of law. What, he asked, was this alcalde system of which he heard? To this query the officials themselves, even including the *de facto* governor, were not able to give a satisfactory answer. To meet the emergencies the governor instructed the alcaldes that for the time being they should be governed by the customs and laws of the country as far as they could ascertain them, and by their own good sense and sound discretion. Considering the fact that the alcalde of San Francisco, after diligent search, reported that he could find no law books except a small Mexican pamphlet and a digest of the Laws of the Indies published in Spain a century earlier, it will be readily seen that the officers were forced to rely almost entirely upon their "own good sense and sound discretion."

In view of this lack of legal works, we are not surprised to find a wide difference in the responsibilities assumed by the different officials. Alcalde Walter Colton, of Monterey, has left us his interpretation of his powers:

"It devolves upon me duties similar to those of a mayor of one of our cities, without any of those judicial aids which he enjoys. It involves every breach of the peace, every case of crime, every business obligation, and every disputed land-title within a space of three hundred miles. From every other alcalde's court in this jurisdiction there is an appeal to this, and none from this to any higher tribunal. Such an absolute disposal of questions, affecting property and personal liberty, never ought to be confided to one man. There is not a judge on any bench in England or the United States, whose power is so absolute as that of the alcalde of Monterey."

To anyone at all familiar with the spirit of the typical American frontiersman, it will readily be apparent that here were the elements of discontent. Instead of self-government, which every American claims as an inherent right, here was an archaic foreign system that no one was able to understand, and even less willing to accept.

We have seen how the men in the mining camps met the situation philosophically by establishing local governments with their own laws and courts. These men did not question the wisdom of this action, for their local government met their needs and the justice meted out, though crude, was efficient. In the cities, especially San Francisco, there arose more difficult problems. There the Mexican system had been established and the newcomers were not so free to set up their own style of government. The need of an efficient government, however, was no less pressing than in the mines, for in the cities were congregated the most vicious elements of society. It is not surprising, therefore, to find the journals of San Francisco very outspoken against the system of government whereby they were ruled. Furthermore, Governor Mason recognized the anomalous position in which he found himself as a military officer endeavoring to administer government over so large a civilian population after the war had both actually and formally ceased. After the news of the peace treaty reached him, Mason waited patiently for the expected news that Congress had provided a civil government for California, and was very much disappointed when he learned that that body had adjourned during the summer of 1848, without making provision for a California government. Appreciating the position in which he was placed, we cannot but sympathize with him when we read his request of November 24, 1848: "The war being over, the soldiers nearly all deserted, and having now been from the states two years, I respectfully request to be ordered home."

Meanwhile the agitation for an efficient civil government was gaining volume and mass meetings of citizens were held in various cities demanding that some action be taken. At the pueblo of San José a meeting held on December 11, 1848, adopted resolutions calling for a convention to organize a civil government for California. A few weeks later a mass meeting of San Francisco citizens likewise endorsed this movement declaring that the frequent murders and other daring outrages committed of late in different parts of the country, especially at the mines, while there was no proper legal protection for the lives and property of the citizens, had forced the people to conclude that Congress had been trifling with them in delaying the long proposed constitution—that there was no more time to wait—and, therefore, that instant steps should be taken to establish a form of government for themselves. Similar meetings at Sacramento, Santa Cruz, Monterey and other parts of the territory gave the movement increasing momentum.

Meanwhile a new administration had been inaugurated at Washington. General Zachary Taylor, a southern Whig, had been elected president, with Millard Fillmore, a former Democrat, as vice-president. The Whig party, although having a large anti-slavery element, had been careful to avoid any positive stand on the slavery issue. Taylor, being a military man, and a Whig, was not in sympathy with many of the political issues that engaged Congress. To him it was a matter of little importance what kind of a government the people of California should have. If they needed a government, why should they not form one to suit themselves? Congress could then do naught else than accept it.

General Bennet Riley, who arrived in California during

April, 1849, probably knew the policy of the President and came with the idea of acting as a civil rather than a military governor and was not unwilling to accede to the desires of the people of California. When, therefore, on May 28th, news arrived that Congress had again adjourned without providing a government for California, Riley issued a call for a convention to be held at Monterey on September 1.

Notwithstanding that this was in harmony with the desires of the people of California, there appeared strong opposition to the idea of the call being issued by the military governor, and only the wise counsel of the more conservative element prevented a general disruption in the plans. The election of delegates was consequently held according to the governor's call, and the members assembled at Monterey during the first days of September, 1849.

The constitutional convention at Monterey was a noteworthy gathering. It was composed of forty-eight delegates, mostly young men, a large majority of them being under forty years of age. Fourteen of the members were lawyers, but farmers and merchants were well represented. The large population of the mines and cities of Northern California elected thirty-eight delegates, while the more sparsely settled grazing country of the south was represented by ten. Twenty-three of the delegates came originally from the North and fifteen from southern states, but the latter were all elected from the northern districts of California. An important element were the twenty-one delegates, nearly one half of the whole number, who had been residents of California before the raising of the American flag, and seven of whom were natives of the province.

The routine of the convention need not concern us here, but its action on two or three issues is of consider-

can territory. The treaty with Mexico in 1848 had, on the other hand, limited the area on the south to what the Spanish called Upper or New California. The eastern boundary, however, had never been fixed either by Spain or Mexico and members of the California Convention were therefore free to set the stakes as wide as they desired.. There was, however, the danger that Congress might either delay or refuse to admit to statehood such a large area, or might divide it by a line which would deprive the new state of some of its seacoast, any of which alterations would be very undesirable. In the endeavor to determine the boundaries many suggestions were made. One proposition would have included all that area west of the one hundred and fifth meridian, a line running just west of Santa Fé, New Mexico. Gwin suggested the line be placed at the one hundred twelfth meridian, or just east of Great Salt Lake. On the other hand, more modest members suggested the summit of the Sierra Nevada and the Colorado River. To complicate the issue were also the claims of New Mexico and Deseret, the latter being the name of the proposed Mormon state, which, if the dream of its promoters had been realized, would have included practically all the coast line and territory of Southern California. After many heated debates the present state boundaries of California were adopted.

The convention completed its task about the middle of October, and because of the approach of the rainy season decided to submit the constitution to the people of the state at an election to be held within thirty days. The voters should then express their desires upon the constitution and also elect the state officers and members of Congress. In the weeks that preceded the election, candidates waged such a campaign as they were able, but in the unsettled condition of the country the men who were running for office were relatively unknown and all attempts to organize political parties were unsuccessful.

November 13, 1849, election day, came in the midst of a rainstorm. Many miners were unable to vote and the number of votes cast was small. The chief issue, however, was regarding the adoption of the constitution, and upon this there was no great division of opinion, for the results show 12,061 votes for its adoption, with only 811 in the negative. Peter H. Burnett, a recent arrival from Oregon, was elected governor while Edward Gilbert and George W. Wright were named as members of Congress.

In accordance with provisions of the constitution the new state legislature convened at San José, December 15, 1849, and on the twentieth of that month General Riley graciously turned over the governorship to the newly elected executive. In his inaugural address Governor Burnett placed before the legislature the query as to what should be the next step in the establishment of statehood—should they await the action of Congress upon the constitution, or should they proceed upon the assumption that the state government had already been established? The governor favored this stand and the legislature accepted his point of view. California was already a state and was resolved to act as such. Two United States Senators, John C. Frémont and William Gwin, were promptly elected and with the members chosen for seats in the lower house, began their journey to Washington to announce the action of the people of California and to ask for the admission of the State of California into the Federal Union.

It is now necessary that we ascertain what was going on in Congress while California had thus been acting in such an independent manner. There the prospect for a satisfactory adjustment of the nation's problems was not reassuring.

Weeks were spent in the organization of the House and

threats of disruption of the Union were openly made. Representative Toombs of Georgia vehemently declared: "I do not hesitate to avow before this House and the country, and in the presence of the living God, that if by your legislation you seek to drive us from the territories of California and New Mexico, purchased by the common blood and treasure of the whole people, and to abolish slavery in this District, thereby attempting to fix a national degradation upon half the States of this Confederacy, *I am for disunion.*"

To this Representative Baker of Illinois came back with the following reply: "In the name of the men of the North so rudely attacked, and speaking what I know to be their sentiments, I say a dissolution of this Union is, must be, shall be, impossible, as long as an American heart beats in an American bosom, or the Almighty sends His wisdom and His goodness to guide and to bless us."

Never before had the members of Congress faced such a grave situation, for the fiercest passions of both North and South seemed to have been let loose. To the anti-slavery people in the North, the moral evil of slavery was not to be tolerated. The entire exclusion of slavery from all the new territory was the least they were willing to accept. On the other hand, the slavery men of the South were equally pronounced in their belief that slavery was not only a necessity but that it was both morally and ethically right. To prevent their expansion into the territory won at the cost of the blood of the South as well as of the North was unfair and without moral basis. If southern rights were to be so wantonly disregarded by abolition fanatics, their only hope was in separation from the Union.

It was at this time that the statesman, Henry Clay, came forward in a last attempt to save the Union. Clay's plan was for compromise, and it won the support of the conservative members of both sides but did not satisfy President Zachary Taylor. The scenes in Congress had never been more tense than during the debates upon the admission of California in 1850. The veteran Clay pleaded with both North and South to lay aside their differences for the sake of unity. Daniel Webster, the veteran orator from Massachusetts, put aside his New England hatred for slavery in order to make a plea for the preservation of the Union. Others joined these great leaders in the cause of harmony.

Opposing forces, however, were strong. The aged John C. Calhoun, now on the edge of the grave, was perhaps the ablest leader of the South. In a last effort for the Southern cause he proclaimed in fiery words his opposition to compromise. If the South gave in, he said, its cause was lost. The North was the aggressor, the abolitionists were the cause of all the discord. Let the North recognize the rights of the South and there would be peace and harmony. Otherwise he saw nothing but dissension. This address, although penned by Calhoun, was read by another, and within a month the South Carolinian had passed to the Great Beyond. There was likewise strenuous opposition to the compromise from Northern anti-slavery men who would not think of accepting a fugitive slave law or other measures sought by the South.

One of the most difficult problems for the leaders of the compromise was the attitude of President Taylor, who did not have any sympathy with the compromise idea. As a soldier, he believed in direct action and he felt that California should be admitted without delay. Meanwhile, passions became more inflamed and at a Southern convention held at Nashville in June, nine states threatened secession if California were admitted under the free state constitution. It looked as if either the compromise effort would fail, or the admission of California would disrupt the Union.

As summer wore on matters changed. On July 9th, the death of President Taylor placed in the presidential chair Millard Fillmore, a man whose convictions favored compromise. With the aid of the new president, Clay and his associates were able to secure the necessary support with the result that on September 9, 1850, President Fillmore signed the act making California the thirty-first state in the Federal Union.

While these stirring events were taking place at the nation's capital, the people of California had been kept in suspense. The uncertainty of the attitude of Congress, combined with the great distance and the inadequate means of communication, all served to give the people of California a feeling of uncertainty which led at times to expressions of independence.

During these months the California legislature had met and performed its functions just as though California were a fully accredited member of the Union. The necessary machinery for setting the state government in operation was soon established; local governments were provided for the counties and cities, and a system of law and courts was adopted. During the spring at the county elections local officials were chosen, and by the summer of 1850 California was well launched upon her career as a state in so far as action on her part would make that possible.

If Congress should stupidly refuse to recognize properly the status of this state, there were many ready to assert with the editor of the San Francisco *Evening Picayune* that California could exist without connection with the Federal government. Had not the settlers raised their own flag at Sonoma in 1846? If they then felt their ability to establish their own government, did not the fact that the Sierra Nevada had been pouring forth her golden treasure furnish still more ample proof of the ability of the natural resources of California to maintain her economic as well as political independence? He further contended, "No people can lay under the uncompensated exactions which have, for two years passed, been forced upon us; and the people are with great plausibility, familiarizing their minds with the idea, long entertained and boldly promulgated, before the close of the Mexican War, by those now in places of executive power and legislative influence at Washington that united with Oregon, and with the inevitable extension of our influence on either hand of us, we may build up here a great western Republic, independent of the world beside. If this idea is treasonable or revolutionary, it is forced upon the minds of our people, by the necessities in which Congress has presumed upon the right to leave us."

Speaking in a similar manner the editor of the *Pacific News*, during the latter part of August, 1850, thus expresses his views: "Suppose California should form an independent government—and we trust our New York contemporary will discern no 'treason' in the bare supposition— what a spectacle she would present! We should indeed be a nation 'born in a day,' the wonder and admiration of the world. Through her mineral resources California would become the richest nation on the face of the globe —the grand attractive circle upon which all eyes would be pointed as if by enchantment. Her institutions would become permanent, the government strong and lasting, impregnable in its own defense and faithful to freedom and equality. We should collect and expend our own revenues without a distant power sending us in officers to perform that pleasing duty and locking up, at five per cent a month, an amount of treasure sufficient to pay off our indebtedness."

These opinions, while being set forth in papers of importance, probably do not reflect the opinion of the greater part of the people, yet the Sacramento *Transcript* felt it necessary to condemn these expressions and to urge the people to remain steadfast in their loyalty to the Union: "Let no one think those remarks extravagant and ill-timed when we hear of Bear Flag sentiments openly avowed and advocated in our streets; when we see a portion of our press with an evident leaning in favor of independence. It is time for those at least who hold with determination different views to speak their sentiments without reserve. Although, there are some in our midst who, in the event of discouraging news by the next two or three steamers are in favor of separation from the Union, we are not only opposed to it ourselves, but we believe the vast majority are opposed to it also."

Fortunately, as we have seen, the news to come was not to be discouraging. On October 18th the steamer *Oregon* approached the Golden Gate with her rigging trimmed with bunting and as she entered the bay she repeatedly fired her signal guns that told the welcome story. From her masthead spread a great banner with the words "California is a State."

Almost immediately the whole city was astir with intense excitement; business was suspended, courts were adjourned and everyone hastened to the streets and wharves to welcome the steamer and to celebrate the occasion. As the day wore on the excitement increased, aided by a brilliant show of flags at all possible places of display and the discharge of guns placed upon the plaza. At night bonfires lighted up the hills surrounding the city and skyrockets rent the air. Everyone made merry until dawn announced another day. Plans were made for a more formal celebration, and on October 29th a grand ball including five hundred men and three hundred ladies was held in San Francisco's grandest public hall to celebrate the admission of California as the thirty-first state.

The admission of California to the Union was an event which the people of California might well celebrate, for the effect of that action was to have a great influence upon our national history. Talk of a separate Pacific Republic was dispelled until the stormy days of the Civil War, and California took her place among the states to build up the resources of the great nation. Before the Compromise of 1850 the balance of power between the slave states and free states had been carefully preserved. Of the thirty states composing the Union in 1849 there were fifteen known as free states and fifteen as slave states. The admission of California as a free state overthrew this balance. For the next decade, however, the effect of this was not noticeable in any marked degree because of the fact that in politics California was Democratic and its representatives in Congress were at most times sympathetic with the aims of Southern politicians. The people of California as a whole were little concerned with the political issues so important to the eastern politician. Distance and lack of means of communication led to a feeling of isolation while the intense economic activity around the mines caused Californians to think particularly of their own affairs. The campaign of 1860 found California conservative but divided between Lincoln, Douglas and Breckenridge. Lincoln, however, held a small lead over his rivals and received California's electoral vote. The secession of South Carolina and the firing upon Fort Sumter came as a shock to the Californians and threw the balance. California came strongly to the Union side, and, during the great war between the states, California remained loyal to the Federal government.

Although California's contributions from a military point of view were not inconsiderable, from an economic standpoint her adherence to the Federal Union was of paramount importance. The mines of California continued to pour their golden stream into the marts of trade. During the years from 1860 to 1865 California produced $172,387,985 in gold. This addition to the country's supply of precious metal helped materially to maintain the value of the Federal currency. Had this gold found a terminus in the South the results would have spelled national disaster. As it was, the loyalty of California insured a strong reserve supply of gold at a time when the nation's credit was being stretched to the breaking point. California gold also assisted in another way, for the state's contribution to the Sanitary Fund reached nearly a million and a quarter of dollars, a sum exceeding one fourth of the combined contribution of all the states. Thus we see that California, one of the youngest members of the Union, demonstrated her loyalty in a most generous manner.

California gold not only sustained the nation's credit and furnished relief to the sick and wounded soldiers of the Federal army during the trying days of the Civil War, but her mineral resources have, during subsequent years, continued to add to the nation's wealth in figures almost beyond belief. Gold stampedes have swept the population to the Washoe Mines, to Fraser River, to Pike's Peak, to Idaho, to the Black Hills, to Arizona and elsewhere. While many of these have flourished for a time and then become exhausted, the mines of California have continued steadily to add to the supply of precious metal. The remarkable thing is that, eighty years after Marshall's discovery, California still leads the states in the production of gold, the output in 1926 being given at $12,000,000, or

approximately thirty per cent of the entire gold production of the United States. This vast mineral wealth of
the state, added to its other resources in soil and climate,
has given California a place of preeminence among
her sister states. Thus has California, a
daughter of the Gold Days, won for
herself the right to be known
as "The Golden State."

Appendix

APPENDIX

OFFICIAL REPORTS OF THE GOLD DISCOVERY, 1848

The following documents constitute the first official reports of the gold discovery to reach the United States in the fall of 1848.

Mr. Thomas O. Larkin was the special agent of the United States in California, having resided in that province since 1831. He served as United States Consul from 1841 to 1845 and just before the war with Mexico was appointed special diplomatic agent of the State Department. His word was therefore considered very reliable. Larkin's letter of June 1, 1848, was probably the first report of the gold discovery sent East by any of the United States officials in California, and it reached the State Department at Washington about September 15th. Larkin's letter of June 28th, was carried by Lieutenant Edward F. Beale on the flagship *Ohio* to La Paz and thence forwarded to Washington with the navy mail.

Colonel R. B. Mason was the commanding officer of the United States forces in California and acting governor of that territory. During July he visited the gold district and August 17, 1848, submitted his report to the War Department. It is more complete than Larkin's previous letters but confirmed the information contained in them. It was sent in the charge of Lieutenant L. Loeser, bearer of dispatches, who left Monterey August 30, 1848, for Washington via South America. In addition to this report he carried with him "a tea caddy" containing two hundred and thirty ounces fifteen pennyweights and nine grains of gold. This reached Washington just before the publication of the President's annual message of December 5, 1848. The text here given follows literally the text of the documents as they were first officially published with the President's message of December, 1848.

LETTER OF THOMAS O. LARKIN, JUNE 1, 1848

San Francisco, Upper California
June 1, 1848.

Sir: . . . I have to report to the State Department one of the most astonishing excitements and state of affairs now existing in this country, that, perhaps, has ever been brought to the notice of the

[317]

Government. On the American fork of the Sacramento and Feather River, another branch of the same, and the adjoining lands, there has been, within the present year, discovered a placer, a vast tract of land containing gold, in small particles. This gold, thus far, has been taken on the bank of the river, from the surface to eighteen inches in depth, and is supposed deeper, and to extend over the country.

On account of the inconvenience of washing, the people have, to this time, only gathered the metal on the banks, which is done simply with a shovel, filling a shallow dish, bowl, basket, or tin pan with a quantity of black sand, similar to the class used on paper, and washing out the sand by movement of the vessel. It is now two or three weeks since the men employed in those washings have appeared in this town with gold, to exchange for merchandise and provisions. I presume nearly twenty thousand dollars ($20,000) of this gold has, as yet, been so exchanged. Some two or three hundred men have remained up the river, or are gone to their homes, for the purpose of returning to the placera, and washing immediately with shovels, picks, and baskets; many of them, for the first few weeks, depending on borrowing from others. I have seen the written statement of the work of one man for sixteen days, which averaged twenty-five dollars ($25) per day; others have, with a shovel and pan, or wooden bowl, washed out ten to even fifty dollars in a day. There are now some men yet washing, who have five hundred to one thousand dollars. As they have to stand two feet deep in the river, they work but a few hours in the day, and not every day in the week.

A few men have been down in boats to this port, spending twenty to thirty ounces of gold each—about three hundred dollars ($300). I am confident that this town (San Francisco) has one-half of its tenements empty, locked up with the furniture. The owners—storekeepers, lawyers, mechanics and laborers—all gone to the Sacramento with their families. Small parties, of five to fifteen men, have sent to this town, and offered cooks ten to fifteen dollars per day for a few weeks. Mechanics and teamsters, earning the year past five to eight dollars per day, have struck and gone. Several United States volunteers have deserted. United States bark Anita, belonging to the army, now at anchor here, has but six men. One Sandwich Island vessel in port lost all her men; engaged another crew at fifty dollars ($50) for the run of fifteen days to the islands.

One American captain having his men shipped on this coast in such a manner that they could leave at any time, had them all on the eve of quitting, when he agreed to continue their pay and food; leaving one on board, he take a boat and carry them to the gold regions; furnishing tools and giving his men one-third. They have been gone a week. Common spades and shovels, one month ago worth one dollar, will now bring ten dollars at the gold regions. I am informed fifty dollars has been offered for one. Should this gold continue as represented, this town and others, would be depopulated. Clerks' wages have risen from six hundred to one thousand dollars per annum, and board; cooks', twenty-five to thirty dollars per month. This sum will not be any inducement a month longer, unless the fever and ague appears among the washers. The "Californian," printed here, stopped this week. The "Star" newspaper office, where the new laws of Governor Mason, for this country, is printing, has but one man left. A merchant, lately from China, has even lost his China servants. Should the excitement continue through the year, and the whale ships visit San Francisco, I think they will lose most all their crews. How Colonel Mason can retain his men, unless he puts a force on the spot, I know not.

I have seen several pounds of this gold, and consider it very pure, worth, in New York, seventeen to eighteen dollars per ounce; fourteen to sixteen dollars, in merchandise, is paid for it here. What good or bad effect this gold region will have on California, I cannot foretell. It may end this year; but I am informed that it will continue many years. Mechanics now in this town are only waiting to finish some rude machinery, to enable them to obtain the gold more expeditiously, and free from working in the river. Up to this time, but few Californians have gone to the mines, being afraid the Americans will soon have trouble among themselves, and cause disturbance to all around. I have seen some of the black sand, as taken from the bottom of the river (I should think in the States it would bring twenty-five to fifty cents per pound), containing many pieces of gold; they are from the size of the head of a pin to the weight of the eighth of an ounce. I have seen some weighing one-quarter of an ounce (four dollars). Although my statements are almost incredible, I believe I am within the statements believed by every one here. Ten days back, the excitement had not reached Monterey. I shall, within a few days, visit this gold mine, and will make another report to you. Inclosed you will have a specimen.

I have the honor to be, very respectfully,

THOMAS O. LARKIN.

Hon. James Buchanan,
Secretary of State, Washington.

P. S. This placer, or gold region, is situated on public land.

LETTER OF THOMAS O. LARKIN, JUNE 28, 1848
Mr. Larkin to Mr. Buchanan:

Monterey, California
June 28, 1848.

Sir: My last dispatch to the State Department was written in San Francisco, the first of this month. In that I had the honor to give some information respecting the new "placer," or gold regions lately discovered on the branches of the Sacramento River. Since the writing of that dispatch, I have visited a part of the gold regions, and found it all I had heard, and much more than I anticipated. The part that I visited was upon a fork of the American River, a branch of the Sacramento, joining the main river at Sutter's Fort. The place in which I found the people digging was about twenty-five miles from the fort by land.

I have reason to believe that gold will be found on many branches of the Sacramento and the Joaquin rivers. People are already scattered over one hundred miles of land, and it is supposed that the "placer" extends from river to river. At present the workmen are employed within ten or twenty yards of the river, that they may be convenient to water. On Feather River, there are several branches upon which the people are digging for gold. This is two or three days' ride from the place I visited.

At my camping place I found, on a surface of two or three miles on the banks of the river, some fifty tents, mostly owned by Americans. These had their families. There are no Californians who have taken their families as yet to the gold regions; but few or none will ever do it. Some from New Mexico may do so next year, but no Californians.

I was two nights at a tent occupied by eight Americans, viz: two sailors, one clerk, two carpenters, and three daily workmen. These men were in company; had two machines, each made from one hundred feet of boards (worth there one hundred and fifty dollars; in Monterey, fifteen dollars—being one day's work), made similar to a child's cradle, ten feet long, without the ends.

The two evenings I saw these eight men bring to their tents the labor of the day. I suppose they made each fifty dollars per day; their own calculation was two pounds of gold a day—four ounces to a man—sixty-four dollars. I saw two brothers that worked together, and only worked by washing the dirt in a tin pan, weigh the gold they obtained in one day; the result was, seven dollars to one and eighty-two dollars to the other. There were two reasons for this difference; one man worked less hours than the other, and by chance had ground less impregnated with gold. I give this statement as an extreme case. During my visit I was an interpreter for a native of Monterey, who was purchasing a machine or canoe. I first tried to purchase boards and hire a carpenter for him. There were but a few hundred feet of boards to be had; for these the owner asked me fifty dollars per hundred ($500 per M), and a carpenter washing gold dust demanded fifty dollars per day for working. I at last purchased a log dug out, with a riddle and sieve made of willow-boughs on it, for one hundred and twenty dollars, payable in gold dust at fourteen dollars per ounce. The owner excused himself for the price, by saying that he was two days making it, and even then demanded the use of it until sunset. My Californian has told me since that himself, partner, and two Indians obtained with this canoe eight ounces the first and five ounces the second day.

I am of the opinion that, on the American Fork, Feather River, and Copimes [Cosumnes] River, there are near two thousand people, nine-tenths of them foreigners. Perhaps there are one hundred families, that have their teams, wagons and tents. Many persons are waiting to see whether the months of July and August will be sickly, before they leave their present business to go to the "placer." The discovery of this gold was made by some Mormons, in January or February, who for a time kept it a secret; the majority of those who are working there began in May. In most every instance the men, after digging a few days, have been compelled to leave for the purpose of returning home to see their families, arrange their business, and purchase provisions. I feel confident in saying there are fifty men in this "placer" who have on an average one thousand dollars each, obtained in May and June. I have not met with any person who had been fully employed in washing gold one month; most, however, appear to have averaged an ounce per day. I think there must at this time be over one thousand men at work upon the different branches of the Sacramento; putting their gains at ten thousand per day, for six days in the week, appears to me not overrated.

Should this news reach the emigration of California and Oregon, now on the road, connected with the Indian wars, now impoverishing the latter country, we should have a large addition to our population; and should the richness of the gold regions continue, our emigration in 1849 will be many thousand, and in 1850 still more. If our countrymen in California as clerks, mechanics, and workmen, will forsake employment at from two dollars to six dollars per day, how many more of the same class in the Atlantic States, earning much less, will leave for this country under such prospects? It is the opinion of many who have visited the gold regions the past and present months, that the ground will afford gold for many years, perhaps for a century. From my own examination of the rivers and their banks, I am of the opinion that, at least for a few years, the golden products will equal the present year. However, as neither men of science, nor the laborers now at work, have made any explorations of consequence, it is a matter of impossibility to give any opinion as to the extent and richness of this part of California. Every Mexican who has seen the place says throughout their republic there has never been any "placer" like this one.

Could Mr. Polk and yourself see California as we now see it, you would think that a few thousand people, on one hundred miles square of the Sacramento Valley, would yearly turn out of this river the whole price our country pays for all the acquired territory. When I finished my first letter I doubted my own writing, and, to be better satisfied, showed it to one of the principal merchants of San Francisco, and to Captain Fulsom, of the quartermaster's department, who decided at once I was far below the reality. You certainly will suppose, from my two letters, that I am, like others, led away by the excitement of the day. I think I am not.

In my last I enclosed a small sample of the gold dust, and I find my only error was in putting a value to the sand. At that time I was not aware how the gold was found; I now can describe the mode of collecting it. A person without a machine, after digging off one or two feet of the upper ground, near the water (in some cases they take the top earth), throws into a tin pan or wooden bowl a shovelful of loose dirt and stones; then, placing the basin an inch under water, continued to stir up the dirt with his hand in such a manner that the running water will carry off the light earth, occasionally, with his hand, throwing out the stones; after an operation of this kind for twenty or thirty minutes, a spoonful of small black sand remains; this is on a handkerchief or cloth dried in the sun, the emerge is blown off, leaving the pure gold. I have the pleasure of enclosing a paper of this sand and gold, which I, from a bucket of dirt and stones, in half hour, standing at the edge of the water, washed out myself. The value of it may be two or three dollars.

The size of the gold depends in some measure upon the river from which it is taken, the banks of one river having larger grains of gold than another. I presume more than one-half of the gold put into pans or machines is washed out and goes down the stream; this is of no consequence to the washers, who care only for the present time. Some have formed companies of four or five men, and have a rough made machine put together in a day, which worked to much advantage, yet many prefer to work alone, with a wooden bowl or tin pan, worth fifteen or twenty cents in the States, but eight to sixteen dollars at the gold region. As the workmen continue and materials can be obtained, improvements will take place in the mode of obtaining gold; at present it is obtained by standing in the water, and with much severe labor, or such as is called here severe labor.

How long this gathering of gold by the handful will continue here, or the future effect it will have on California, I cannot say. Three-fourths of the houses in the town on the bay of San Francisco are deserted. Houses are sold at the price of the ground lots. The effects are this week showing themselves in Monterey. Almost every house I had hired out is given up. Every blacksmith, carpenter and lawyer is leaving; brick yards, saw mills, and ranches are left perfectly alone. A large number of the volunteers at San Francisco and Sonoma have deserted; some have been retaken and brought back; public and private vessels are losing their crews; my clerks have had one hundred per cent advance offered them on their wages to accept employment. A complete revolution in the ordinary state of affairs is taking place; both of our newspapers are discontinued from want of workmen and the loss of their agencies; the alcaldes have left San Francisco, and I believe Sonoma likewise; the former place has not a justice of the peace left.

The second alcalde of Monterey today joins the keepers of our principal hotel, who have closed their office and house, and will leave tomorrow for the golden rivers. I saw on the ground a lawyer who was last year attorney general of the king of the Sandwich Islands, digging and washing out his ounce and a half per day; near him can be found most all his brethren of the long robe, working in the same occupation.

To conclude; my letter is long, but I could not well describe what I have seen in less words, and I now can believe that my account may be doubted; if the affair proves a bubble, a mere excitement; I know not how we can all be deceived, as we are situated. Governor Mason and his staff have left Monterey to visit the place in question, and will I suppose soon forward to his department his views and opinions on this subject. Most of the land, where gold has been discovered, is public land; there are on different rivers some private grants. I have three such purchased in 1846 and '47, but have not learned that any private lands have produced gold, though they may hereafter do so.

I have the honor, dear sir, to be, very respectfully,

Your obedient servant,

THOMAS O. LARKIN.

Hon. James Buchanan, *Secretary of State, Washington City.*

REPORT OF COLONEL R. B. MASON, AUGUST 17, 1848

HEADQUARTERS TENTH MILITARY DEPARTMENT,
Monterey, California
August 17, 1848.

Sir: I have the honor to inform you that, accompanied by Lieutenant W. T. Sherman, 3rd artillery, acting assistant adjutant general, I started on the 12th of June last to make a tour through the northern part of California. My principal purpose, however, was to visit the newly-discovered gold placer in the valley of the Sacramento.

I had proceeded about forty miles when I was overtaken by an express, bringing me intelligence of the arrival at Monterey of the United States storeship Southampton, with important letters from Commodore Shubrick and Lieutenant-Colonel Burton. I returned at once to Monterey, and despatched what business was most important, and on the 17th resumed my journey. We reached San Francisco on the 20th, and found that all, or nearly all, its male population had gone to the mines. The town, which a few months before was so busy and thriving, was then almost deserted. On the evening of the 24th, the horses of the escort were crossed to Sausolito in a launch, and on the following day we resumed the journey, by way of Bodega and Sonoma, to Sutter's Fort, where we arrived on the morning of the 2nd of July. Along the whole route mills were lying idle, fields of wheat were open to cattle and horses, houses vacant, and farms going to waste. At Sutter's there was more life and business. Launches were discharging their cargoes at the river, and carts were hauling goods to the fort, where already were established several stores, a hotel, &c. Captain Sutter had only two mechanics in his employ—a wagon-maker and blacksmith—whom he was then paying ten dollars per day. Merchants pay him a monthly rent of one hundred dollars per room, and whilst I was there a two-story house in the fort was rented as a hotel for five hundred dollars a month.

At the urgent solicitation of many gentlemen, I delayed there to participate in the first public celebration of our national anniversary at that fort, but on the 5th resumed the journey and proceeded twenty-five miles up the American Fork, to a point on it now known as the lower mines, or Mormon diggings. The hillsides were thickly strewn with canvas tents and bush arbors. A store was erected, and several boarding shanties in operation. The day was intensely hot; yet about two hundred men were at work in the full glare of the sun, washing for gold, some with tin pans, some with close-woven Indian baskets, but the greater part had a rude machine known as the cradle. This is on rockers six or eight feet long, open at the foot, and at its head has a coarse grate and sieve; the bottom is rounded, with small cleets nailed across. Four men are required to work this machine; one digs the gravel in the bank close by the stream, another carries it to the cradle and empties it on the grate, a third gives a violent rocking motion to the machine, whilst a fourth dashes water on from the stream itself. The sieve keeps the coarse stones from entering the cradle, the current of water washes off the earthy matter, and the gravel is gradually carried out at the foot of the machine, leaving the gold mixed with a fine heavy black sand above the first cleets. The sand and gold, mixed together, are then drawn off through auger holes into a pan below, are dried in the sun, and afterwards separated by blowing off the sand. A party of four men thus employed at the lower mines averaged a hundred dollars a day. The Indians, and those who have nothing but pans or willow baskets, gradually wash out the earth and separate the gravel by hand, leaving nothing but the gold mixed with sand, which is separated in the manner before described. The gold in the lower mines is in fine bright scales, of which I send several specimens.

As we ascended the south branch of the American Fork, the country became more broken and mountainous, and at the saw-mill, twenty-five miles above the lower washings, or fifty miles from Sutter's, the hills rise to about a thousand feet above the level of the Sacramento plain. Here a species of pine occurs, which led to the discovery of the gold. Captain Sutter, feeling the great want of lumber, contracted, in September last, with a Mr. Marshall, to build a saw-mill at that place. It was erected in the course of the past winter and spring—a dam and race constructed; but when the water was let on the wheel, the tail race was found to be too narrow to permit the water to escape with sufficient rapidity. Mr. Marshall, to save labor, let the water directly into the race, with a strong current, so as to wash it wider and deeper. He effected his purpose, and a large bed of mud and gravel was carried to the foot of the race. One day Mr. Marshall when walking down the race to this deposit of mud, observed some glittering particles at its upper edge; he gathered a few, examined them, and became satisfied of their value. He then went to the fort, told Captain Sutter of his discovery, and they agreed to keep it secret until a certain grist-mill of Sutter's was finished. It however got out, and spread like magic. Remarkable success attended the labors of the first explorers, and in a few weeks hundreds of men were drawn thither. At the time of my visit, but little more than three months after its first discovery, it was estimated that upwards of four thousand people were employed. At the mill there is a fine deposit, or bank of gravel, which the people respect as the property of Captain Sutter, although he pretends to no right to it, and would be perfectly satisfied with the simple promise of a preemption, on account of the mill which he has built there, at considerable cost. Mr. Marshall was living near the mill, and informed me that many persons were employed above and below him, that they used the same machines as at the lower washings, and that their success was about the same, ranging from one to three ounces of gold per man daily. This gold too is in scales, a little coarser than those of the lower mines. From the mills Mr. Marshall guided me up the mountain, on the opposite or north bank of the South Fork, where, in the beds of small streams, or ravines, now dry, a great deal of the coarse gold has been found. I there saw several parties at work, all of whom were doing very well. A great many specimens were shown me, some as heavy as four or five ounces in weight; and I send three pieces, labelled No. 5, presented by a Mr. Spence. You will perceive that some of the specimens accompanying this hold, mechanically, pieces of quartz, that the surface is rough, and evidently moulded in the crevice of a rock. This gold cannot have been carried far by water, but must have remained near where it was deposited from the rock that once bound it. I inquired of many people if they had encountered the metal in its matrix, but in every instance they said they had not, but that the gold was invariably mixed with washed gravel, or lodged in the crevices of other rocks. All bore testimony that they had found gold in greater or less quantities in the numerous small gullies or ravines that occur in that mountainous region. On the 7th of July I left the mill and crossed to a small stream emptying into the American Fork, three or four miles below the saw-mill. I struck this stream (now known as Weber's Creek) at the washings of Suñal & Co. They had about thirty Indians employed, whom they pay in merchandise. They were getting gold of a character similar to that found in the main fork, and doubtless in sufficient quantities to satisfy them. I send you a small specimen, presented by this company, of their gold. From this point we proceeded up the stream about eight miles, where we found a great many people and Indians; some engaged in the bed of the stream, and others in the small side valleys that put into it. These latter are exceedingly rich, and two ounces were considered an ordinary yield for a day's work. A small gutter, not more than a hundred yards long by four feet wide and two or three feet deep, was pointed out to me as the one where two men, William Daly and Perry McCoon, had, a short time before, obtained in seven days $17,000 worth of gold.

Captain Weber informed me that he knew that these two men had employed four white men and about a hundred Indians, and that, at the end of one week's work, they paid off their party and had left with $10,000 worth of gold. Another small ravine was shown me, from which had been taken $12,000 worth of this gold. Hundreds of similar ravines, to all appearances, are as yet untouched. I could not have credited these reports had I not seen, in the abundance of the precious metal, evidence of their truth. Mr. Neligh, an agent of Commodore Stockton, had been at work about three weeks in the neighborhood, and showed me, in bags and bottles, over $2,000 worth of gold; and Mr. Lyman, a gentleman of education and worthy of every credit, said he had been engaged, with four others, with a machine, on the American Fork, just below Sutter's saw-mill, that they worked eight days, and that his share was at the rate of fifty dollars a day; but, hearing that others were doing better at Weber's place, they had removed there, and were then on the point of resuming operations.

I might tell of hundreds of similar instances; but to illustrate how plentiful the gold was in the pockets of common laborers, I will mention a simple occurrence which took place in my presence when I was at Weber's store. This store was nothing but an arbor of bushes, under which he had exposed for sale, goods and groceries suited to his customers. A man came in, picked up a box of seidlitz powders, and asked its price. Captain Weber told him it was not for sale. The man offered an ounce of gold, but Captain Weber told him it only cost fifty cents, and he did not wish to sell it. The man then offered an ounce and a half, when Captain Weber *had* to take it. The prices of all things are high; and yet Indians, who before hardly knew what a breech-cloth was, can now afford to buy the most gaudy dresses.

The country, on either side of Weber's creek, is much broken up by hills, and is intersected in every direction by small streams or ravines, which contain more or less gold. Those that have been worked are barely scratched, and, although thousands of ounces have been carried away, I do not consider that a serious impression has been made upon the whole. Every day was developing new and rich deposits, and the only apprehension seemed to be that the metal would be found in such abundance as seriously to depreciate in value.

On the 8th of July I returned to the lower mines, and on the following day to Sutter's, where, on the 10th, I was making preparations for a visit to the Feather, Yubah, and Bear rivers, when I received a letter from Commodore A. R. Long, United States Navy, who had just arrived at San Francisco from Mazatlan, with a crew for the sloop-of-war Warren, and with orders to take that vessel to the squadron at La Paz. Captain Long wrote to me that the Mexican Congress had adjourned without ratifying the treaty of peace, that he had letters for me from Commodore Jones, and that his orders were to sail with the Warren on or before the 20th of July. In consequence of these, I determined to return to Monterey, and accordingly arrived here on the 17th of July. Before leaving Sutter's, I satisfied myself that gold exists in the bed of the Feather river, in the Yubah, and Bear, and in many of the small streams that lie between the latter and the American Fork; also, that it had been found in the Cosumnes, to the south of the American Fork. In each of those streams the gold is found in small scales, whereas in the intervening mountains it occurs in coarse lumps.

Mr. Sinclair, whose rancho is three miles above Sutter's, on the north side of the American, employs about fifty Indians on the North Fork, not far from its junction with the main stream. He had been engaged about five weeks when I saw him, and up to that time his Indians had used simply closely-woven willow baskets. His net proceeds (which I saw) were about $16,000 worth of gold. He showed me the proceeds of his last week's work—fourteen pounds avoirdupois of clean washed gold.

The principal store at Sutter's Fort, that of Brannant & Co., had received in payment for goods $36,000 worth of this gold from the 1st of May to the 10th of July; other merchants had also made extensive sales. Large quantities of goods were daily sent forward to the mines, as the Indians, heretofore so poor and degraded, have suddenly become consumers of the luxuries of life. I before mentioned that the greater part of the farmers and rancheros had abandoned their fields to go to the mines; this is not the case with Captain Sutter, who was carefully gathering his wheat, estimated at 40,000 bushels. Flour is already worth at Sutter's $36 a barrel, and soon will be $50. Unless large quantities of bread-stuffs reach the country, much suffering will occur; but as each man is now able to pay a large price, it is believed the merchants will bring from Chili and Oregon a plentiful supply for the coming winter.

The most moderate estimate I could obtain from men acquainted with the subject was, that upwards of four thousand men were working in the gold district, of whom more than half were Indians, and that from $30,000 to $50,000 worth of gold, if not more, was daily obtained. The entire gold district, with very few exceptions of grants made some years ago by the American [Mexican] authorities, is on land belonging to the United States. It was a matter of serious reflection with me how I could secure to the government certain rents or fees for the privilege of procuring this gold; but upon considering the large extent of country, the character of the people engaged, and the small scattered force at my command, I resolved not to interfere, but permit all to work freely, unless broils and crimes should call for interference. I was surprised to learn that crime of any kind was very unfrequent, and that no thefts or robberies had been committed in the gold district. All live in tents, in bush houses, or in the open air, and men have frequently about their persons thousands of dollars' worth of this gold; and it was to me a matter of surprise that so peaceful and quiet a state of things should continue to exist. Conflicting claims to particular spots of ground may cause collisions, but they will be rare, as the extent of country is so great, and the gold so abundant, that for the present there is room and enough for all; still the government is entitled to rents for this land, and immediate steps should be devised to collect them, for the longer it is delayed the more difficult it will become. One plan I would suggest is to send out from the United States surveyors, with high salaries, bound to serve specified periods; a superintendent to be appointed at Sutter's Fort, with power to grant licenses to work a spot of ground, say 100 yards square, for one year, at a rent of from $100 to $1,000 at his discretion; the surveyors to measure the grounds and place the renter in possession. A better plan, however, will be to have the district surveyed and sold at public auction to the highest bidder, in small parcels, say from 20 to 40 acres. In either case there will be many intruders, whom for years it will be almost impossible to exclude.

The discovery of these vast deposits of gold has entirely changed the character of Upper California. Its people, before engaged in cultivating their small patches of ground and guarding their herds of cattle and horses, have all gone to the mines, or are on their way thither; laborers of every trade have left their work-benches, and tradesmen their shops; sailors desert their ships as fast as they arrive on the coast, and several vessels have gone to sea with hardly enough hands to spread a sail; two or three are now at anchor in San Francisco with no crews on board. Many desertions, too, have taken place from the garrisons within the influence of the mines; 26 soldiers have deserted from the post of Sonoma, 24 from that of San Francisco, and 24 from Monterey. For a few days the evil appeared so threatening that great danger existed that the garrisons would leave in a body; and I refer you to my orders of the 25th of July to show the steps adopted to meet this contingency. I shall spare no exertions to apprehend and punish deserters; but I believe no time in the history of our country has presented such temptations to desert as now exist in California. The danger of apprehension is small, and the prospect of higher wages certain; pay and bounties are trifles, as laboring men at the mines can now earn in *one day* more than double a soldier's pay and allowances for a month, and even the pay of a lieutenant or captain cannot hire a servant. A carpenter or mechanic would not listen to an offer of less than fifteen or twenty dollars a day. Could any combination of affairs try a man's fidelity more than this? And I really think some extraordinary mark of favor should be given to those soldiers who remain faithful to their flag throughout this tempting crisis. No officer can now live in California on his pay. Money has so little value, the prices of necessary articles of clothing and subsistence are so exorbitant, and labor so high, that to hire a cook or servant has become an impossibility, save to those who are earning from thirty to fifty dollars a day. This state of things cannot last forever; yet from the geographical position of California, and the new character it has assumed as a mining country, prices of labor will always be high, and will hold out temptations to desert. I therefore have to report, if the government wish to prevent desertions here on the part of men, and to secure zeal on the part of officers, their pay must be increased very materially. Soldiers both of the volunteer and regular service discharged in this country should be permitted at once to locate their land warrants in the gold district. Many private letters have gone to the United States giving accounts of the vast quantity of gold recently discovered, and it may be a matter of surprise why I have made no report on this subject at an earlier date. The reason is, that I could not bring myself to believe the reports that I heard of the wealth of the gold district until I visited it myself. I have no hesitation now in saying that there is more gold in the country drained by the Sacramento and San Joaquin rivers than will pay the cost of the present war with Mexico a hundred times over. No capital is required to obtain this gold, as the laboring man wants nothing but his pick, shovel, and tin pan, with which to dig and wash the gravel; and many frequently pick gold out of the crevices of rock with their butcher knives in pieces from one to six ounces.

Mr. Dye, a gentleman residing in Monterey, and worthy of every credit, has just returned from Feather river. He tells me that the company to which he belonged worked seven weeks and two days, with an average of fifty Indians (washers), and that their gross product was 273 pounds of gold. His share, one-seventh, after paying all expenses, is about 37 pounds, which he brought with him and exhibits in Monterey. I see no laboring man from the mines who does not show his two, three, or four pounds of gold. A soldier of the artillery company returned here a few days ago from the mines, having been absent on furlough twenty days; he made by trading and working during that time $1,500. During these twenty days he was travelling ten or eleven days, leaving but a week, in which he made a sum of money greater than he receives in pay, clothes, and rations during a whole enlistment of five years. These statements appear incredible, but they are true.

Gold is believed also to exist on the eastern slopes of the Sierra Nevada; and when at the mines, I was informed by an intelligent Mormon that it had been found near the Great Salt Lake by some of his fraternity. Nearly all the Mormons are leaving California to go to the Salt Lake, and this they surely would not do unless they were sure of finding gold there in the same abundance as they now do on the Sacramento.

The gold "placer" near the mission of San Fernando has long been known, but has been but little wrought for want of water. This is a spur that puts off from the Sierra Nevada (see Fremont's map), the same in which the present mines occur. There is, therefore, every reason to believe that in the intervening space of five hundred miles (entirely unexplored) there must be many hidden and rich deposits.

The placer gold is now substituted as currency of this country; in trade it passes freely at $16 per ounce; as an article of commerce its value is not yet fixed. The only purchase I made was of the specimen No. 7, which I got of Mr. Neligh at $12 the ounce. That is about the present cash value in the country, although it has been sold for less. The great demand for goods and provisions made by this sudden development of wealth has increased the amount of commerce at San Francisco very much, and it will continue to increase.

I would recommend that a mint be established at some eligible point on the bay of San Francisco, and that machinery, and all the apparatus and workmen, be sent by sea. These workmen must be bound by high wages, and even bonds, to secure their faithful services; else the whole plan may be frustrated by their going to the mines as soon as they arrive in California. If this course be not adopted, gold to the amount of many millions of dollars will pass yearly to other countries, to enrich their merchants and capitalists. Before leaving the subject of mines, I will mention that on my return from the Sacramento I touched at New Almoden, the quicksilver mine of Mr. Alexander Forbes, consul of her Britannic Majesty at Tepic. This mine is in a spur of mountains 1,000 feet above the level of the bay of San Francisco, and is distant in a southern direction from the Pueblo San José about twelve miles. The ore (cinnabar) occurs in a large vein dipping at a strong angle to the horizon. Mexican miners are employed in working it, by driving shafts and galleries about six feet by seven, following the vein.

The fragments of rock and ore are removed on the backs of Indians in raw-hide sacks. The ore is then hauled in an ox wagon from the mouth of the mine down to a valley well supplied with wood and water, in which the furnaces are situated. These furnaces are of the simplest construction, exactly like a common bake-oven, in the crown of which is inserted a whaler's trying kettle; another inverted kettle forms the lid. From a hole in the lid a small brick channel leads to an apartment or chamber, in the bottom of which is inserted a small iron kettle. This chamber has a chimney.

In the morning of each day the kettles are filled with mineral (broken in small pieces), mixed with lime; fire is then applied, and kept up all day. The mercury, volatilized, passes into the chamber, is condensed on the sides and bottom of the chamber, and flows into the pot prepared for it. No water is used to condense the mercury.

During a visit I made last spring, four such ovens were in operation and yielded in the two days I was there 656 pounds of quicksilver, worth at Mazatlan $1.80 per lb. Mr. Walkinshaw, the gentleman now in charge of this mine, tells me that the vein is improving, and that he can afford to keep his people employed even in these extraordinary times. This mine is very valuable of itself, and becomes the more so, as mercury is extensively used in obtaining gold. It is not at present used in California for that purpose, but will be at some future time. When I was at this mine last spring, other parties were engaged in searching for veins but none have been discovered that are worth following up, although the earth in that whole range of hills is highly discolored, indicating the presence of this ore. I send several beautiful specimens, properly labelled. The amount of quicksilver in Mr. Forbes' vats on the 15th of July was about 25,000 pounds.

I enclose you herewith sketches of the country through which I passed, indicating the position of the mines, and the topography of the country in the vicinity of those I visited.

Some of the specimens of gold accompanying this were presented for transmission to the department by the gentlemen named below; the numbers on the topographical sketch, corresponding to the numbers on the labels of the respective specimens, show from what part of the gold region they were obtained:

1. Captain J. A. Sutter.
2. John Sinclair.
3. William Glover, R. C. Kirby, Ira Blanchard, Levi Fairfield, Franklin H. Ayer; Mormon diggings.
4. Chas. Weber.
5. Robert Spence.
6. Sunal & Co.
7. Robert D. Neligh.
8. C. E. Picket; American Fork, Columa.
9. E. C. Kemble.

10. T. H. Green, from San Fernando, near Los Angeles.

    A. Two ounces purchased from Mr. Neligh.

    B. Sand found in washing gold, which contains small particles.

11. Captain Frisbie; Dry diggings, Weber's creek.

12. Cosumnes.

13. Cosumnes; Hartnell's ranch.

14. A small specimen, supposed to be platina, found mixed with the finer particles of the gold.

I have the honor to be your obedient servant,

R. B. Mason,
Colonel 1st Dragoons, commanding.

General R. Jones,
Adjutant General U. S. A., Washington, D. C.

STATEMENTS OF JOHN A. SUTTER AND JAMES W. MARSHALL NOVEMBER, 1857

One of the first attempts to get from Sutter and Marshall their own accounts of the gold discovery was made by Mr. M. Hutchings, editor of *Hutchings' Illustrated California Magazine.* During the year 1857 he visited both of these men and obtained their own narratives which were printed in his magazine for November, 1857. These accounts have been referred to so frequently that they are here quoted in full in order that the reader may be able to have them before him in their original form. It should be noted that, during the nine years since the discovery, both of the writers had become indefinite and confused regarding some of the detailed facts.

STATEMENT OF JOHN A. SUTTER, NOVEMBER, 1857

It was in the first part of January, 1848, when the gold was discovered at Coloma, where I was then building a saw-mill. The contractor and builder of this mill was James W. Marshall, from New Jersey. In the fall of 1847, after the mill seat had been located, I sent up to this place Mr. P. L. Wimmer with his family, and a number of laborers, from the disbanded Mormon Battalion; and a little later I engaged Mr. Bennet from Oregon to assist Mr. Marshall in the mechanical labors of the mill. Mr. Wimmer had the team in charge, assisted by his young sons, to do the necessary teaming, and Mrs. Wimmer did the cooking for all hands.

I was very much in need of a saw-mill, to get lumber to finish my large flouring mill, of four run of stones, at Brighton, which was commenced at the same time, and was rapidly progressing; likewise for other buildings, fences, etc., for the small village of Yerba Buena, (now San Francisco). In the City Hotel, (the only one), at the dinner table this enterprise was unkindly called "another folly of Sutter's," as my first settlement at the old fort near Sacramento City was called by a good many, "a folly of his," and they were about right in that, because I had the best chances to get some of the finest locations, near the settlements; and even well-stocked rancho's had been offered to me on the most reasonable conditions; but I refused all these good offers, and preferred to explore the wilderness, and select a territory on the banks of the Sacramento. It was a rainy afternoon when Mr. Marshall arrived at my office in the Fort, very wet. I was somewhat surprised to see him, as he was down a few days previous; and when, I sent up to Coloma a number of teams with provisions, mill irons, etc., etc. He told me then that he had some important and interesting news which he wished to communicate secretly to me, and wished me to go with him to a place where we should not be disturbed, and where no listeners could come and hear what we had to say. I went with him to my private rooms; he requested me to lock the door; I complied, but I told him at the same time that nobody was in the house except the clerk, who was in his office in a different part of the house; after requesting of me something which he wanted, which my servants brought and then left the room, I forgot to lock the doors, and it happened that the door was opened by the clerk just at the moment when Marshall took a rag from his pocket, showing me the yellow metal: he had about two ounces of it; but how quick Mr. M. put the yellow metal in his pocket again can hardly be described. The clerk came to see me on business, and excused himself for inter-rupting me, and as soon as he had left I was told, "Now lock the doors; didn't I tell you that we might have listeners?" I told him that he need fear nothing about that, as it was not the habit of this gentle-man; but I could hardly convince him that he need not to be suspicious. Then Mr. M. began to show me this metal, which consisted of small

[336]

pieces and specimens, some of them worth a few dollars; he told me that he had expressed his opinion to the laborers at the mill, that this might be gold; but some of them were laughing at him and called him a crazy man, and could not believe such a thing. After having proved the metal with aqua fortis, which I found in my apothecary shop, likewise with other experiments, and read the long article "gold" in the Encyclopedia Americana, I declared this to be gold of the finest quality, of at least 23 carats. After this Mr. M. had no more rest nor patience, and wanted me to start with him immediately for Coloma; but I told him I could not leave, as it was late in the evening and nearly supper time, and that it would be better for him to remain with me till the next morning, and I would travel with him, but this would not do: he asked me only, "Will you come to-morrow morning?" I told him yes, and off he started for Coloma in the heaviest rain, although already very wet, taking nothing to eat. I took this news very easy, like all other occurrences good or bad, but thought a great deal during the night about the consequences which might follow such a discovery. I gave all my necessary orders to my numerous laborers, and left the next morning at 7 o'clock, accompanied by an Indian soldier, and vaquero, in a heavy rain, for Coloma. About half way on the road I saw at a distance a human being crawling out from the brushwood. I asked the Indian who it was; he told me, "The same man who was with you last evening." When I came nearer I found it was Marshall, very wet; I told him that he would have done better to remain with me at the fort than to pass such an ugly night here; but he told me that he went up to Coloma (54 miles), took his other horse and came half way to meet me; then we rode up to the new Eldorado. In the afternoon the weather was clearing up, and we made a prospecting promenade. The next morning we went to the tail-race of the mill, through which the water was running during the night, to clean out the gravel which had been made loose, for the purpose of widening the race; and after the water was out of the race we went in to search for gold. This was done every morning: small pieces of gold could be seen remaining on the bottom of the clean washed bed rock. I went in the race and picked up several pieces of this gold, several of the laborers gave me some which they had picked up, and from Marshall I received a part. I told them that I would get a ring made of this gold as soon as it could be done in California;

and I have had a heavy ring made, with my family's coat of arms engraved on the outside, and on the inside of the ring is engraved, "The first gold, discovered in January, 1848." Now if Mrs. Wimmer possesses a piece which has been found earlier than mine Mr. Marshall can tell, as it was probably received from him. I think Mr. Marshall could have hardly known himself which was exactly the first little piece, among the whole.

The next day I went with Mr. M. on a prospecting tour in the vicinity of Coloma, and the following morning I left for Sacramento. Before my departure I had a conversation with all hands: I told them that I would consider it as a great favor if they would keep this discovery secret only for six weeks, so that I could finish my large flour mill at Brighton, (with four run of stones,) which had cost me already about from 24 to 25,000 dollars—the people up there promised to keep it secret so long. On my way home, instead of feeling happy and contented, I was very unhappy, and could not see that it would benefit me much, and I was perfectly right in thinking so; as it came just precisely as I expected. I thought at the same time that it could hardly be kept secret for six weeks; and in this I was not mistaken, for about two weeks later, after my return, I sent up several teams in charge of a white man, as the teamsters were Indian boys. This man was acquainted with all hands up there, and Mrs. Wimmer told him the whole secret; likewise the young sons of Mr. Wimmer told him that they had gold, and that they would let him have some too; and so he obtained a few dollars' worth of it as a present. As soon as this man arrived at the fort he went to a small store in one of my outside buildings, kept by Mr. Smith, a partner of Samuel Brannan, and asked for a bottle of brandy, for which he would pay the cash; after having the bottle he paid with these small pieces of gold. Smith was astonished and asked him if he intended to insult him; the teamster told him to go and ask me about it; Smith came in, in great haste, to see me, and I told him at once the truth— what could I do? I had to tell him all about it. He reported it to Mr. S. Brannan, who came up immediately to get all possible information, when he returned and sent up large supplies of goods, leased a larger house from me, and commenced a very large and profitable business; soon he opened a branch house of business at Mormon Island.

Mr. Brannan made a kind of claim on Mormon Island, and put a tolerably heavy tax on "The Latter Day Saints." I believe it was thirty per cent, which they paid for some time, until they got tired of it, (some of them told me that it was for the purpose of building a temple for the honor and glory of the Lord.)

So soon as the secret was out my laborers began to leave me, in small parties first, but then all left, from the clerk to the cook, and I was in great distress; only a few mechanics remained to finish some very necessary work which they had commenced, and about eight invalids, who continued slowly to work a few teams, to scrape out the mill race at Brighton. The Mormons did not like to leave my mill unfinished, but they got the gold fever like everybody else. After they had made their piles they left for the Great Salt Lake. So long as these people have been employed by me they have behaved very well, and were industrious and faithful laborers, and when settling their accounts there was not one of them who was not contented and satisfied.

Then the people commenced rushing up from San Francisco and other parts of California, in May, 1848: in the former village only five men were left to take care of the women and children. The single men locked their doors and left for "Sutter's Fort," and from there to the Eldorado. For some time the people in Monterey and farther south would not believe the news of the gold discovery, and said that it was only a '*Ruse de Guerre*' of Sutter's, because he wanted to have neighbors in his wilderness. From this time on I got only too many neighbors, and some very bad ones among them.

What a great misfortune was this sudden gold discovery for me! It has just broken up and ruined my hard, restless, and industrious labors, connected with many dangers of life, as I had many narrow escapes before I became properly established. From my mill buildings I reaped no benefit whatever, the mill stones even have been stolen and sold.

My tannery, which was then in a flourishing condition, and was carried on very profitably, was deserted, a large quantity of leather was left unfinished in the vats; and a great quantity of raw hides became valueless as they could not be sold; nobody wanted to be bothered with such trash, as it was called. So it was in all the other mechanical trades which I had carried on; all was abandoned, and work commenced or nearly finished was all left, to an immense loss for me. Even the Indians had no more patience to work alone, in harvesting and threshing my large wheat crop out; as the whites had all left, and other Indians had been engaged by some white men to work for them, and they commenced to have some gold for which they were buying all kinds of articles at enormous prices in the stores; which, when my Indians saw this, they wished very much to go to the mountains and dig gold. At last I consented, got a number of wagons ready, loaded them with provisions and goods of all kinds, employed a clerk, and left with about one hundred Indians, and about fifty Sandwich Islanders (Kanakas) which had joined those which I brought with me from the Islands. The first camp was about ten miles above Mormon Island, on the south fork of the American river. In a few weeks we became crowded, and it would no more pay, as my people made too many acquaintances. I broke up the camp and started on the march further south, and located my next camp on Sutter creek (now in Amador county), and thought that I should there be alone. The work was going on well for a while, until three or four traveling grog-shops surrounded me, at from one and a half to two miles distance from the camp; then, of course, the gold was taken to these places, for drinking, gambling, etc., and then the following day they were sick and unable to work, and became deeper and more indebted to me, and particularly the Kanakas. I found that it was high time to quit this kind of business, and lose no more time and money. I therefore broke up the camp and returned to the Fort, where I disbanded nearly all the people who had worked for me in the mountains digging gold. This whole expedition proved to be a heavy loss to me.

At the same time I was engaged in a mercantile firm in Coloma, which I left in January, 1849—likewise with many sacrifices. After this I would have nothing more to do with the gold affairs. At this time, the Fort was the great trading place where nearly all the business was transacted. I had no pleasure to remain there, and moved up to Hock Farm, with all my Indians, and who had been with me from the time they were children. The place was then in charge of a Major Domo.

It is very singular that the Indians never found a piece of gold and brought it to me, as they very often did other specimens found in the ravines. I requested them continually to bring me some curiosities from the mountains, for which I always recompensed them. I have received animals, birds, plants, young trees, wild fruits, pipe clay, stones, red ochre, etc., etc., but never a piece of gold. Mr. Dana, of the scientific corps of the expedition under Commodore Wilkes' Exploring Squadron, told me that he had the strongest proof and signs of gold in the vicinity of Shasta Mountain and further south. A short time afterwards, Doctor Sandels, a very scientific traveler, visited me, and explored a part of the country in a great hurry, as time would not permit him to make a longer stay. He told me likewise that he found sure signs of gold, and was very sorry that he could not explore the Sierra Nevada. He did not encourage me to attempt to work and open mines, as it was uncertain how it would pay, and would probably be only profitable for a government. So I thought it more prudent to stick to the plow, notwithstanding I did know that the country was rich in gold, and other minerals. An old attached Mexican servant who followed me here from the United States, as soon as he knew that I was here, and who understood a great deal about working in placers, told me he found sure signs of gold in the mountains on Bear Creek, and that we would go right to work after returning from our campaign in 1845, but he became a victim to his patriotism and fell into the hands of the enemy near my encampment, with dispatches for me from General Micheltorena, and he was hung as a spy, for which I was very sorry.

By this sudden discovery of the gold, all my great plans were destroyed. Had I succeeded with my mills and manufactories for a few years before the gold was discovered, I should have been the richest citizen on the Pacific shore; but it had to be different. Instead of being rich, I am ruined, and the cause of it is the long delay of the United States Land Commission, of the United States Courts, through the great influence of the squatter lawyers. Before my case will be decided in Washington, another year may elapse, but I hope that justice will be done me by the last tribunal—the Supreme Court of the United States. By the Land Commission and the District Court it has been decided in my favor. The Common Council of the city of Sacramento, composed partly of squatters, paid Alpheus Felch (one of the late Land Commissioners, who was engaged by the squatters during his office), $5,000, from the fund of the city, against the will of the tax-payers, for which amount he has to try to defeat my just and old claim from the Mexican Government, before the Supreme Court of the United States in Washington.

J. A. SUTTER.

STATEMENT OF JAMES W. MARSHALL, NOVEMBER, 1857

Being a millwright by trade, as there was a ready cash sale for lumber, I concluded to seek a location in the mountains and erect a mill, to supply the valley with lumber. Some time in April, 1847, I visited New Helvetia, commonly known as the "Fort," where I made my resolution known to John A. Sutter, sen., and requested of him an Indian boy, to act as an interpreter to the mountain Indians in the vicinity of the American river—or Rio del los Americanos, as it was then called. At first he refused, because, he said that he had previously sent several companies, at various times, and by different routes, for that purpose, all of whom reported that it was impossible to find a route for a wagon road to any locality where pine timber could be procured, and that it was the height of folly to attempt any such thing.

Capt. Sutter at length, however, promised me the desired interpreter, provided I would stock some six or eight plows for him first, of which he was in immediate want, which I readily agreed to do. While I was employed upon this job there was much talk at the Fort concerning my contemplated trip to the mountains; and Messrs. Gingery, P. L. Wimmer and McLellan having resolved also to take a trip, with the same object in view, came where I was working, and asked me where I expected to find a road and timber, and I promptly gave them my views and directions.

They departed, I believe in company, but finally separated, and P. L. Wimmer found pine timber and a road, on what is now known as the Sacramento and Diamond Springs road, and about the 12th of May, Gingery and Wimmer commenced work, about thirteen miles west of the (now called) Shingle Spring House.

On the 16th of May, having completed my work for Capt. Sutter, I started, with an Indian boy—Treador, and W. A. Graves (who is now residing in Butte County, and who had assisted me in my work, and heard the conversation between myself, Gingery, Wimmer and McLellan,) accompanied me for the purpose of seeing the mountains. On the 18th of May we entered the valley of Culluma [Coloma]; and on the 20th Gingery joined our company. We then traveled up the stream now called Weber Creek—the Indian name which is Pul-Pul-Mull—to the head of the creek; thence higher in the mountains until we arrived at the South Fork of the American river, where it divides into two branches of about equal size; from whence we returned by Sly Park and Pleasant Valley to the Fort.

On my arrival I gave Capt. Sutter an account of my trip, and what I had discovered. He thereupon proposed to me a partnership; but before we were ready to commence operations, some persons who had tried, in vain, to find Culluma, reported to Sutter that I "had made a false representation, for they could find no such place." To settle matters, Capt. Sutter furnished me with a Mission Indian, who was Alcalde of the Cosumnes tribe, as an interpreter and guide —trusting partly to the Indian's report, as to the propriety of the proposed co-partnership.

The report which I had made on my first trip having been fully confirmed by observations on the second, the co-partnership was completed, and about the 27th of August we signed the agreement to build and run a saw-mill at Culluma. On the third day (I think) afterwards, I set out, with two wagons, and was accompanied by the following persons, employed by the firm of Sutter & Marshall, viz,: P. L. Wimmer and family, James Barger, Ira Willis, Sidney Willis, Alexander Stephens, Wm. Cunce, James Brown, and Ezekiah Persons.

On our arrival in the Valley we first built the double log cabin, afterwards known as Hastings & Co.'s store. About the last of September, as Capt. Sutter wanted a couple of capable men to construct a dam across the American river at the grist-mill—near where the Pavilion now stands—I sent the two Willis', as the most capable; (Wm. Cunce being in feeble health, left about the same time;) and I received Henry Bigler, Israel Smith, Wm. Johnston and —— Evans in return; and shortly afterwards I employed Charles Bennet and Wm. Scott, both carpenters. The above named individuals, with some ten Indians, constituted my whole force.

While we were in the habit at night of turning the water through the tail race we had dug for the purpose of widening and deepening the race, I used to go down in the morning to see what had been done by the water through the night; and about half past seven o'clock on or about the 19th of January—I am not quite certain to a day, but it was between the 18th and 20th of that month—1848, I went down as usual, and after shutting off the water from the race I stepped into it, near the lower end, and there, upon the rock, about six inches beneath the surface of the water, I DISCOVERED THE GOLD. I was entirely alone at the time. I picked up one or two pieces and examined them attentively; and having some general knowledge of minerals, I could not call to mind more than two which in any way resembled this—*sulphuret of iron*, very bright and brittle; and *gold*, bright, yet malleable; I then tried it between two rocks, and found that it could be beaten into a different shape, but not broken. I then collected four or five pieces and went up to Mr. Scott (who was working at the carpenter's bench making the mill wheel) with the pieces in my hand, and said, "I have found it."

"What is it?" inquired Scott.

"Gold," I answered.

"Oh! no," returned Scott, "that can't be."

I replied positively—"I know it to be nothing else."

Mr. Scott was the second person who saw the gold. W. J. Johnston, A. Stephens, H. Bigler, and J. Brown, who were also working in the mill yard, were then called up to see it. Peter L. Wimmer, Mrs. Jane Wimmer, C. Bennet, and J. Smith, were at the house; the latter two of whom were sick; E. Persons and John Wimmer, (a son of P. L. Wimmer), were out hunting oxen at the same time. About 10 o'clock the same morning, P. L. Wimmer came down from the house, and was very much surprised at the discovery, when the metal was shown him; and which he took home to show his wife, who, the next day, made some experiments upon it by boiling it in strong lye, and saleratus; and Mr. Bennet by my dirertions beat it very thin.

Four days afterwards I went to the Fort for provisons, and carried with me about three ounces of the gold, which Capt. Sutter and I tested with *nitric acid*. I then tried it in Sutter's presence by taking three silver dollars and balancing them by the dust in the air, then immersed both in water, and the superior weight of the gold satisfied us both of its nature and value.

About the 20th of February, 1848, Capt. Sutter came to Coloma, for the first time, to consummate an agreement we had made with

this tribe of Indians in the month of September previous, to wit :—
that we live with them in peace, on the same land.

About the middle of April the mill commenced operation, and,
after cutting a few thousand feet of lumber was abandoned; as all
hands were intent upon gold digging. In December, '48, Capt.
Sutter came again to Coloma, and some time in that month sold his
interest in the mill to Messrs. Ragley & Winters, of which new firm
I became a member. The mill was soon again in operation, and cut
most of the lumber of which the town Coloma was built.

The *first piece of gold*, which I found, *weighed about fifty cents*. Mr.
Wimmer, having bought a stock of merchandise some time about
May or June, 1848; and Mrs. Wimmer being my treasurer, used four
hundred and forty dollars of my money to complete the purchase; and
among which was the first piece of gold which I had found. Where
that went, or where it is now, I believe that nobody knows.

J. W. MARSHALL.

Bibliography

BIBLIOGRAPHY

Abbott, C. S., *Recollections of a California pioneer*. New York: Neale Publishing Company. 1918.

Allen, W. W., and Avery, R. B., *California gold book*. San Francisco: Donohue & Henneberry. 1893.

Atherton, Gertrude, *California, an intimate history*. New York: Boni & Liveright. 1927.

Avery, B. P., "The Trinity diamond," *Overland*, vol. VI.

Ayers, J. J., *Gold and sunshine*. Boston: R. G. Badger. 1922.

Babek, "The first gold in Merced," *Golden Era*, vol. XXXIV (October, 1885).

Bancroft, Hubert Howe, *California inter pocula*. San Francisco: The History Company. 1888.

Bancroft, Hubert Howe, *History of California*, vol. VI. San Francisco: The History Company. 1888.

Bancroft, Hubert Howe, *Popular tribunals*. San Francisco: The History Company. 1887.

Bandini, Helen Elliott, *History of California*. New York: American Book Company. 1908.

Bates, Mrs. D. B., *Incidents on land and water: or four years on the Pacific coast*. Boston: James French & Company. 1857.

Bekeart, Philip Baldwin, "James W. Marshall, discoverer of gold," *Society of California Pioneers Quarterly*, vol. I, no. 3 (September, 1924).

Bell, Major Horace, *Reminiscences of a ranger: or early times in southern California*. Santa Barbara: W. Hebberd. 1927.

Berry, Mrs. J. Van Antwerp, "A letter from the mines," *Annual Publications Historical Society of Southern California*, vol. V, no. 3 (September, 1926).

Borthwick, J. D., *Three Years in California*. Edinburgh: William Blackwood & Sons. 1857.

Borthwick, J. D., *The gold hunters: a first-hand picture of life in California mining camps in the early fifties*. New York: The Macmillan Company. 1922.

Bowman, Mary M., "California's first American school and its Teacher," *Annual Publications Historical Society of Southern California*, vol. X, Part II (1916).

Brooks, Elisha, *A Pioneer Mother of California*. San Francisco: Harr Wagner Publishing Company. 1922.

Brooks, J. T., *Four months among the gold-finders in Alta California*. New York: D. Appleton & Company. 1849.

Browne, J. Ross, *Report of the debates in the convention of California, on the formation of the state constitution, in September and October, 1849*. Washington. 1850.

Bryant, Edwin, *What I saw in California*. New York: D. Appleton & Co. 1848.

Buffum, E. Gould, *Six months in the gold mines*. Philadelphia. 1850.

Burnett, Peter H., *Recollections and opinions of an old pioneer*. New York: D. Appleton & Company. 1880.

"California gold," *Hutching's California Magazine*, vol. IV (1859).

Capron, E. S., *History of California*. Boston: John P. Jewett & Company. 1854.

Chamberlain, J. F., "Lure of gold; story of the gold rush of 1849," *Overland*, vol. LXXXI (October, 1923). *Ibid.*, vol. LXXXVI (July, 1928).

Church, A. S., "Memoirs," *Society of California Pioneers Quarterly*, vol. III (1925).

Clappe, Mrs. Louise A. K. (Smith), *Shirley letters from California mines in 1851-52.* San Francisco: T. C. Russell. 1922.

Cleland, Robert Glass, *A history of California: The American period.* New York: The Macmillan Company. 1922.

Cole, Cornelius, *Memoirs.* New York: McLoughlin Brothers. 1908.

Colton, Walter, *Three Years in California.* New York and Cincinnati: Cleaves, McDonald & Co. 1850.

Connelly, T. A., "San Francisco in '49," *Monitor*, vol. LIX, no. 4 (November 12, 1904).

Coy, Owen C., *California county boundaries.* Berkeley: California Historical Survey Commission. 1923.

Coy, Owen C., *The Humboldt Bay region, 1850-1875: a study in the American colonization of California.* Los Angeles: California State Historical Association. 1929.

Coy, Owen C., *Pictorial history of California.* Berkeley: University of California Extension Division. 1925.

Cronise, Titus Fey, *The natural wealth of California.* San Francisco: H. H. Bancroft & Company. 1868.

Davidson, W. A., "Letters from Sear's diggings," *Pacific*, vol. II: 282 (January 28, 1853).

Davis, John F., *Historical sketch of mining laws.* Los Angeles. 1902.

Davis, William Heath, *Seventy-five years in California.* San Francisco: John Howell. 1929.

Davis, William Heath, *Sixty years in California.* San Francisco: A. J. Leary. 1889.

"Days of Gold," *Land of Sunshine*, vol. XIII (July, 1900).

Degelman, C. F., "Leaves from a '49 ledger," *Argonaut*, vol. XVIII, no 4 (January 9, 1886.)

Delano, Alonzo, *Life on the plains and at the diggings: being scenes and adventures of an overland journey to California*. Auburn and Buffalo: Miller, Orton & Mulligan. 1854.

Downie, Major William, *Hunting for gold*. San Francisco. 1893.

Dunbar, Edward E., *The romance of the age*. New York. 1867.

"Early mining laws," *Grizzly Bear*, vol. I (October, 1907).

Eldredge, Zoeth Skinner, *The beginnings of San Francisco*. San Francisco: Z. S. Eldredge. 1912.

Eldredge, Zoeth Skinner, *History of California*, vol. IV. New York: The Century History Company. (n. d.)

Ellison, Joseph, *California and the nation 1850-1869*. Berkeley: University of California Press. 1927.

Evans, A. S., "A waif of the Pogony," *Overland*, vol. VI.

Evans, Taliesin, "Shakes," *Overland*, vol. VII.

Fairchild, Frances, "As told by a forty-niner," *Grizzly Bear*, vol. IX, no. 1 (May, 1911).

Fairchild, Frances, "Historical sketch of pioneer who founded Stockton," *Grizzly Bear*, vol. XII, no. 1 (September, 1912).

Farley, A. J., "Rose's bar," *Overland*, vol. VII.

Farnham, Mrs. Eliza W., *California in-doors and out*. New York. 1856.

Foster, M. M., "An account of the '49 movement," *Grizzly Bear*, vol. XXI (September, 1917).

Foster, M. M., "From a '49 ledger," *Overland*, vol. LXXXIV (February, 1926).

Frost, John, *History of the state of California*. New York: Hurst & Company. (n. d.)

Goodwin, Cardinal, *The establishment of state government in California*. New York: The Macmillan Company. 1914.

Guinn, James Miller, "The gold hunters," *Argonaut*, vol. XLI, no. 5 (August 2, 1897).

Guinn, James Miller, "Gold placers of Los Angeles," *Annual Publications Historical Society of Southern California*, vol. VIII, part III.

Guinn, James Miller, "In the days of '49," *Grizzly Bear*, vol. I, 17 (July, 1907).

Guinn, James Miller, "In the days of '49," *Annual Publications Historical Society of Southern California*, vol. VI, p. 71. 1903.

Guinn, James Miller, "The myth of Gold Lake," *Annual Publications Historical Society of Southern California*, vol. VI, p. 82. 1903.

Guinn, James Miller, "The poetry of the Argonauts," *Annual Publications Historical Society of Southern California*, vol. V, 1902.

Guinn, James Miller, "San Francisco in 1849," *Grizzly Bear*, vol. I (September, 1907).

Hall, S. M., "In the land of the forty-niners," *Out West*, vol. XXX (January, 1909).

Haskins, C. W., *The Argonauts of California*. New York: Howard & Hurlbert. 1890.

Hastings, L. W., *Emigrant's guide to Oregon and California*. Cincinnati. 1849.

Heaven, L. P., *History of California*. San Francisco: A. Roman. 1883.

Helper, Hinton Rowan, *Land of gold: reality vs. fiction*. Baltimore. 1855.

Hines, Rev. J. W., *Pioneer life on the Pacific coast*. San José. 1911.

Hittell, John S., *Marshall's gold discovery, a lecture delivered before the Society of California Pioneers . . . 1893.* San Francisco, 1893.

Hittell, John S., "The mining excitements of California," *Overland*, vol. II.

Hittell, John S., *The Resources of California* . . . San Francisco. 1863.

Hittell, Theodore H., *History of California*, vol. III, book VIII. San Francisco: N. J. Stone & Company, 1897.

Hittell, Theodore H., "Oration delivered on the 9th of September, 1869 . . ." *Society of California Pioneers Quarterly*, vol. II (1925).

Howe, Octavius Thorndike, *Argonauts of '49: history and adventures of the emigrant companies from Massachusetts, 1849-1850.* Cambridge: Harvard University Press. 1923.

Hunt, Rockwell D., *California, the golden.* New York: Silver, Burdett & Company. 1911.

Hunt, Rockwell D., *California, an American commonwealth.* (California and the Californians, vol. II). Chicago: The Lewis Publishing Company. 1926.

James, Alfred, "Early days in Washoe," *Annual Publications Historical Society of Southern California*, vol. V.

Jarvis, Clarence, "Alpine state highway preserves historic trail," *Grizzly Bear*, vol. XII (March, 1913).

Jenkins, W. W., "History of the development of placer mining in California," *Annual Publications Historical Society of Southern California*, vol. VII (1906).

Johnson, Solomon, "Gold coast of California and Oregon," *Overland*, vol. II.

Kelly, William, *An excursion to California . . . with a stroll through the diggings and ranches of that country.* 2 vols. London. 1851.

Kelly, William, *A stroll through the diggings of California*. London. 1852.

Kerr, Thomas, "Journal," *California Historical Society Quarterly*, vols. VII and VIII (1928-1929).

Larkin, Thomas O., "Letter to James Buchanan, secretary of state," in *House Executive Documents*, 30 congress, 2 session, no. 1. Washington. 1848-49.

Letts, J. M., *California illustrated*. New York: Young. 1852.

Lyman, G. D., "The scalpel under three flags in California: the American period," *California Historical Society Quarterly*, vol. IV, no. 2 (June, 1925).

McGroarty, John S., *California, its history and romance*. Los Angeles: Grafton Publishing Company. 1911.

McIlhany, E. W., *Recollections of a '49er*. Kansas City, Missouri: Hailman Printing Company. 1908.

McLean, Louise, "Discovery of Humboldt Bay," *Overland*, vol. LXX (August, 1917).

Madison, James, "Some shadows of the San Francisco stage," *California Historical Society Quarterly*, vol. IV, no. 1 (March, 1925).

Manly, William Lewis, *Death Valley in '49*. San José: Pacific Tree and Vine Company. 1894.

Markham, Edwin, *California, the wonderful*. New York: Edwin Markham Press. 1923.

Marryat, Frank, *Mountains and molehills*. New York: Harper Brothers. 1855.

Marshall, James W., "The discovery of gold in California," *Hutchings' California Magazine*, vol. II, no. 5 (November, 1857).

Marye, G. T., Jr., *From '49 to '83 in California and Nevada*. San Francisco: Robertson. 1923.

Mason, Richard B., "Report of the gold fields of California," in *House Executive Documents*, 31 congress, 1 session, no. 17. Washington. 1849-50.

Massey, Ernest de, "Journal translated by M. E. Wilbur," *California Historical Society Quarterly*, vol. V (1926). *Ibid.*, vol. VI (1927).

"Memories of '49," *California World*, II: 742 (October 14, 1910).

Miller, Joaquin, "The story and glory of Shasta," *Sunset Magazine*, vol. XI (October, 1903).

"Mining for gold in California," *Hutchings' California Magazine*, vol. II.

"Mining scenes and sketches," *Hayes Collection*, Bancroft Library.

Morrow, William W., *Historical Introduction to California Jurisprudence*. San Francisco: Bancroft-Whitney Company. 1921.

Morse, Edwin Franklin, "Reminiscences," *California Historical Society Quarterly*, vol. VI (1927).

Mulford, Prentice, "The bed of the river," *Overland*, vol. VI.

Mulford, Prentice, "California culinary experiences," *Overland*, vol. II.

Mulford, Prentice, "Early schools in mining camps," *Overland*, vol. VII.

Muzzy, F. E. D., "Log of a forty-niner," *Harper's Magazine*, November, 1906.

Neal, Mrs. James, "Spilled milk," *Overland*, vol. V.

Norton, Henry K., *The story of California*. Chicago: A. C. McClurg & Company. 1925.

Nye, B. H., "Extracts from the letters of a Nantucket forty-niner," *History Teachers' Magazine*, vol. VI (September, 1915).

"An old time California book," *Pacific*, LV: 3 (1905).

Oldtimer, E. Z., "Placer mines of early days," *Grizzly Bear*, vol. XII (April, 1913).

O'Meara, James, "Reminiscences of the gold period," *Californian*, vol. VI (October, 1882).

Parsons, George F., *Life and adventures of James W. Marshall*. Sacramento. 1870.

Peabody, Alfred, "Early days and rapid growth of California," *Essex Institute Historical Collection*, vol. XII, no. 2. Massachusetts. 1874.

"Pioneer's first letter home, June 14, 1849," *Overland*, August, 1925.

Prouty, W. H., "Some pioneer reminiscences," *Grizzly Bear*, vol. X (February, 1912).

Purdy, H. T., *San Francisco*. San Francisco: Paul Elder & Company, 1912.

Revere, J. W., *A tour of duty in California*. New York. 1849.

Rickard, T. A., "The discovery of gold in California," *University of California Chronicle*, vol. XXX (1928). Berkeley.

"River mining," *Hutchings' California Magazine*, vol. III (1859).

Robinson, Fayette, *California and its gold region*. New York. 1849.

Robinson, Henry, "Pioneer days of California," *Overland*, vol. VIII.

Robinson, Henry, "The pioneers of '49," *Grizzly Bear*, vol. I (August, 1907).

Rochester, "Praying Abe Slocum: a mining sketch," *Argonaut*, vol. I (November 24, 1877).

Royce, Josiah, *California, from the conquest in 1846 to the second vigilance committee in San Francisco* . . . Boston. 1886. (American Commonwealths.)

Ryan, William Redmond, *Personal adventures in upper and lower California*. Vol. II. London. 1850.

"San Francisco, 1850," *Society of California Pioneers Quarterly*, vol. II (1925).

Scherer, James A. B., *The first forty-niner*. New York: Minton, Balch & Company. 1925.

Schoonover, T. J., *Life and times of General John A. Sutter*. Sacramento: Bullock-Carpenter Printing Company. 1907.

Shaw, Pringle, *Ramblings in California*. Toronto: James Bain. 1856.

Shaw, William, *Golden dreams and waking realities*. London. 1851.

Shinn, Charles Howard, *Mining camps: a study in American frontier government*. New York: Charles Scribner's Sons. 1885.

Shirley, *pseudonym*, see Clappe.

Smith, G. H., "Bodie, the last of the old-time mining camps," *California Historical Society Quarterly*, vol. IV, no. 1 (March, 1925).

Smith, G. W., "The light of other days: dueling in the southern mines twenty years ago," *Argonaut*, vol. I (November 24, 1877).

Smith, G. W., "Representative men: Major M. B. Duffield—a representative ruffian," *Argonaut*, vol. I (November 17, 1877).

Soulé, Frank, Gihon, J. H., and Nisbet, James, *Annals of San Francisco*. New York: D. Appleton & Company. 1855.

Stafford, Mallie, *March of empire*. San Francisco: Geo. Spaulding & Company. 1884.

Steele, James, *Old California days*. Chicago: Homewood Publishing Company. 1893.

Stillman, J. D. B., *Seeking the golden fleece*. San Francisco: A. Roman & Company. 1887.

Sutter, John Augustus, "The discovery of gold in California," *Hutchings' California Magazine*, vol. II, no. 5 (November, 1857).

Swett, John, "An evening in the California mines," *Pacific*, vol. IV (February 23, 1855).

Taylor, Bayard, *Eldorado, or adventures in the path of empire*. New York: G. P. Putnam's Sons. 1907.

Taylor, Father, "California in 1849," *Land of Sunshine*, vol. XIII (August, 1900).

Taylor, Father, "Some typical incidents and pictures," *Land of Sunshine*, vol. XIII (September-October, 1900).

Taylor, William, *California life illustrated*. New York: Carlton & Porter. 1848.

Taylor, William, *Seven years' street preaching in San Francisco*. New York. 1857.

Teggart, Frederick J. (editor), "Diary of Nelson Kingsley, a California Argonaut of 1849," *Publications Academy of Pacific Coast History*, vol. III, no. 3. Berkeley. 1914.

Teggart, Frederick J. (editor), "The gold rush, extracts from the diary of Chester Smith Lyman, 1848-49," *California Historical Society Quarterly*, vol. II, no. 3 (October, 1923).

Thomson, M., "The gravel ranges of the gold belt," *Overland*, vol. XI.

Tuthill, Franklin, *History of California*. San Francisco: H. H. Bancroft & Company. 1886.

Tyson, James L., *Diary of a physician in California . . . including notes of the journey by land and water.* New York. 1850.

Victor, Frances F., "What they told me at Wilson's Bar," *Overland*, vol. VIII.

Wheeler, O. C., *The story of early Baptist history in California.* California Baptist Historical Society, 1888.

White, Laura L., "Spades," *Overland*, vol. VIII.

White, Stewart Edward, *The forty-niners.* New Haven: Yale University Press. 1918.

Wicher, Edward Arthur. *The Presbyterian church in California, 1849-1927.* New York: The Grafton Press. 1927.

Wierzbicki, F. P., *California as it is, and as it may be, or, a guide to the gold region.* San Francisco. 1849.

Willey, Rev. S. H., *Thirty years in California . . . 1849 to 1879.* San Francisco: A. L. Bancroft. 1879.

Williams, Mary Floyd, *History of the San Francisco Committee of Vigilance of 1851.* Berkeley: University of California Press. 1921.

Woodhams, A. R., "A trip to California in the early days," *Grizzly Bear*, vol. XVIII (November 1915 to January 1916).

Woods, J. L., *California pioneer decade of 1849: the Presbyterian church.* San Francisco: Hansen Company. 1922.

Woolley, L. H., *California, 1849-1913.* Oakland: De Witt & Snelling. 1913.

Yount, G. C., "Chronicles," *California Historical Society Quarterly*, vol. II, no. 1 (April, 1923).

FICTION

Adventures of a gold finder, written by himself. 3 vols. 1850.

Aimard, Gustave, *The gold seekers, a tale of California.* 1888.

Barra, Ezekiel I., *A tale of two oceans; a new story by an old Californian.* 1893.

Brunner, Jane W., *Free prisoners.* Philadelphia: R. & H. Claxton. 1887.

Canfield, Chauncey L., *The city of six.* Chicago: A. C. McClurg & Co. 1910.

Canfield, Chauncey L., *The diary of a forty-niner.* Boston: Houghton, Mifflin Co., 1920.

Cendrars, Blaise, *Sutter's gold.* New York: Harper & Brothers. 1926.

Delano, Alonzo, *Old Block's sketch-book; or tales of California life.* Sacramento. 1856.

Dietrich, Dr., *The German emigrants; or Frederick Wohlgemuth's voyage to California.* Trans. by Leopold Wray. (n. d.)

Harte, Francis Bret, "The Illiad of Sandy Bar," *Overland*, vol. II.

Harte, Francis Bret, *The luck of Roaring Camp.*

Harte, Francis Bret, *The goddess of Excelsior.*

Harte, Francis Bret, *The outcasts of Poker Flat.*

McNeil, Everett, *The cave of gold; a tale of California in '49.* New York: E. P. Dutton. 1911.

Miller, Joaquin, i. e., Cincinnatus Heine, *'49, the gold-seeker of the Sierras.* New York: Funk & Wagnalls. 1884.

Munroe, Kirk, *Golden days of '49; a tale of the California diggings.* New York: Dodd, Mead & Company. 1889.

Sabin, E. L., *Goldseekers of '49.* New York: J. B. Lippincott Company. 1915.

Spurr, G. G., *The land of gold; a tale of '49, illustrative of early pioneer life in California and founded upon fact.* Boston: A. Williams & Company. 1881.

White, Stewart Edward, *Gold.* New York: Doubleday, Page & Company. 1913.

Index

INDEX

A

C

Calaveras County, Mother Lode in, 138.
Calaveras River, map 74; neocene, 100, 104.
Calaveritas, map 74.
Calhoun, John C., 307.
California Gold Book, 41.
California, origin of name, 1.
California Star, early newspaper, mentions gold discovery, 56; suspends publication, 61, 319; staff deserts, 319.
California, state of, statutes of 1851, mining district laws quoted, 181; boundaries of, 303; legislature of, 305, 308.
California, steamship, 244.
Californian, first newspaper in California, announces gold discovery, 55; condemns gold fever, 60; suspends publication, 61, 319.
Cameron at Weaverville, 199.
Camp Far West, on Bear River, 25; map 72.
Campo Seco, map 74.
Camptonville, map 72.
"Canoe," term used for "tom," 321.
Cape Cod Bar, 238; map 74.
Carquinez Straits, 68.
Carson Creek, town of, established 1848, 78; mines near, 149; on map as Carson Flat, 74.
Carson, J. H., hears of gold discovery, 59; on Carson Creek, 78; quoted, 174, 188.
Castañares, report of quoted, 10.
Cathay, 239, map 74.
Catholic fathers, Franciscans, in early gold rumors, 8-9; Jesuits in Baja California, 8; clergy in California, 285.
Caton at Weaverville, 199.
Cave City, map 74.
Centerville, Alameda County, map 74.
Centerville (Pilot Hill), Eldorado County, map 74.
Central Wharf built, 248.
Chana, Claude, discovers gold at Auburn, 75.
Charlie's Ranch (Veazie City), 227.
Cherokee, map 72.
Cherokee Flat, map 72.
Chico Creek, explorations to, 12; Bidwell settles on, 25, 81.
"Chile mill" used by Sonorans in quartz mines, 139.
Chilean miners, 205.
Chili Bar, map 72.

Chili Camp, map 74.
China, granite from, in San Francisco buildings, 260.
Chinese Camp, 238; map 74.
Chinese miners, 130, 206; use rocker, 122.
Civil War, California loyal in, 311; contributions during, 312.
"Claim" explained, 112; laws, 192.
Clark, W. S., builds wharf at Clark's Point, 248.
Clarksville, map 72.
Clay, Henry, 306.
Clay Street Wharf, San Francisco, 250.
Clear Creek, gold discovered on by Reading, 1848, 83; 228.
Clergymen in San Francisco, 285-287.
Coal discovered on Mt. Diablo, 55.
Cold Springs, map 72.
Colfax, 75; map 72.
Coloma, site of Sutter's sawmill, 27; gold discovery at, 31-45; Swiss teamster at, 54; mining at, 75; mentioned, 86, 94, 91, 340; map 72.
Coloma Indians, 50.
"Color," mining term explained, 112.
Colton, Walter, alcalde of Monterey, describes gold fever, 62; Congregational chaplain, 285; quoted from his *Three Years in California*, 297.
Columbia, on Feather River, 1849, map 72.
Columbia (Hildreth's Diggings) Tuolumne County, map 74.
Columbia Hill (North Columbia), map 72.
Columbia River, Ft. Vancouver on, 18.
Columbia, steamer, 230.
Colusa, agricultural town of 1849, 25, 228.
Compromise of 1850, 306-308.
Congress fails to pass mining legislation, 1849-50, 169; debates on slavery, 296.
Conness, Senator John, quoted, 183.
Constitutional convention, mass meetings at San José and elsewhere call for, 299; called by Governor Riley, 300; assembles at Monterey, 300; work of, 300-304; composition of, 300.
Corcoran, May, 206.
Corcoran, Judge John M., 206.
Cordelia, map 74.
Cordua, Theodore, 25.
Coronel, Antonio, at mines, 1848, 81.

G

Geologists look for gold in California, 11.
Georgia Slide, 238; map 72.
Gibsonville, map 72.
Gilbert, Congressman Edward, 305.
Gilded man (El Dorado), 2.
Gingery, Mr., 342.
Glacial period of Sierra, 103.
Gold, myths and rumors of before 1848, 1-8, 341; discovery of by Marshall, 31-45, 342-345, recorded by Bigler, 31, 38, date of, 37-39, kept secret, 37, made known in California, 49-64; testing of at Coloma and Sutter's Fort, 35; digging of begun by Mormons, 52; in Baja California, 7; at San Luís Obispo, 8; from San Fernando (San Feliciano) to Philadelphia, 10 f.; in Sacramento Valley, 7; at Mountain House, 69; on American River, 75; on Feather River, 82; on Trinity River, 83; geologists look for, 12; stories about finding, 137, 147; gravel deposits, 105; "Mother Lode" deposits, 106; dredging, 140; amalgam of, 124; specific gravity of, 115; Wimmer Nugget of, 40; production of, see Mineral. See also Mines and Mining.
Gold belt defined, 104.
Gold Bluffs excitement, 230.
Gold dust as currency, 333.
Gold Hill, 137.
Gold Lake, map 72.

Gold mines of 1848, 67-91.
Gold region, geological history of, 97-107.
Gold Spring, map 74.
Goldometer at Murphy's, 148.
Goodyear's Bar, 106; map 72.
Gordon at Weaverville, 199.
Gouge Eye (Pleasant Grove), Yuba County, 238; map 72.
Gouge Eye (Hunt's Hill), Nevada County, map 72.
Governors of California—See Mason, Riley, Burnett.
Government and law in the mines, 165-183, 191.
Graham, alcalde at Ford's Bar, 203.
Gran Quivira, Kingdom of, 5.
Graves, W. A., 342.
Grass Valley, 150, map 72.
Gregg, Josiah, discovers Humboldt Bay in 1849, 229.
Green Springs House, map 74.
Grist mill, at Brighton, 26; at Sutter's Fort, 24.
Grizzly Flat, 237; map 74.
Ground sluicing, at Sutter's mill, 32; defined, 133.
Guadalupe, map 74.
Guadalupe Hidalgo, Treaty of, 90, 166.
Groveland (First Garrotte), map 74.
Gwin, Dr. William, member of Constitutional convention, 303; elected United States Senator, 305; quoted on state boundaries, 304.

H

Halfway House, map 72.
Halleck, Major H. W., quoted, 179.
Halls, J., surveys Boston, 224.
Hamilton, Bidwell discovers gold at, 82; county seat of Butte County, 227; map 72.
Hanging, penalty of in Jacksonville code, 193; at Hangtown, 203; described, 209.
Hangtown, early name for Placerville, 76, 203; map 72.
Hank's Exchange, map 72.
Happy Camp on Klamath River, 233.
Hartman Bar, map 72.
Hastings, L. W., author of *Emigrant's Guide*, quoted 11-12.
Hastings & Co. store at Coloma, 343.
Hawaiian Islands, 285. See also Sandwich Islands, Kanakas.
Hawkeye, map 74.

Hecox, A. A., Methodist clergyman, 285.
Helltown, 238; map 72.
Hock Farm, Sutter's, 24, 81, 215; Sutter retires to, 92, 340; map 72.
Honcut Creek, 227.
"Hopper," part of miner's rocker, 118.
Hornitos, 206; map 74.
Horseshoe Bar, map 72.
Horseshoe Bend, map 74.
Hudson's Bay Company, 18, 25.
Humboldt Bay, discovery of, 1849, 229; occupied, 229-231.
Humboldt City, 229, 230-233.
Humboldt County created 1853, 231; county seat election, 232.
Humbug (North Bloomfield), map 72.
Humbug Bar, map 72.
Humbug Creek, Little, 179.

H

Humphrey, Isaac, Georgia miner, hears of gold discovery, 55; returns to Coloma with Bennett—constructs miner's cradle, 86, 118.
Hungry Hollow, map 72.
Hunt, T. Dwight, Chaplain of San Francisco, 285.

Hunt's Hill (Gouge Eye), map 72.
Hutchings, J. M., publisher of *Hutchings' California Magazine*, quoted, 37.
Hydraulic mining described, 132-137.

I

Ide, William B., 25.
Illinoistown, 75; map 72.
Indians, at Sutter's Fort, 20-24; give titles to Sutter, 50; consider gold "bad medicine," 51; work at gold digging, 70, 84; employment of, opposed by Americans, 84, 93; explore Southern mines, 77; at Weber Creek, 78; in Trinity mines, 84; did not know value of gold, 84; defrauded with "digger ounce,"

85; effect of gold discovery on, 329; Coloma (Culuma, Kulumah), 50; Cosumnes, 343.
Indian Bar, 156; map 74.
Indian baskets used for washing gold, 70.
Indian Diggings, maps 72, 74.
Indian Gulch, map 74.
Interest rates in San Francisco, 272.
Ione, map 74.
Iowa Hill, 75; map 72.
Iron and zinc houses, 272.

J

Jackass Gulch, 174.
Jackson, 236; map 74.
Jackson, Colonel, at Jacksonville, 191.
Jackson Creek, map 74.
Jacksonville, 191; mining laws quoted, 191-194; map 74.
Jails and prisons, lack of, 200.
Jamestown (American Camp), on Wood's Creek, established in 1848, 78; map 74.
Jamison Creek, map 72.
Jenny Lind Theatre opened, 1849, 282.
Jesuits, gold mines of, in Baja California, 8.

Jesus, José, ex-Mission Indian, discovers gold in Stanislaus region, 77.
Joaquin, used for San Joaquin, 320.
Johnson, William, on Bear River, 24.
Johnson, William, Mormon soldier employed at Sutter's mill, 31; called Johnston, 343.
Johnson Bar, map 72.
Johnson Ranch, map 72.
Jones, Commodore T.A.C., 329.
Juanita hanged at Downieville, 204-205.
Jurassic Sea, 99.
Jury, miners', 187-211, 195, 205, 200, 210.

K

Kanakas, employed by Sutter, 19, 20, 24, 84; diving for gold, 125. See also Sandwich Islands.
Kearny, General Stephen W., 31; grants beach and water lots to city of San Francisco, 248.
Kelly, William, author of *Stroll through the Diggings*, quoted 125, 157, 274.
Kelsey's, or Kelsey's Diggings, discovered 1848, 75; map 72.
Kemble, E. C., editor of *California Star*, mentions gold discovery, 56;

visits Sutter's mill, 56; fails to report gold, 59; withstands gold fever, 60; quoted, 51.
Kentucky House, map 74.
King's Store, map 72.
Klamath County, 230, 233.
Klamath gold mines, 105, 231.
Knight, Captain, 231.
Knight, William, rancho of, on Feather River, 25; establishes Knight's Ferry, 78.
Knight's Ferry, on Stanislaus River, 77, 78, 237; map 74.

S

T

U

Union (Uniontown), early name for Arcata, 229.
Union Bar, map 72.
Union Valley House, map 72.
United States Army, headquarters at Benicia, 219; at Far West Camp, 25; Stephenson's Regiment, 44, 174, 217; Mormon Battalion, 31; soldiers desert, 89, 318, 323.
United States, admission of California to, 308-311; Congress, 305-308, 166, 169, 181-183; Department of State, Larkin reports to, 317, 320; Department of War, Mason reports to, 324; General Land Office, 178;

Land Commission, 341; land policies, 89, 166-168, 181-183; Law of Mines, 166, 169, 181 f.; Mint, 11, 333; National Museum (Smithsonian), 43; Postmaster of San Francisco, 244; Presidents of, see see Polk, Taylor, Fillmore, Lincoln; Consul, Vice-Consul, see Larkin, Leidesdorff.
United States Exchange, gambling hall, fire starts in, 257.
Upper Rancheria, map 74.
Upham, Samuel C., author of *Notes of a Voyage to California*, quoted, 251.

V

Vacaville, map 74.
Valle, Ignacio del, appointed *juez de policia* at San Feliciano, 10.
Vallecito, map 74.
Vallejo, General Mariano G., 8; visited by Sutter, 19; pays little attention to reports of gold, 56; erects capitol building, 220.
Vallejo as state capital, 220; map 74.
Valley Springs, map 74.

Veazie City (Charlie's Ranch), 227; map 72.
Verandah, The, gambling house, 279.
Ver Mehr, J. L., Episcopalian clergyman, 286.
Vernon, described by Buffum, 224; map 72.
Volcano, Amador County, map 74.
Volcanoville, Eldorado County, map 72.
Volunteer fire companies, 260.

W

Wages in 1849, 319, 322, 331.
Walkinshaw at New Almaden, 334.
Walnut Creek, map 74.
Ware, Dr., water rights of in Trinity County, 196 ff.
Washington, Yolo County, opposite Sacramento in 1849, 221.
Washington, Nevada County, map 72.
Washington City, Sacramento County 224, map 72.
Washington, D. C., first gold from Coloma sent to, 43.
Washoe Mines, 312.
Water companies, 135.
Water lots in San Francisco, 248, 261.
Weaver (Creek), East and West, 196 ff.
Weaverville, 236; miners' meetings at, 196-200.
Weber, Captain Charles M., settles at French Camp Rancho, 25; promotes Tuleburg, 1847, 215; organizes Stockton Mining Company, 76; employs Indians, 84; profits in

mines of 1848, 86; changes name of Tuleburg to Stockton, 77; store of, 328; mentioned, 91.
Weber (Webber, Weber's) Creek, named for Captain Weber, 76; visited by Mason in 1848, 327; Sutter's activities on, 78; map 72.
Webster, town of, 1849, 221; map 74.
Webster, Daniel, 307.
Weimer—See Wimmer.
Wheeler, O. C., Baptist clergyman, 286.
Whipping of criminals, 200, 208, 210.
Whisky Bar, map 71.
Whisky Diggings, map 72.
Whisky Flat, Butte County, map 72.
Whisky Flat, Mariposa County, map 74.
Wild Yankee Ranch, map 72.
Wilke's expedition, 341.
Willey, S. A., Congregational clergyman of 1849, 286.
Williams, Albert, Presbyterian clergyman, 286; private school of, in San Francisco, 291.

W

Williams, Dr. Mary Floyd, author of *History of the San Francisco Committee of Vigilance of 1851*, quoted, 169, 187.
Willis, Ira and Sidney, 343.
Willow Springs, 237, map 74.
Wilson, Colonel Charles L., builds plank road to Mission Dolores, 253.
Wimmer, Peter L., foreman at Coloma, 31, 36, 40, 41, 335, 342-345; Elizabeth Jane, wife of Peter L., 31, 40, 41, tests gold, 35; sons of, 31, 36.

Wimmer Nugget, 40-42, 338.
"Wing dams" described, 126.
Wisconsin Bar, map 74.
Wisconsin Hill, 238; map 72.
Wolfskill, John R., 25.
Woods, James, discovers gold on Wood's Creek, 1848, 78.
Wood's Creek, 78; mining laws at, 174; map 74.
Wood's Diggings, map 74.
Woodbridge, Sylvester, Presbyterian clergyman of 1849, 286.
Women, lack of, in California, 288.
Wright, George W., 305.

Y

Yankee Hill, Tuolumne County, map 74.
Yankee Hill, Butte County, map 72.
Yankee Jim's, origin of name, 75; map 72.
Yankee traders at Sutter's Fort, 24.
Yeomet, maps, 72, 74.
Yerba Buena, early name for San Francisco, 243; name changed, 219; Sutter at, 19; mentioned, 218, 336.

Y.M.C.A., in San Francisco, 287.
You Bet, 238; map 72.
Yount's, map 74.
Yuba City, 226; map 72.
Yuba River, cañon formed, 103; mines on, 82; neocene, 100-104; mentioned, 25, 146, 174, 329; map 72.
Yubah—See Yuba River.
Yreka established in gold era, 236.

Z

Zinc and iron houses in 1849, 272.